ONE WEEK LOAN

2 5 AUG 2009

Toxic Tourism

Toxic Tourism

Rhetorics of Pollution, Travel, and Environmental Justice

PHAEDRA C. PEZZULLO

THE UNIVERSITY OF ALABAMA PRESS

Tuscaloosa

Typeface: Perpetua

∞

The paper on which this book is printed meets the minimum requirements of American National Standard for Information Sciences-Permanence of Paper for Printed Library Materials, ANSI Z39.48-1984.

Library of Congress Cataloging-in-Publication Data

Pezzullo, Phaedra C.
Toxic tourism : rhetorics of pollution, travel, and environmental justice /
Phaedra C. Pezzullo.
p.   cm. — (Rhetoric, culture, and social critique)
Includes bibliographical references and index.
ISBN-13: 978-0-8173-1550-4 (cloth : alk. paper)
ISBN-10: 0-8173-1550-0 (alk. paper)
1. Tourism—Environmental aspects. 2. Tourism—Social aspects. 3. Hazardous waste sites—Political aspects. 4. Environmental justice. I. Title.
G155.A1P47 2007
338.4′791—dc22

2006022572

This book is dedicated to all the environmental justice and environmental activists, advocates, and tourists whom I have met and have yet to meet—for never giving up.

Contents

Illustrations

Acknowledgments

As I was growing up on a hill in Abington, Pennsylvania, there were four views from my kitchen window: closest in my line of sight was my mother's bird feeder; a bit beyond was the township dump; above that, I could see the top of the local high school's swimming pool; and on the horizon was the skyline of Philadelphia. Some days, I think that location shaped me as much as anything else in my life. It embodied the value of other-than-human animals my mother instilled in me, the stench of human waste (that my family could sometimes smell before we ever looked), the privilege and value of a well-funded suburban public education system (where my father taught and my brother and I attended), and the significance of sprawling urban centers (which continue to place stress on and blur the liminal boundaries of city life). The proximity of these interrelated scenes of nature, waste, education, and culture appropriately embodied the material and symbolic flows between these dynamic and interdependent facets of the world.

In a sense, this book was written as my way of sharing that location. Birds fly over everyone's heads. We all make waste that ends up in landfills. At some level, everyone seeks education and pleasure. And each city's dreams and nightmares continue to sprawl outward and inward across the country as people and goods migrate, air blows, and water flows. The "toxic tours" described in this book remind us what is at stake in this perspective: the distance between us is much more fragile than we tend to admit.

Moving homes across the country and touring different parts of the world, I have met many people who generously have shared their own homegrown views of the planet and their sense of interconnection. First,

I feel honored to have the opportunity to publicly acknowledge my professional debt to the social movement activists and advocates who inspired and contributed to this project in various ways, particularly those who took time out of their busy schedules for interviews and sharing resources, namely, Bradley Angel, Judith Brady, Dollie Burwell, John Delicath, Domingo González, Kim Haddow, Reginald Harris, Charlotte Keys, Neal Livingston, Darryl Malek-Wiley, Elizabeth May, John McCown, Kristopher Michel, Catherine Murray, Kirstin Replogle, Jim Warren, Adam Werbach, Sue Williams, and J. Wil Wilson.

I want to thank the Department of Communication Studies at the University of North Carolina, Chapel Hill, from 1996 to 2002 for their encouragement and stimulation, including graduate students Bernadette Calafell, Lisa Calvente, Nina Lozano-Reich, and Jules Odendahl; the staff, especially Sharon Riley; and the faculty—particularly my exceptional mentors V. William Balthrop, Carole Blair, Lawrence Grossberg, D. Soyini Madison, Della Pollock, and Julia T. Wood. The humble spirit who persuaded me to study with him at UNC and to join the Sierra Club undoubtedly has influenced my professional life more than any other; thank you, J. Robert Cox.

For fostering my ongoing research, I want to acknowledge the Environmental Communication Network (www.ecn.org). I feel fortunate to be a part of this sympathetic and committed community of invaluable interlocutors online and at conferences where I have presented this work, including at the National Communication Association Convention from 2001 to 2004, at COCE (Conference on Communication and Environment) in 2001 and 2003, and at the Crossroads in Cultural Studies Conference in 2004.

I am grateful to the journal editors who have helped me develop and circulate my scholarship, namely, Michael Bowman, Karlyn Kohrs Campbell, Stephen Depoe, and David Henry. Although expanded, chapter 3 draws heavily on my earlier essay "Touring 'Cancer Alley,' Louisiana: Performances of Community and Memory for Environmental Justice," *Text and Performance Quarterly* 23, no. 3 (2003): 226–52. Some of chapter 4 draws on my essay "Resisting 'National Breast Cancer Awareness Month': The Rhetoric of Counterpublics and Their Cultural Performances," *Quarterly Journal of Speech* 89, no. 4 (2003): 345–65. All reproductions from these journals have been done with permission from Taylor and Francis (http://www.tandf.co.uk). Throughout, with permission, I also reproduce brief excerpts from my essay "Toxic Tours: Communicating the 'Presence' of Chemical Contamination" in *Communication and Public Participation in Environmental Decision-Making,* ed. Stephen P. Depoe, John W. Delicath, and Marie-France Aepli Elsenbeer, the State of New York University Press, ©2004, 235–54 (All Rights Reserved). Overall, this previously published research has been revised, expanded, and integrated thoroughly in the original arguments presented in this book.

The faculty and students at Indiana University, Bloomington, in the Department of Communication and Culture provided a nourishing home as this project developed, particularly my spring 2004 undergraduate "Environmental Tourism" class, my graduate students, the staff, my growing cohort of untenured (and increasingly becoming tenured) friends—especially Yeidy Rivero and Michael Kaplan—and my mentor-colleagues Joan Hawkins, Robert L. Ivie, John L. Lucaites, Robert Terrill, and Gregory Waller. Drafts of this book in various stages were improved as a result of profoundly generous and insightful feedback from Bob Ivie, Ted Striphas, and Rachel Hall. My appreciation goes to two anonymous reviewers and to the staff at The University of Alabama Press.

Finally, I want to acknowledge my gratitude to my loving biological and socially constructed family, particularly my parents, Vincent and Carmen Pezzullo; my godparents, Gerald and Virginia Alpaugh; my brother and his partner, Alexis and Summer Pezzullo; my extended family (of which there remain too many to name); my sister-friends, Rachel Hall (whom I can't thank enough), Stacy Farr, Christina Kowalchuk, Stephanie O'Brien, Elaine Vautier, and Maria Willett; my four-legged family members, Ecco and Neptune; and the one who has spent time reading, listening, and supporting me more than anyone else in the past decade, my partner, Ted Striphas.

Introduction

A Challenge

Before the judicial body here makes a decision, we strongly urge that
you come to our city and meet with us and see where we live and see
what we're exposed to. Right now, I'm offering that invitation. I would
very much like an answer.

> —Zulene Mayfield, on behalf of
> Chester Residents Concerned for
> Quality Living, in her remarks to
> the Pennsylvania State Environ-
> mental Hearing Board

Would you accept Zulene Mayfield's invitation? Can you imagine traveling
to a place that local residents claim is polluted by toxins to witness the
bodies and landscapes that supposedly have been affected? Would—or
could—you risk exposing your own body? Or would you instead refuse,
given the chance that the smells, sounds, contagions, and stories would
be too much? Mayfield's invitation, like countless others across the Americas, is not innocent.[1] It is a challenge that awaits an answer.

When an invitation like this is accepted, community activists organize
and facilitate what they call a "toxic tour." Such a name enhances the irony
of the invitation: who would want to *tour* toxins? Tours, normally linked
with vacation, leisure, and picturesque beauty, seem an odd match for
chemicals that are synonymous with poison. How could any good come
from an invitation to travel to such a site?

Beyond the undesirability of toxins and the perhaps unexpected pairing
of them with tours, the use of tourism for politically progressive ends may
seem odd for still another set of reasons. As Dean MacCannell writes,
"tourists dislike tourists."[2] Further, many of the people who are toured
dislike tourists.[3] Even scholars of tourism tend to dislike tourists.[4] After
all, what is there to like? By definition, tourists are invasive and ignorant

of their surroundings. Tourists make waste, take resources, destroy—or, at minimum, transform—places, and encourage local communities literally to sell themselves and to commodify their culture for money. So, for the most part, it's not just that we don't like tourists or find tourism pointless. Our disdain belies a stronger, more powerful, underlying cultural belief: *tourism is toxic*. Tourism contaminates the people and the places where it occurs. Tourism corrodes. Tourism offends. Tourism exploits. In a sense, some might even conclude, tourism kills.

Tours hosted under the rubric of "environmental tourism" or "ecotourism" only seem to exacerbate people's cynicism about the practice of touring.[5] Skeptics often sound either amused or disgusted by the proposition that touring might help to improve the world ("What self-righteous arrogance!" "How hypocritical!" "The irony!"). A consistent economic trend within the United States and abroad helps foster such suspicious responses; communities that turn to the tourist industry as their primary source of revenue often find that this choice is predicated on sustaining financially, environmentally, and culturally precarious positions. Consider, for example, the depressing and complicated dynamics illustrated in films such as Michael Moore's *Roger & Me,* documenting desperate tourist initiatives to boost the local economy in Flint, Michigan, and John Sayle's *The Sunshine State,* dramatizing a scenario common in economically depressed areas of the Florida coast, in which residents and local business owners must decide what to do with their land and lives in response to offers from wealthy corporate land developers. As these two films attest, decisions about tourism as a means of helping the local economy or preserving local environments are rarely straightforward.[6]

But, disliking tourists and believing tourism is toxic have a price. At the very least, there is every indication that tourism is here to stay. It is an international phenomenon that we cannot avoid or ignore with much success. Tourism, in fact, is the largest industry in the world.[7] Globally, we spend more on touring than we do on eating. Think about that for a moment. Consider all of those trips to a grocery store or to a restaurant or even to a field to harvest crops. Now, try to imagine more money, time, and resources. That's how massive the tourist industry is. And our appetite for touring seems to keep growing.

This leads to the primary reason we should question our dislike of tourists: most of us have been or will be tourists at some point in our lives. We will travel to someplace at some moment in time in which we are visitors and are not planning to settle. It might be a trip to the coast or to the mountains or to a city, but we will be touring. Disliking tourists, therefore, is really a way to express a dislike for ourselves, our culture, and who we have become. Tourists dislike tourists because people dislike people. We dislike the fact that we cannot always already belong wherever we go. We dislike the fact that we always appear to want to consume more. We dislike the fact that we love the same cultures and places that we seem to be killing every day.

In a sense, then, claiming that tourism is toxic is about giving up on the hope that we as a people and as tourists can expect more from ourselves. It is to resign to life as it is. Yet, of course, when stated so definitively, we know we can change. We begin to distance ourselves from the tourist, the tourist who dislikes the tourist, the person who dislikes the people, and we think that this conversation must be about someone else. Unless you are one of the few who has never glared at a tourist, thought poorly of a tourist, or laughed at a tourist's expense, however, this conversation is about each one of us. The labeling of tourism as "toxic," either explicitly or implicitly, implicates all of us who are invested in believing that our practices and beliefs can and should change.

This book is written, in part, with the hope of engaging the many overlapping conversations about the value of tourism and, in particular, the possibility that people, even tourists, can resist toxicity. While it is important to acknowledge that tourism is capable of unpleasant, offensive, and harmful effects, I contend that it is equally significant to recognize how and when practices of tourism may be motivated by our more admirable desires for fun, connection, difference, civic spirit, social and environmental change, and education. In this book I draw from examples across the United States and its borders in the late twentieth and early twenty-first century to show how noncommercial tours can serve as embodied rhetorics of resistance aimed at mobilizing public sentiment and dissent against material and symbolic toxic patterns. By weaving together social critiques of tourism and the responses of communities to the burdens of literal chemical toxicity, this book aims to bring into focus and hold accountable deeply embedded and highly problematic assumptions about travel, pollution, and democracy.

Touring Toxins

Tours of toxins generally fall into either of two categories: tours of toxic sites provided by industries, or "toxic tours." The former might be considered an outgrowth of industrial plant tours more broadly, which have existed since at least the early 1960s. In 1962, for example, *Life* magazine offered a "welcome to U.S. industry's spectaculars," inviting readers to "hop in your car and have a look at the biggest show of all—U.S. industry at work."[8] Charmed by the ingenuity of these experiences and the companies that host them, a writer in *Reader's Digest* defined a "plant tour" in 1966 as "a tour of an industrial plant or office, one of the vast array in the United States that feeds, clothes, houses, transports, insures, guards the health of or otherwise caters to the nation's nearly 200 million people."[9] Today, plant tours designed for public consumption continue to boast of "American know-how," tend to be free because "factory tours are good publicity for the company," and include a wide range of industries, such as Binney and Smith's Crayola, Boeing, the Denver Mint, and Hershey's.[10]

Some of the more notorious plant tours that draw millions of visitors are located at sites of well-known environmental disasters, such as the Three Mile Island tourist center, the bus tour of the Alaskan pipeline terminal along which the *Exxon Valdez* sailed, and the Chernobyl nuclear facility, where employees who continue to work there pass out calendars with the slogan: "Safety culture, effectiveness, social progress." Since toxin-producing companies or polluting government agencies typically sponsor this type of tour destination, these institutions tend to frame their narratives for tourists within discourses of safety and containment, industrial progress, and objective science.[11]

A very different kind of tour about toxins is the one this book primarily considers, the type Zulene Mayfield and growing numbers of North American activists are inviting people to attend. These tours differ, in part, from the more institutionalized tours of toxic sites by drawing on discourses of uncertainty and contamination, of social justice and the need for cultural change. "Toxic tours," as they are called by those who host them, are noncommercial expeditions into areas that are polluted by toxins, spaces that Robert D. Bullard calls "human sacrifice zones."[12] More and more of these communities have begun to invite outsiders in, providing tours as a means of educating people about and, it is hoped, transforming their situation. For, although "all communities, at least in the United States in the [new millennium], . . . are contaminated to some extent," some communities are "toxically assaulted."[13] These toxic assaults tend to occur in or on communities that historically have been segregated from elite centers of power, areas Robert R. Higgins argues are deemed culturally to be "appropriately polluted spaces," such as neighborhoods of people of color and low-income communities.[14] There exists, in turn, both a psychological and geographical distance between dominant public culture and the cultures of those who live in places where both waste and people are articulated together as unnecessary, undesirable, and contaminating.[15] The creation of these "separate areas of existence"[16] enables our culture more readily to dismiss the costs of toxic pollution because the waste and the people most affected by the waste appear hidden within their proper place.

It is this cultural and physical distance—between those hosting the tours and those, often more privileged, tourists traveling to toxically assaulted sites—that has led many activists to testify to the value of toxic tours. As Rita Harris, a toxic tour guide in Memphis, Tennessee, attests: "Some people that do not frequent the parts of town that are included in the tour are always shocked at the nearness of homes, playgrounds, schools, and parks. They get to see firsthand the environmental insult to residents (of having these polluters so close to homes), as well as the noxious odors that permeate the neighborhood. Toxic tours can give the best close-up and personal view of what poor communities are faced with and cause some participants to want to do more to help in some way. And most participants say they cannot imagine living with these conditions daily."[17] Consider, further, the reactions shared in this newspaper report of a toxic tour in 1998: "'This part of Baltimore is not perceived by many people who live in Baltimore—it's a section of the city that isn't part of the city,' said Maeve Hitzenbuhler [a schoolteacher of environmental history and an advocate for Health Care Without Harm], as the chartered bus rambled past one industrial plant after another. 'The community in Baltimore doesn't have a good idea of what's going on here.' "[18] A local toxic tour guide, Terry Harris, further explains: "The area, despite being only several miles from downtown Baltimore, is very isolated and most people on the tour have no idea of the scale of the operations, or the environmental and public health threats involved. A common reaction of tour-goers is 'I had no idea.' "[19] It is within this context of living in alienated "worlds apart" that grassroots communities engaged in anti-toxic struggles have turned to tours as a tactic of resistance.[20]

Nevertheless, there are many constraints toxins themselves pose to limit the ways that a community may raise questions about toxic pollution in public debates. Michael R. Reich argues, for example, that any attempt to construct a counterdiscourse to toxic production is restricted by the invisibility of the toxic agent, the nonspecificity of toxic symptoms, and difficulties of identification.[21] In addition to their obscure material characteristics, toxins may appear to most of us as excessively dangerous and overwhelming in scale. Due to economic and cultural disparities, the dissenting messages of toxically assaulted communities are unlikely to be heard as loudly as or to be perceived as authoritative as those produced by polluting industries. Tours face the challenge, therefore, of reframing hegemonic pubic discourses about chemical contamination perpetuated by popular and catchy corporate tag lines, such as Monsanto's "Without chemicals, life itself would be impossible," DuPont's "Better living through chemistry," General Electric's "We bring good things to life," and the industry's more recent "Essential2" campaign, launched in 2005.[22]

Invented as a creative response to this wide range of constraints, toxic tours are motivated by community members' collective desire to survive and to resist toxic pollution through active participation in public life. In the name of environmental and social justice, grassroots groups offer tours for and with a broad range of audiences, such as academics, more traditional environmental groups, industrial representatives, government officials, and journalists. Typically, one or more "guides" walk or drive block to block, pointing out where polluting industries are located in relation to the residents, stopping to allow the "tourists" to witness the stories of various residents' ailments and struggles, and providing information they have gathered regarding the violations and the apparent effects of these industries on the surrounding land and people. Sometimes, local communities and older, more established environmental organizations such as Greenpeace and the Sierra Club collaborate in order to pool resources and energy together. In addition, toxic tours have become incorporated increasingly in public participation gatherings facilitated by the U.S. Environmental Protection Agency (EPA) as a means to increase awareness of toxic hazards, identify environmental justice concerns, gather additional information, and provide hands-on experience for problem solving and critical skills.[23] As environmental justice leader Rose Marie Augustine testified at an EPA meeting subsequent to a toxic tour, for those involved in these decisions on a national level, the proliferation of toxic tours highlights toxic pollution as a systemic challenge: "And then you look and you do tours, the toxic tours, and you see these communities and the people are sick and dying—and we're talking about thousands of communities, we are talking about a sick and dying nation."[24]

Historically, however, conversations about public participation in environmental decision making more broadly tend not to recognize tourism as a relevant or serious practice. Admittedly, by definition, tourism is conducted by outsiders who visit places for short periods of time. Further, tourism is what many consider to be "low culture" (as in, "That's such a tourist trap!"; "It's just tourist schlock"; or "Stop acting like such a tourist!"), whereas public participation usually is perceived as more official, more important, and involving more consistent engagement over a more sustained period of time.[25] Yet, the subsequent pages will follow cues from cultural studies by illustrating how toxic tours blur the lines between the official and the vernacular, "high" and "low" public culture. Raymond Williams traces these distinctions and has debunked the notion that "low" or "bad" culture inevitably drives out or dilutes "high" or "good" culture. Instead, he suggests that we acknowledge how "culture is ordinary" and, as such, recognize that "we live in an expanding culture, and all of the elements in the culture are themselves expanding."[26] Likewise, expanding more conventional understandings of tourism, toxic tours not only place everyday life and public culture on display but also constitute a discourse of political dissent against the power relations that enable lethal patterns of toxic pollution to persist.

Complicating what we consider "high" and "low" culture is more than just a philosophical or semantic exercise. Doing so, as Robin D. G. Kelley reminds us, challenges the very way we understand and, therefore, identify what is allowed to count as "politics" and "resistance": "We have to step into the complicated maze of experience that renders 'ordinary' folks so extraordinarily multifaceted, diverse, and complicated. Most importantly, we need to break away from traditional notions of politics. We must not only redefine what is 'political' but question a lot of common ideas about what are 'authentic' movements and strategies of resistance."[27] In this spirit, I engage not only concrete political goals of toxic tours but also the possibilities that they more generally offer for redefining what is relevant to public participation and environmental politics.

As such, toxic tours are negotiations of power. Giovanna Di Chiro argues that toxic tours "challenge the remoteness of the 'tourist gaze,' a kind of museumlike looking from afar, and instead seek to create the conditions for an interactive form of sightseeing."[28] Through the interactions they invite, toxic tours complicate and trouble the simplistic binary opposition often constructed between "nature" and "culture." They repudiate traditional concepts of the "environment" as somewhere "out there" and, instead, highlight the racial, economic, and gendered cultural politics enabled and limited by the environments of which humans are a part. This book aims to examine these dynamic relations in order to explore how and why toxic tours perform as embodied rhetorical tactics to resist material and symbolic toxicity—a sensual effort, I would add, through which more than just the eyes are engaged.

Communicating Pain

I think that . . . it has something to do with the emotional response. When folks actually see the problem and make the link of the degradation activities that is going on and how they can assist the community with better or more—I'm—I'm searching for a certain word to give to you, because it's so important that folks really understand that when communities have suffered severely for decades that nobody has actually made an attempt to look at ways of solving the problems. But, when they make the physical connection—or interaction—with the problems, with the people, that is suffering and impacted the most, it sometimes does something to their emotions and causes them to have more affection and compassion on the people that's living under these certain kinds of conditions and they, in turn, will have enough compassion in their hearts to render assistance or services that lies within their powers as a means of doing something.

—Charlotte Keys, 2001,
environmental justice leader
from Columbia, Mississippi[29]

Initially, my study of toxic tours led me to examine how they function rhetorically as creative or inventional acts of political dissent. Why travel? How does this mode of resistance communicate something that might not be shared otherwise? What is being attempted by these ways of operating? What is being produced by this kind of performance? Which discursive frames are informed by and constitute these tours? Why name this practice a "tour" and not a protest or a march or lobbying or a pilgrimage or some other seemingly appropriate act? In order to overcome the distance— literally and figuratively—between communities that are severely affected by toxins and those that are not, my assumption from interactions and conversations with environmental justice activists such as Keys (above) was—and is—that an invitation to a toxic tour is a request for outsiders to travel in order *to be present* and, perhaps more importantly, *to feel present*.

More than simply "showing up," being present as a mode of advocacy suggests that the materiality of a place promises the opportunity to shape perceptions, bodies, and lives with respect to the people and places host- ing the experience. Being "present," like roll call in school, indicates the significance of someone literally coexisting with another in a particu- lar space and time. Yet, a rhetorical appreciation of "presence" also can indicate when we *feel as if* someone, someplace, or something matters, whether or not she/he/it is physically present with us.[30] Presence also refers, then, to the *structure of feeling* or one's *affective* experience when certain elements—and, perhaps, more importantly, relationships and communities— in space and time appear more immediate to us, such that we can imagine their "realness" or "feasibility" in palpable and significant ways.[31] Through the rhetorical performance of a toxic tour, for example, people, places, processes, and things may seem more tangible to us and, thus, we may be more persuaded to identify with or believe in their existence, their significance, and their consequence. Communicating a sense of presence, in other words, offers a means for marginalized communities to challenge feelings of alienation from the land and each other. It is *sensual*.[32]

On toxic tours, this sense of presence is not performed to invite some sense of the sublime or the picturesque, as is common on most commercial tours. Rather, toxic tours invoke the uglier sensualities of our world: the disgusting and the grotesque. Tourists are asked to expose themselves to the costs of human greed: poisoned air, polluted water, degraded land, and bodies that are diseased, deformed, or dying.

Yet, as important as feeling a sense of presence is to toxic tours and to my initial efforts to examine them, participating in toxic tours began to make me feel that I needed to take a step backward, in a way, from my initial theoretical assumptions and to consider the conditions of possibility that led host communities to attempt to create a feeling of presence in the first place. This shift in my perspective eventually led me to consider the relevance of feminist writings on corporeality to anti-toxic activism.

On every toxic tour, bodies are at stake. More specifically, what is to be won or lost through toxic tours as a rhetorical practice is nothing short of, to borrow Caren Kaplan's phrase from *Questions of Travel,* "bodies of knowledge, physical bodies, and bodies of land."[33] Bodies, understood in this expanded sense, are not pre-given, "natural" entities with boundaries that are beyond questioning and whose "truth" is somehow transparently understood. Bodies are defined rhetorically, within specific contexts of power and history, and their value is constantly contested.

Although Kaplan does not elaborate on the concept "bodies of land," imagining land as a body resonates with Aldo Leopold's holistic and ethical conception of "land" as exceeding the literal soil of our Earth. "The land ethic," according to Leopold, "simply enlarges the boundaries of the community to include soils, waters, plants, and animals, or collectively: the land."[34] This ecological sense of interconnectedness, more colloquially referred to today as "the environment," runs counter to hegemonic Western, liberal, and capitalistic epistemological legacies, such as anthropocentrism and autonomous individuality; thus, environmentalism continues to struggle to find acceptance in contemporary politics.

Physical human bodies, like tourism itself, historically have been marginalized by dominant culture as too peripheral to take into account when discussing politics, too sensational for bearing any relevance to meaningful public dialogue, and often simply just "too much." The Western bias against bodies and corresponding privileging of the disembodied human agent can be traced back at least as early as Plato's writings on how corporeal appearances can deceive one's judgment of another's "true" soul and was reinforced by, among other thinkers and beliefs in history, Descartes's stance that the body was something merely to be mastered by the mind.[35] This perception of bodies both reinforces and is reinforced by a larger, binary system of thought, whose structures cast the land and women in a similar, negative light. In other words, this dualistic system of thinking typical of Western modernity and Enlightenment theory places bodies, the land, and women at the bottom of a value hierarchy in which minds, technology (or that which is created by Man), and men are privileged as somehow superior, independent, more rational, and, thus, more important. In turn, this rigid hierarchy influences and is influenced by our perceptions of specific bodies of thought. To offer some general examples of this ongoing legacy, "objective" science remains taken more seriously than the admittedly more subjective humanities, rational norms of debate continue to be privileged over more overtly emotional testimonies of experience, and the written word is persistently fetishized in contrast to oral performances.[36]

Despite this history, as I will elaborate throughout this book, bodies powerfully and undeniably do inform our experiences, our beliefs, and our judgments in socially meaningful ways. Further, as Kaplan's broader sense of "bodies" helps us appreciate, thought, land, and humanity are intimately interconnected through the trope of corporeality. These interconnections suggest the need to account for and to reassess the blurred and interdependent categories of the material and the symbolic, the organic and the inorganic, the emotional and the reasonable.[37]

On toxic tours, the fundamental motive to engage and to mobilize rhetorical bodies most often is pain—pain that some answers are not definite, pain that some ways of knowing have not protected us, pain that some people are dying from this uncertainty and set of assumptions, pain that other people are not, and pain that our air, water, and land are suffering to a degree that we have yet to comprehend. Compounding these feelings, the inexpressibility of corporeal pain, as Elaine Scarry observes, is constitutive of pain itself: "To have pain is to have *certainty;* to hear about pain is to have *doubt.*"[38] Toxic tours, therefore, turn on a leap of faith, or an assumption, that the pain of others—though seemingly incoherent—can be made to feel more present to those who might otherwise doubt its existence.

Moreover, Richard Hofrichter argues that we live in a "toxic culture," which need not be limited to the "economic, social, and spiritual" consequences of the "harmful materials and processes" that exist in our environment, but also might be used as "a metaphor for the way language, concepts, rituals, valuation processes, and politics frame the debates over major issues, ignoring the political conflict and relations of power that influence human and community health. These power relations," he explains, "generate their own logic, ideology, myths, symbols and cultural norms. Most important, we are often unaware of their existence."[39] Indeed, to emphasize that the construction of our toxic culture *is a process* that is ongoing, incomplete, and, therefore, not inevitable, I believe it is useful to examine pain as a crucial part of the *toxification* of our culture, or the processes through which people are persuaded (and sometimes compelled) to accept the ongoing pollution of our bodies with toxic chemicals.[40]

It is precisely the lack of recognition of the processes and practices Hofrichter discusses, that is, the ongoing, dynamic power relations enabling the perpetuation of toxification, which toxic tours attempt to make present and to remedy. Part of the motivation for this book is to illustrate how such efforts to engender presence through touring are not isolated to one particular community or one set of decision makers and actors. Rather, this book aims to follow and to explore the range of practices called "toxic tours," to articulate their systemic arguments about and through bodies with each other, to synthesize their collective critique of pain, and to bring these disparate voices and struggles together in the hopes of helping to move their democratic efforts forward.

Democratic Movements for Environmental Justice

While it may seem counterintuitive, tourism has a long relationship with democracy and civic life.[41] Although tourism often is associated with leisure, it also creates opportunities for a wider range of people (*demos*) to gain access and opportunity to interact with each other and unfamiliar places. For reasons such as these, tours increasingly are mobilized to bring various communities together in the name of democratic movements for "environmental justice."

According to most accounts, the environmental justice movement was born during the summer of 1982 in Warren County, North Carolina, after the state decided to construct a toxic waste landfill against the wishes of local citizens, who felt that the predominantly black, poor, and rural Warren County was chosen for political, not ecological, reasons.[42] Warren County's story brought heightened awareness on an international level that suggested patterns of environmental degradation had been—and continued to be—predicated upon social discrimination over ecological considerations. In particular, Warren County's story helped set the stage for activists who were fighting what became known as "environmental racism": "racial discrimination in environmental policymaking, the enforcement of regulations and laws, the . . . targeting of communities of color for toxic waste facilities, the official sanctioning of the life-threatening presence of poisons and pollutants in our communities [i.e., those of people of color], and the history of excluding people of color from leadership of the environmental movement."[43]

This last point, a critique of what is more traditionally understood as the environmental movement, has sparked a transformation in environmental discourses, practices, and agents. Environmentalists have long been identified with the preservation of scenic areas, such as Yosemite or Grand Canyon National Parks, and with predominantly affluent, white environmental organizations such as the Sierra Club, the National Wildlife Federation, the Natural Resources Defense Council, and the Environmental Defense Fund.[44] In addition, most of these organizations were (and are) led by men.[45] Although the mid-twentieth century signaled the potential beginnings of a significant shift in focus and leadership, the environmental movement *predominantly* remained constituted by affluent whites with higher education degrees and focused primarily on campaigns such as promoting clean water and preserving endangered species.[46]

In a sense, the shift encouraged by the environmental justice movement has been to insist on the insertion of "justice" into the middle of the environmental movement. As environmental justice advocate Dana Alston argues: "For us, the issues of the environment do not stand alone by themselves. They are not narrowly defined. Our vision of the environment is woven into an overall framework of social, racial and economic justice. The environment, for us, is where we live, where we work, and where we play."[47] Given the environmental justice struggles to protect Native American sacred sites and family graveyards in Appalachia, environmental justice activism also includes "where we pray." From this perspective, "the environment" is not some abstract place "out there," void of human activity, but the dynamic elements that make up life itself. This expanded definition of "environment" requires environmentalists to foreground cultural and political questions about bodies of land or "the environment," such as *who* has clean water, *who* doesn't, and *why?* What is endangering life—human and nonhuman—and how can we stop these threats in every habitat?

Remembrance of Warren County as the catalyst for this historical transformation in the definition and mission of environmental activism, of course, is granted with an appreciation for its value as a symbolic birthplace. As is true with most stories of origin, the roots of the environmental justice movement belie a more complicated appreciation for history and social change. Luke W. Cole and Sheila R. Foster suggest that it is more useful "to think metaphorically of the movement as a river, fed over time by many tributaries," such as the civil rights movement, the anti-toxics movement, academics, Native American struggles, the labor movement, and, of course, the environmental movement.[48] Irreducible to one race or one struggle, the environmental justice movement has grown to represent countless communities fighting grievances in the nexus between environmental and social justice concerns. Its goals, Bunyan Bryant states, are "served when people can realize their highest potential, without experiencing the 'isms' [racism, classism, etc.]."[49]

Hofrichter maintains, moreover, that "[e]nvironmental justice is therefore closely related to the practice of democracy."[50] Environmental justice academic and activist Robert D. Bullard explains how these struggles are related closely to a more democratic society: "The goal of an environmental justice framework is to make environmental protection more democratic. More important, it brings to the surface the *ethical* and *political* questions of 'who gets what, why, and in what amount.' Who pays for, and who benefits from, technological expansion?"[51] Environmental justice activist and writer Lois Marie Gibbs similarly calls for the following environmental justice agenda: "We can't shut down the sources of dioxin [i.e., toxic pollution] without finding the courage to change the way government works. To begin this process of change, we have to create a national debate, community by community, on the nature of our government and society. We have to explore how people became powerless as the corporations became powerful. We have to discuss why our government protects the right to pollute more than it protects our health. We have to figure out how to speak honestly and act collectively *to rebuild our democracy.*"[52]

The environmental justice movement includes controversies that span a wide range of people and issues, such as anti-pesticide struggles of migrant farmworker unions, anti-CAFO (Concentrated Animal Feeding Operations) efforts in rural communities, attempts to achieve redress for uranium mining on tribal lands, and urban neighborhoods contesting medical waste incinerators. Creating what Ernesto Laclau and Chantal Mouffe call "chains of equivalence" among a plurality of communities resisting conditions of oppression promises to "deepen and expand" our democracy.[53]

In the early 1990s, broad support of the U.S. environmental justice movement reached a peak of political mobilization.[54] As journalists Fred Setterberg and Lonny Shavelson wrote at the time, "The 1990s, they [the movement] hoped, would be their decade."[55] In many ways, this wish came true. As growing numbers of communities and individuals were moved to find ways to mobilize against their interconnected experiences of social and environmental degradation, the environmental justice movement became recognized and institutionalized in national venues. In 1991 the First National People of Color Environmental Leadership Summit met in Washington, D.C., and established a set of "Principles of Environmental Justice," a document that delineates a coherent platform to foster the primary goals and ethics of the movement. One year later, the Office of Environmental Equity was created, and in 1994 President Clinton issued Executive Order 12898, creating the Interagency Working Group on Environmental Justice, thus officially recognizing the importance of environmental justice for people of color and low-income communities.

Unfortunately, despite this national momentum and ongoing grassroots activism, environmental injustices persist. To commemorate the fifteenth anniversary of the groundbreaking 1987 study by the United Church of Christ's Commission on Racial Justice, "Toxic Wastes and Race," the board of directors of that church's Justice and Witness Ministries facilitated a toxic tour of East St. Louis, Illinois, in June 2002 to highlight ongoing local struggles.[56] In October of that year, the Second National People of Color Environmental Leadership Summit convened again in Washington, D.C., to celebrate past achievements and explore future goals. Particularly disappointed by the policies of the George W. Bush administration, environmental justice activist Vernice Miller-Travis emphasized that "there's absolutely no comparison between the efforts that were put forth by the Clinton-Gore administration vs. the Bush-Cheney administration in advancing environmental justice and increasing protection for underrepresented communities. . . . This has been a dismal, dismal time for people of color and environmental protection."[57]

Given the setbacks enabled by the Bush administration, the related and growing lack of corporate accountability, and the challenges faced by all social movements when they become institutionalized, democratic efforts to achieve environmental justice continue into the twenty-first century. It is important to remember, however, that the Bush administration is not an aberration; rather, it is the culmination of three decades of environmental and civil rights backlash in the United States, a backlash born not of the Republican Party but from entities such as the "Wise Use" movement and the new Right. Despite the consistent popularity of "the environment" in polls, this powerful minority of neoconservatives has resisted new environmental and civil rights legislation, degraded old policies, and thus enabled the continued toxification of the nation. Furthermore, some level of toxic pollution has been deemed acceptable and, therefore, has been sanctioned by Democrats and Republicans alike.[58] The critique presented by toxic tours is therefore one that exceeds political party labels and the current administration's approach to toxic pollution.

Studying Toxic Tours

In addition to the people I have met in the environmental justice movement, my own research on toxic tours is inspired by at least two passions: tourism and environmentalism. Tourism itself has always fascinated me. I confess: I love to tour. Since I was two, my parents brought my brother and me on their road trips to visit family across the United States from New Jersey to Colorado, through battlefields and cornfields. As teachers, they found an organization that would pay for our costs to tour Europe on ten-day "spring break" trips for every seven students they could sign up. I loved those "packaged" fast-paced tours, too. Not many my age had the privilege of experiencing Michelangelo's artwork in person or were able to witness the way time and acid rain had begun to take their toll on the Parthenon.

Although I had encountered some negative perceptions of U.S. tourists while in Europe, it wasn't until I spent a semester abroad in Kenya and Tanzania as an undergraduate away from my family that I became conscious of negative perceptions of tourists in general. We were students, and most of us automatically assumed that made us better than the tourists who would wander into Nairobi with big backpacks traveling in taxis (instead of the local buses, or *matutus*), speaking only English or German (instead of Kiswahili). There I launched my first study of tourists, more specifically, of ecotourism at Amboseli National Park (now Amboseli National Reserve).[59] At the time, as is still the case today, tourism was Kenya's number one foreign exchange earner. Particularly interesting to me was how safari tourists would talk about wanting to check off "the Big Six" on their lists of "sitings": buffalo, cheetah, elephant, lion, rhino—and Maasai.[60] Even as a visitor myself, this crass categorization of a people (Maasai) as exotic attractions for gazing or for hire struck me as insensitive at best.[61] Although I needed much more background on interviewing techniques, theory, and simply time in the area, this study marked the beginning of my more focused academic interest in examining environmentalism, social justice, and travel.

I first decided to study toxic tours deliberately in 1998 as a graduate student of rhetoric, performance, and cultural studies. As someone who had participated in "toxic tours" as an activist, the responses I received about my trips intrigued me. Knowing I was traveling, my family, friends, and colleagues often would ask, "Where are you going this weekend?" Inevitably, when I would explain I was going on a toxic tour, a curious expression of simultaneous amusement and confusion often would come over their faces and a response something like the following would be offered: "Have fun . . . if that's the appropriate thing to say." It was in this repeated stuttering or moment of hesitation that my desire to write about toxic tours was born. Are toxic tours "fun"? Are they more serious than the usual tourist fare? Or was this type of traveling a mixture of both entertainment and education? Why has this practice come about? And why now?

To explore answers to these questions in this book, I have drawn on and will attempt to foreground many voices: tour guides and tourists whom I've interviewed (who do not necessarily agree with each other—even on whether or not they are part of the same movement), textual documents from popular media (which often indicate multiple conclusions), multi-disciplinary theoretical texts (which almost always indicate multiple conclusions), and my own perspective about toxic tours. The subsequent pages thus draw from my fieldwork experience as a participant-observer, an interviewer, an activist, an academic, and a reader of books, newspapers, and other archival sources, including the internet. This experiential approach to rhetorical and cultural analysis is, I believe, particularly useful in studying an "emergent" practice such as toxic tours,[62] because it provides the opportunity to examine a side of public discourse that tends to be marginalized in traditional written records.[63]

It is worth emphasizing how toxic tours challenge researchers to respond, at least in part, ethnographically.[64] For example, on a follow-up phone interview with Judith Brady, a toxic tour organizer in the San Francisco Bay Area, we shared the following exchange:

Brady: Did you happen to go to Hunter's Point when you were here?
Pezzullo: I didn't, and I wish I had planned for that.
Brady: I wish you had too, because it's an astonishing place. It's almost totally African American. It's left over from World War II, from the shipyard building. And it's geographically a *gorgeous* site— you know, it sits right over the Bay, with hills that look right across the Bay; it's amazing; it's beautiful—except that in that six square miles, there are *three hundred and twenty-five* toxic sites. . . . This year . . . I went on a tour of Hunter's Point. And it was *amazing*. It totally changed my relationship with that geographic area.
Pezzullo: *That's interesting.* Even with all your background experience, you felt the tour made that difference.

Brady: Oh, yes. It's *not* that I didn't know. I *did* know. And I've heard *many* people from that community talk. But, *being there* made a difference.[65]

This project, however, is not a traditional ethnography. I have been studying and supporting the environmental justice movement since 1995 and participating in toxic tours since 1996. My stay in each tour location has varied from an afternoon excursion to monthly visits over a period of as many as four years. Following the practice with this multi-sited approach to participant observation is more indicative of the experiences of tourists than those of the community members who organize and facilitate toxic tours.[66] I joined the Sierra Club, the oldest environmental advocacy organization in the United States, as part of its national Environmental Justice Committee in 1999. Demographically, one could say that I represent an "average" Sierra Club volunteer, insofar as I am female, middle class, white, and have at least one higher education degree.[67]

Although I do not dwell heavily on my personal experiences in this book, some still consider this project a kind of auto-ethnography insofar as I describe and discuss tours that I both observed as a researcher and participated in as an activist. Yet I should pause to explain what I mean when I claim to be a part of the environmental justice movement. The environmental justice movement, in part, is based on a sense of location. It began in communities that felt they were or still are disproportionately targeted for pollution because of their racial identity and/or economic status. Many residents of these areas argue that they have had no choice about their activism—they have to do something in order to survive. As environmental justice activist Les Ann Kirkland of Reveilletown, Louisiana, testifies: "I spent 1,017.75 hours last year doing environmental activism work because I *had* to, *not* because I liked it. I don't like it. But, our situation is crucial."[68] I, on the other hand, am not poor, nor am I a person of color. I don't live in a grassroots community of the movement. I am middle class and live with white privilege. I *choose to visit* places that have been polluted and to struggle for environmental justice. There is a difference.

Still, my sense of identification and my identity as an "outsider" are not necessarily contradictory. Perhaps it can be said of all social movements that there have been those who have supported movements without sharing a common history with those who inspired the movement. To name a few who have been particularly notable "outsiders": Frederick Douglass was part of the women's liberation movement; Michael Schwerner and Andrew Goodman were part of the civil rights movement; and Fred Ross was part of the farmworkers' movement. Yet for those of us who literally go out of our way to participate in a movement, our "belonging" does mean something different. There is something distinct at stake in the performances of those of us who are able to choose our associations more freely. We do not have the "privilege" of belonging as readily (if ever) as those closer to the location and identities of struggle. Conversely, those of us who are literally farther from the location or identities of struggle are more open to accusations of falsely claiming membership, because we tend to have more choice as to whether or not to leave the movement.

Since my research and activism are dialectically related, it is sometimes difficult and usually undesirable to say when one or the other of these impulses drives my actions and perceptions; yet I believe it is less helpful to try to create some artificial line between the two than it is to ask whether the results of my efforts are viable as one or the other or both. Rather than romanticizing "critical distance" as a criterion of academic research, I prefer to adhere to an epistemological stance that aims to achieve what Dwight Conquergood calls "genuine conversation" in a "dialogical performance," a position located somewhere within and between the tensions of detachment and commitment, objectivity and subjectivity.[69] Likewise, as D. Soyini Madison points out, performance in its many forms is "a communicative act in which you basically have people saying: I want to connect my body and my voice to this story that is not mine, or yet that could be."[70] As I have indicated already, despite the embodied economic, racial, gendered, and political differences between people, part of the goal of this book is to trouble false assumptions that we are not implicated in each other's stories.

Overall, this book assumes that more people should know what toxic tourism is and why it has come about, because it is a provocative response to a disturbingly persistent situation. It is a step in the process called for by James Clifford to "take travel knowledges seriously," an attempt to consider what dwelling in a place—even temporarily—might teach us.[71] In a sense, the limits of my approach to studying toxic tours reflect the constraints toxic tourists face themselves. Time shared and knowledge learned is relatively little compared to the experience of one who resides in an area. Still, by the end of this book I hope to have shown that, despite these constraints, touring also opens possibilities for enriched democratic forums of engagement and ethical entanglement.

This book also presumes that people who do organize and participate in toxic tours should record and analyze the purpose, practice, and efficacy of this tactic for the aim of becoming more persuasive, since, as opposed to commercial tourism, the goal of toxic tour guides would seem to be putting themselves "out of business," or making their roles unnecessary. I do not presume to write for the environmental justice movement. People from environmental justice communities continue to "speak for themselves"—and they do so quite well.[72] Rather, this project is undertaken with the belief that toxic tours have something to teach those of us who are not necessarily from environmental justice communities, particularly those of us who are interested in tourism as a mode of acting in the world. The lessons toxic tours offer, thus, exceed their most practical and important intention: to bring an end to the toxic assault of communities. The subsequent pages aim to engage what some of those insights might be.

A Map

The benefit of interdisciplinary work, one would hope, is the way it offers a more nuanced account of the complexity of our world, despite the recognition that no one version can include everything. By making connections across various spheres of public discourse, such research refuses the insularity of any one community and challenges us to imagine how we might find ways to work across intellectual and political borders. The uncertainty of this approach, of course, is that when one travels more than one path, one risks losing some or all of those who try to follow, because the journey can become so unpredictable. A brief map seems a fitting aid in these moments.

Chapters 1 and 2 parse out terms, cultural perceptions, historical trends, and theoretical debates that inform and are informed by the practice of "toxic tours." Written to foreground broader academic and cultural discourses, they engage popular culture, which, as Stuart Hall reminds us, "is the arena of consent and resistance. It is partly where hegemony arises, and where it is secured."[73] In chapter 1, "Tourist Itineraries," I engage four main characteristics of tourism that often are raised in tourist studies when considering the politics of this practice: the primacy of vision, the privilege of having a home, the role of tourism as education, and the more recent trend involving the pleasure of touring sites of tragedy. Chapter 2, "Toxic Baggage," shifts to U.S. culture's love/hate relationship with the toxic and examines how attempts to counter toxic production and distribution face the challenge of breaking silences about pain, our bodies, and the limits of communication more broadly. This conversation leads me to trace the persistent toxic metaphor of "social pollution," which informs hegemonic attitudes regarding women, people of color, lower-income communities, and the ill.

Chapters 3, 4, and 5 foreground specific toxic tour practices. Although they build on the overall arguments of the book, each chapter also detours through an additional theoretical dialogue and particular historical context that informs the politics of each particular tour. This structural pattern reflects the dialectic between theory and practice and between local and national struggles inherent to this project. Rather than offering an exhaustive account of toxic tours, I want to provide more nuanced interpretations of three in-depth examples to illuminate the cultural practices and meanings at stake in these toxic tours. Chapter 3, "Sites and Sacralization," travels through the area between Baton Rouge and New Orleans, Louisiana, to introduce an example of a "typical" toxic tour to illustrate how it both enacts what Dean MacCannell calls the tourist practice of "sight sacralization" and contests conventional tourist representations as a tactic to subvert oppressive environmental and social practices. In chapter 4, "Cancer and Co-optation," rather than touring at the site of the pollution's most extreme impacts, an example of a tour performed at the site of the polluters' corporate headquarters is explored to analyze how such a shift in the location of touring helps highlight concerns about accountability, public relations, and bodies in protest. Although this book examines toxic tourism primarily from the perspective of the United States, chapter 5, "Identification and Imagined Communities," explores toxins and toxic tours that travel across national borders between the United States and Mexico. Since toxic tours are offered not only in person but also and increasingly through various media technologies, such as websites and film, this chapter draws on a short video, participant observation, interviews, and the previous two chapters to interrogate how much "going there" matters in a globalized world.

Although toxic tours clearly share a democratic politics of space, in which communal experiences in a given place are valued, toxic tours also involve shared time. In the conclusion, "All the Time in the World," I engage the theme of time to foreground the potential roles that toxic tourists, tourists in general, and, therefore, people more broadly might have in constituting a democracy that is more inclusive than the one in which we currently live. Drawing on cultural theorists Michel de Certeau and Henry Giroux, I contend that toxic tourism encourages us to reimagine the value and practice of "public time" in environmental decision making so that we can think and act more deliberately.

On the toxic tour I re-present in chapter 3, the guide emphasized that "a toxic tour is not just about the chemical plants. It's about the history, the culture, everything that goes on." Indeed, toxic tours are an attempt to address publicly not just local struggles, but also the larger symbolic and material patterns of pollution and injustice that enable these unjust situations. As cultural performances, they provide the opportunity for a meaningful and sensual communicative exchange in which to share stories, feelings, experiences, physical ailments, living conditions, and arguments in a way that is more visceral, immediate, and, I hope, engaging than traditional political venues for environmental decision making.[74] Toxic tours, therefore, are a call to democratic action. They invite participants to find cultural, economic, technical, and, perhaps most emphatically, practical solutions for communities that are suffering as the result of ongoing toxic pollution. In the subsequent pages I hope to make more apparent these promises and how toxic tours can teach us about ourselves, our planet, and our way of living.

I

Tourist Itineraries

This book began, in part, by recalling the prevalent disdain with which tourists often are referred. It is remarkable, given how many of us tour, that "acting like a tourist" is so often an insult, a prevalent euphemism for looking out of place, making inappropriate remarks, and generally display-ing cultural ignorance without subtlety. In addition to the more toxic undercurrents of this perception, the stigma of the tourist also has served as fodder for comedy, as in the *National Lampoon Vacation* films starring Chevy Chase (1983, 1985, 1987, 1989) and the *Crocodile Dundee* series star-ring Paul Hogan (1986, 1988, 2001).[1] In these repeated, popular depic-tions, the tourist is represented as an uneducated, crass stereotype of a country's citizens, as well as a humorous personality who is noticeably and awkwardly unable to assimilate or "blend in" with local cultures and environments. Indeed, the neophyte tourist—or at least the tourist who appears to be a novice—is usually portrayed as one of the most embar-rassing, obnoxious, and amusing characters in popular culture.

At times, of course, some view tourists and tour destinations quite romantically—especially once a person seems to have become an experi-enced, adaptable tourist. These tourists are admired as noble explorers, danger seekers, risk takers, and those who are willing to place their bodies "on the line" to learn new things and to meet new people. Rather than representing the epitome of "low culture" and a lack of education, a well-traveled tourist is sometimes perceived as a person who exemplifies what it means to act "worldly," thus serving as a kind of multicultural diplo-mat between nations. In this sense, the tourist possesses the opportunity not only to purchase souvenirs on her or his journey but also to accrue what Pierre Bourdieu calls "cultural capital," or the accumulation of experiences that may raise one's status in bourgeois circles (and, arguably, beyond).[2] From this more favorable perspective, the tourist is capable of becoming savvier than the nontourist—a "citizen of the world," not just of one country or government. Amidst more banal examples, recall how performances of international spies like James Bond or Sydney Bristow are admired for their ability to travel to foreign lands, assess the local scene, adapt, and then escape.[3]

These more romanticized depictions of tourist figures might also include the benevolent, more laid-back and carefree individual who welcomes new experiences. Perhaps one of the more famous and nuanced depictions in the United States of this type of tourist is Pulitzer Prize–winning novelist Anne Tyler's acclaimed book that was turned into a Hollywood film of the same title: *The Accidental Tourist*.[4] The protagonist of this drama is appropriately named Macon Leary (as is the cinematic star cast in the role, William Hurt). Leary writes travel guides for U.S. businessmen who frequently—and reluctantly—have to leave their homes and families for their jobs. His instructions help the man on the go to create an individualized version of what Tim Edensor calls an "enclavic space," in which the tourist is able to isolate him- or herself from any spontaneous and unpredictable experiences. Leary advises travelers on planes to "always bring a book, as protection against strangers. Magazines don't last. Newspapers from home will make you homesick, and newspapers from elsewhere will remind you you don't belong. You know how alien another paper's typeface seems." In Paris at the Champs-Elyseés, he chooses a Burger King as an ideal eating place, but warns his date: "Careful, . . . these are not the Whoppers you are used to. You'll want to scrape the extra pickle and onion off." Following Leary's precautions, tourists are promised the ability "to pretend they had never left home."[5] The irony of this narrative, of course, is that by the end of the story we realize that the protagonist's own happiness lies in rejecting all the advice he has written for years and, instead, in embracing a wider variety of touristic experiences by learning from and valuing differences, change, and impulsiveness.

These contrasting projections of the tourist are predicated on the choices a tourist makes. Will the tourist fall into a "tourist trap"? How might the tourist negotiate local customs of language, dress, and decorum? Is the tourist interested in communicating with or ignoring host communities, tourist operators, and other tourists? When the tourist risks experiencing the "new," will it be with eager grace or reluctant awkwardness?

The characteristics that enable these various portrayals and their ability to resonate with mass audiences provide a glimpse into the choices and distinctions raised by tourist practices and cultural perceptions of them. In this chapter I interrogate both negative and positive interpretations of tourists primarily put forth by scholars of tourism as a context for better understanding the cultural politics of toxic tours. In short, toxic tours are an appropriation of tourism as a discourse, a pragmatic mode of communication, and a way of acting in the world. As such, this chapter's broad overview aims to begin to help readers unfamiliar with tourist studies to appreciate more fully how toxic tours reinforce, challenge, and transform common assumptions about our tourist imaginaries.

"Touring" includes a wide variety of practices, from going on a day trip to a local historical monument to vacationing abroad for a month, from experiencing one's last hike in the woods to living through one's first safari in a savannah, and from walking through a potential home to stopping at an art museum.[6] Given the range of experiences these ways of operating enable, almost every book or article written on tourism provides a different definition. Rather than surveying all of these arguments here, let me offer a very basic, working definition: "tourism" generally connotes the traveling from place to place, in a sequence. Hence, as one toxic tour guide explained to me when asked why her coalition of grassroots activists calls their toxic tour a "tour": "It's semantics: a march goes from point a to point b; we go from a to b to c to d to [etc.]."[7]

Yet, beyond purely formal considerations, the naming, facilitating, and enacting of tours implicates much broader social patterns and trajectories. Tours negotiate power relations between the people, places, and values involved. By placing tourist scholarship into dialogue with the practice of toxic touring, this chapter highlights four often-noted and interrelated characteristics about the cultural politics of tourism: the primacy of vision, the privilege of having a home, the role of tourism as education, and the more recent trend involving the pleasure of touring sites of tragedy. These traits, I believe, become particularly salient by the end of the chapter as they lead me to a discussion of toxic tours as modalities that constitute, at least in part, public participation in civic decision making.

Embodying the Visual

The visual stubbornly tends to take center stage of tourist research. This focus is unsurprising, since in most tourist scholarship and in Western culture more broadly, the visual has long been privileged above other embodied ways of sensing the world. Metaphors and references to sight still pervade academic and nonacademic ways of knowing. "Seeing is believing," after all. Add the mode of *sight*seeing to the pursuit of knowledge, and it is no wonder that ocularcentrism abounds. Snap a photograph. Buy a "picture perfect" postcard. Stop at a scenic vista. All of these tourist activities appear to revolve around one's ability to see, or, perhaps more specifically, as some academics would negatively describe it, on one's privilege to exert "the gaze."

"The gaze" implies that in our looking we come no closer to whom or what we are looking at and, in fact, that we may move further away affectively as a result of our look. Film scholar Laura Mulvey is best known in cinema studies for theorizing when scopophilia (the pleasure of looking) is constituted by a voyeuristic male gaze and, as a result, transforms a woman into a spectacle on screen. This process of becoming an erotic object for the pleasure of another's consumption, she argues, positions the female as passive and the male as active.[8] Similarly, Carol Adams and Steve Baker ask us to consider how the ways that we visualize animals as objects (e.g., "meat"), parts (e.g., "breast" or "leg"), or symbolic representations in our everyday lives (e.g., cartoon characters) might enable us to distance ourselves more readily from the subjectivity of nonhuman animals and, thus, further enable the objectification, exploitation, and extinction of other species.[9]

Perhaps best known for illuminating the politics of sight to tourist practices is *The Tourist Gaze,* in which John Urry claims that the visual is the primary or most fundamental sense involved in tourist practices.[10] Through emphasizing the social or collective dimensions of touring, Urry argues that what tourists "gaze at" or expect to "gaze upon" is central to tourist experiences as romantic individuals or part of larger collectives. Seven years after putting forth his initial argument about the primacy of sight, Urry revisits his initial argument in an essay coauthored with Carol Crawshaw on the relationship between tourism and photography. Together they clarify a collective position on tourism and vision, one that responds in part to criticisms of Urry's initial perspective. Although they acknowledge Michel Foucault's critiques of the visual gaze as a disciplining technology of spectacle, science, and punishment, they go on to suggest that such a position is too easily reduced to fodder for tourist scholars to denigrate the role of vision in tourist experience—as though sight were somehow more "superficial" than the other senses. Further, although they admit that other senses are involved in tourist experiences, they claim that a completely pejorative perspective on the visual ignores its role not just as part of these experiences but also as central to them. "It is the visual images of places," they insist, "that give shape and meaning to the anticipation, experience and memories of travelling."[11]

Without a doubt, as Urry, Crawshaw, and others have observed, the visual plays an important role in most tourist practices, as it does in most ways of operating for most people. Sight can be a valuable sense to assess who we have been, are, and want to be. However, I disagree with their privileging of sight and, instead, wish to emphasize that there is more to tourist performances and the performances that tourists consume.[12] Too often, an ocularcentric approach suggests an image of tourists somehow transformed into walking eyeballs, without bodies attached. Yet, looking is itself an embodied experience—one that influences the rest of the body's ability to experience the world, and vice versa. When we look, we peer over the edge of a canyon to feel a sense of the fragility of our position, or we lean backward so that we can admire the top of a tall building. We hold binoculars to catch a glimpse of a bird that we heard in a tree, or we grab onto a safety bar to ensure that we don't fall out of an amusement park ride when we close our eyes. We smell the uniquely colored flower that "caught our eye," and we hold our breath as we dive into a scenic lake.

Narrowing our appreciation of tourist experiences to sight not only ignores how our senses work in conjunction with one another but also excludes the wider range of sensations involved, including perhaps the most obvious one, sound. For those who can hear, how can we imagine touring without guides or hotel staff telling us where to sleep, eat, or even look? What would a vacation be without the sounds offered by our particular tourist destinations, such as ocean waves, winter winds, lion roars, roller-coaster screams, or steel drums? Fetishizing and singling out the visual aspects of touring leaves out all of these audible encounters and much, much more. Simply stated, there are some experiences, some memories, and some knowledges that are not limited to sight. Perhaps, in fact, there are none.[13] Sometimes, we communicate without looking at all. Sometimes, what is most striking or telling to us is a smell, a sound, a touch, a taste, or a sensation we feel because of our proximity to another animal, place, or event. As such, we would do well to heed Adrian Franklin's call to address those instances when senses other than sight serve as the primary motivation for a whole range of popular tourist practices, such as taste (e.g., wine tasting), smell (e.g., a perfume factory), sound (e.g., a music festival), and adrenalin rushes (e.g., bungee jumping or gambling).

When touring toxins, the limits of the visual become all the more apparent. In fact, one of the primary constraints for anti-toxic activists is a lack of visual evidence. If you are familiar with toxins, you know that their detection often is not predicated on sight. Many people who see a toxic dump for the first time are surprised at how benign it looks. Likewise, communities are frequently unaware of the fact that they are polluted by toxins until their bodies start to manifest pain—in those moments when they find themselves, for example, struggling to breathe as a result of respiratory complications, feeling their eyes begin to water after going outside, or finding out from a doctor that they have cancer.

Compounding the frequent invisibility of toxins is the troubling fact that the visibility of this pollution and its environmentally unjust effects often are excluded from elite sight due to racial and economic residential segregation. Limiting our epistemologies of travel and tourism to what we can see exacerbates these power differentials. By refusing to explore beyond what hegemonic relationships help make invisible, we provide further, albeit indirect, consent to the distance necessary to alienate us from each other. We enable ourselves to believe in the false presumption that our lives do not affect or depend on anyone or any place that we cannot see, even though our increasingly global and industrialized world belies a different truth.

In addition, as Dwight Conquergood claims, when a researcher engages people and practices that have historically been marginalized by Western biases, decentering sight and script becomes even more critical. An ocularcentric or scriptocentric approach, he argues, limits the researcher to "the [colonial] powers to see, to search, and to seize."[14] In other words, sensitivity to a much wider range of communicative symbols, practices, and effects would enable researchers to be more attentive to those people who have been pushed into the margins, such as women and people of color, and to the communicative practices that have been marginalized by Western biases of so-called high culture. Consequently, focusing our research solely on the visual facets of touring has much more at stake than merely being incomplete.

Remedying the dominance of the visual in tourist scholarship thus entails at least three changes. First, a less ocularcentric perspective requires us to realize that even when we are looking, we are looking from an embodied subjectivity. Merely focusing on what we can see (or not see), at minimum, excludes the way the ability to see, like any other sense, interacts with and is conditioned by the rest of our bodies. Second, such a perspective reminds us that any tour involves more of our bodies than just looking. This focus on the body need not involve a naive move away from conversations about or understandings of power; in fact, it should expand them. Oppression, for example, can be enabled as much—if not, at times, more—by a tourist's disaffected distance or nonconsensual touching as it is by sight. Third, decentering the visual as the primary focus of all tour experiences may enable those who study tours to be more aware of our own capacities to privilege and to perpetuate Western or colonial sensibilities. Embracing reflexivity toward our corporeal practices and the ways we study them, we might find ourselves more open to becoming what Ruth Behar calls "vulnerable observers."[15] This would involve putting our own cameras and notebooks down—at times—in order to appreciate more fully our significance as "outsiders" *feeling present* within a specific place and time and how we might be implicated in what we are witnessing.

On toxic tours, this sense of presence or willingness to feel connected to the people and places toured is particularly important to the political efficacy of the practice. When limited solely to "the gaze," a toxic tour certainly does risk objectifying the people and the places toured. Some of the people with whom I have discussed toxic tours have likened toxic tours, in their worst possible imagined and practiced scenarios, to visiting a zoo. For example, when asked in an interview if he had any concerns about the use of toxic tours, one environmental activist shared that he lives in a neighborhood where toxic tours are held.[16] Those tours, he said, appear to be a very insulting performance of "the exoticism of poverty," in which he senses an attitude akin to: "Let's go visit the poor people, the poor people in the zoo."[17] Similarly, on two different occasions when I have presented my research on toxic tours in academic forums, one specific colleague (who, like the aforementioned activist, is a European American, middle class, higher educated male) has expressed concern about toxic tours. He continues to wonder if toxic tours function as exploitative zoos, with predominantly white and wealthier tourists quickly passing by the neighborhoods of people of color and low-income communities as if they were exotic animals on display. This tension between engagement and objectification will rear its head repeatedly throughout this book. For now, though, it seems helpful to highlight the role sight plays in this process of negotiation and to delve further into the genuinely disconcerting analogy suggested between zoos and toxic tours.

Historically, the exploitation of people and of the land have been intertwined. The rise in the popularity of zoos, or what Bob Mullan and Gary Marvin call "zoo culture," reflects this enmeshed sensibility. In the midnineteenth- to mid-twentieth-century exhibitions of Great Britain and France, for example, natives of these countries' colonies were brought in to build replicas of their homes and then to "inhabit them, putting on displays of their arts and crafts . . . religious ceremonies, dances and theatrical presentations. The exhibition of exotic people and exotic animals both in the zoo world and in the colonial exhibitions had a commercial purpose but it also enhanced the exhibiting nation's prestige."[18] Hence, not only were humans and nonhuman animals both abducted from their homes and kinship communities, but their mutual forced imprisonment and performance of "acting naturally" served as fodder for amusement and national fantasies. As such, their pain of dislocation and exploitation was deemed insignificant compared to the colonial desire for differentiation, namely, to position humans and nonhumans as "exotic" or "foreign." Further, recent research has found that despite the continued popularity of zoos as venues centered on the "display of 'genetically pure' specimens,"[19] zoo culture is becoming increasingly invested in providing an atmosphere of entertainment, often articulating—or linking—live animals with the animated ones that currently proliferate our cultural landscape.[20] In addition, Third World peoples continue to be marketed to tourists as "unchanged, unrestrained, and uncivilized,"[21] and the ideal "native" desired remains predominantly anonymous, female, and brown.[22]

Despite the importance of reflexively considering the similar motivations and tropes involved in the stubbornly oppressive legacies of "zoo culture" while analyzing the politics of toxic tours, it is vital to emphasize two fundamental differences between toxic tours and zoos as tourist experiences. First, unlike zoos, toxic tours do not construct artificial "homes" or "workplaces" for the sole purpose of a mass-marketed tourist industry. The hosts of a toxic tour do live, work, play, pray, and bury their dead in the spaces toured prior to the tour and, in most cases, subsequent to the tour. In fact, their attachment to the spaces they inhabit tends to be a primary motivator in seeking to improve the environmental conditions of those spaces. Second, unlike those who are involuntarily drugged, captured, and transported to a zoo (and not necessarily in that order), the people who host toxic tours are the ones extending the invitation to visit. Although some are ancestors of slaves, they are not acting in the capacity of a slave when they organize a toxic tour. They have asked, challenged, and hoped for "outsiders" to tour. I do not mean to imply that some toxic tours or specific tourists might not appear obnoxious or invasive to some residents; indeed, some toxic tours that I have participated in have included tourists who have been bored, tired, insensitive, or distracted. Toxic tours, however, crucially involve consent on the part of the hosts. If there is discomfort on the part of those who are not from these communities, that may be more a cause to look inward than a reason to refuse the invitation. The oppressive tendencies of "the gaze" are not in the act of looking per se but in the choice to look only when the chances that the Other will look back have virtually been eliminated.

Mobilizing the Home

In addition to the ambivalent role of "the gaze," one of the primary privileges assumed of the tourist is the freedom to end the tour where he or she began: at home. More than any other characteristic, this one perhaps provokes the most cynicism and disdain for tourists and touristic ways of operating. Zymunt Bauman writes: "The tourist is a conscious and systematic seeker of experience. . . . The tourists want to immerse themselves in a strange and bizarre element (a pleasant feeling, a tickling and rejuvenating feeling, like letting oneself be buffeted by sea waves)—on condition, though, that it will not stick to the skin and thus can be shaken off whenever they wish. They choose the elements to jump into according to how strange, but also how innocuous, they are. . . . [And, in the end,] the tourist has a home."[23] The possibility of returning "whenever they wish," seemingly without barriers, to a "home" clearly marks the privilege of tourists. For the tourist, the existence of a home implies the possibility that a tourist is not *from there* and, therefore, can exercise the power both to visit and to leave. This dual movement arguably distinguishes the tourist from other traveling subjectivities, such as a person forced to migrate from her or his home.[24]

Home also is invoked, as mentioned earlier, with characters such as Macon Leary, who wish to construct what Edensor calls an "enclavic space." Edward M. Bruner describes this promise of many commercial, packaged elite tours as follows: "Tourists, then, experience home while away, a home created by the tourist industry in the accommodations and modes of travel, and a home constructed by the tourists themselves in conversation."[25] In this formulation, the tourist is not only presumed to have a home to which to return but also has the privilege of never feeling like one has left home.

But what is a "home"? As Bauman implies, home often is conceived as a concrete place of origin or, in more illusive terms, a feeling of stability and of belonging, where one may return with certainty when an experience is over. Yet, increasingly, this sense of home seems rather simplistic, both historically and theoretically. In what Lucy R. Lippard calls as "multicentered society," does anyone really come from one place that never changes?[26] Assuming that the world and those of us living in it frequently are in flux, it seems that "home" need not be limited to such a static sense of material or geographic constancy (e.g., "I live in that house in x town"). As the cliché goes, sometimes "home is where the heart is." Alternatively, as Bruner implies, home is what we construct through practices and conversations. Hence, a sense of self, special person, smell, token of affection, or habit might induce *the sense* that one is home.[27] Conversely, one could imagine a person abused by someone in her or his "home" or persecuted by the state under "house arrest" as not feeling "at home" for several years or more, whether or not she or he slept in the same bed every night.

In this more accessible, mobile, fluid, and less nostalgic formulation, "home" still tends to signify one's ability to feel "centered" or "grounded" in a particular space and time. Yet even this structure of feeling of "home" is more or less difficult to achieve, depending on one's privilege. Creating a sense of home varies, for example, between the tenured university professor who has recently migrated across the country to a new job, the military solider who is stationed abroad, and the refugee fleeing for her or his life from a bloody civil war. In other words, the politics and compulsions involved in leaving, returning, and creating a feeling of "home" may be too complex to generalize in any meaningful way.

Further, women and men tend to relate to the privilege of tourism differently, because women and men generally have experienced their relationships to home and travel differently. For example, women of "developing" or Third World nations historically have been packaged as attractions for "developed" or First World heterosexual male tourists to see, exploit, and leave. In addition, with a relatively small number of notable exceptions, Western women of privilege from a very young age have historically been encouraged to stay at home in the kitchen and with the children, while men and boys of privilege have historically been goaded to travel on great adventures for work and play.[28]

Despite what might seem like a fundamental difference between male and female histories of travel and home, gender has also shaped and con-

tinues to be shaped by race, class, nationality, ability, and many other identities that are privileged or oppressed by what MacCannell calls "social
structural differentiation."[29] Enloe, thus, insists that we also recognize that
"[n]o matter how good the feminist tourist's intention, the relationship
between the British woman on holiday and the working women of Portu-
gal seems to fall short of international sisterhood."[30] Tourism may exacerbate preexisting tensions produced by differentiation, because it brings
together diverse populations who often live separate lives. Tourism entails
contact. Although it tends to shine a spotlight on the front stage of the
lives of those who are hosts, tourism still poses opportunities to heighten
our awareness of hierarchies. The moment the tourist and the maid see
each other as they pass in the hallway of a hotel, for example, serves as a
reminder of social hierarchies. It does not necessarily enable the tourist
to know where the maid lives or plays (or vice versa), but this moment
does throw into relief how one's pleasure may be predicated on the labor
of another.

In a scathing critique of the tension between tourists and hosts, Kincaid
shares why, from her experiences growing up in Antigua, she believes
there exists a belief that "a tourist is an ugly human being":

> That the native does not like the tourist is not hard to explain. For
> every native of every place is a potential tourist, and every tourist is
> a native of somewhere. Every native everywhere lives a life of over-
> whelming and crushing banality and boredom and desperation and
> depression, and every deed, good and bad, is an attempt to forget
> this. Every native would like a rest, every native would like a tour.
> But . . . they are too poor to escape the reality of their lives; and
> they are too poor to live properly in the place where they live, which
> is the very place you, the tourist, want to go—so when the natives
> see you, the tourist, they envy you, they envy your ability to leave
> your own banality and boredom, they envy your ability to turn their
> own banality and boredom into a source of pleasure for yourself.

Kincaid's analysis hones in on the privilege of the tourist to have a place
called "home" with "all its nice house things," including a backyard and "all
its nice back-yard things," and to be able to return to it after visiting some-

place else.[31] Even Kincaid, however, does not describe "tourists" and "natives" as static, binary categories. Rather, she theorizes the resentment of the tourist (the always-already native) by the native (the always-already potential tourist) as one of envy over the ability of the tourist to escape or evade her or his everyday life (of banality and boredom) in the name of pleasure at that particular juncture.[32] In other words, she emphasizes the differences between the tourist and the native while simultaneously challenging the tourist to identify with the native as someone not only capable but actively feeling similar (though often unfulfilled) desires to escape her or his banality.

Like Kincaid, I want to emphasize that a primary characteristic of tourist practices is that it tends to entail what I would call a "counterexperience" of *everyday life,* something different (or perceived as different) from one's daily routine.[33] Although we all are immersed in the ways we operate in our everyday lives, tourism involves the visiting of *someone else's* everyday life. Tourism offers the opportunity to make what someone else may take for granted feel more present to the tourist. In other words, tourism pivots on at least the perception of difference between one's home and one's tour. Thus, if one lives in a tropical rain forest or works at a theme park, one is not considered a tourist of that forest or park. Touring a battlefield also presumes that you are not on a military "tour" at the time or living in an active war zone. Naming these practices "tourism" presumes that you can afford—in addition to the cost of traveling and the freedom not to have to work during that time—the energy and desire that are required to travel to a marker of horror. As Kincaid observes, it assumes that what the tourist takes for granted in her or his own life is somehow qualitatively different.[34]

Punctuating the tourist's privilege of home is the unfortunate circumstance that tourism is often born out of desperation and disaster, where alternative economies are scarce, historical legacies of colonialism remain grossly palpable, and oppression persists. Scholars have called this global legacy of trade-offs and exploitation "the devil's bargain," "a mixed blessing," and "a vicious circle."[35] No matter the name, the idea is that tourism usually promises local jobs and revenue; yet, in transforming a community or place into a "tourist attraction," that community and place are inevitably altered, and not necessarily for the better. When such a transformation is financially successful, for example, traffic, pollution, and cultural commodification tend to follow. Perhaps the most cited environmental example of this double bind in the United States is Yosemite National Park. From the sawyers in 1881 who cut a massive hole through the base of a giant sequoia tree allegedly to enhance tourist experiences to the approximately 3.5 million people who will visit the park this year alone (many in their own cars), the effects of tourism on Yosemite have evoked concern that tourism not only helped justify its birth as a protected site but might just help bring about its demise as anything close to what was originally so cherished.[36] Similarly, the "Keep It Hawaii" campaign sponsored by the Hawaiian Visitors Bureau was founded to encourage tourist vendors to maintain what is imagined as "traditional" Hawaiian culture rather than continuing to adapt to the times.[37]

Again, tourist industry desires to exacerbate distinctions between "home" and "away," self and Other, often reinforces a sense of exoticization and alienation. Bruner describes the cultural politics of this relationship between geographical segregation and tourism as follows: "The Other in *our* geography is a source of disgust; the Other in *their* geography is a source of pleasure. In *our* place the Other is pollution; in *their* place the Other is romantic, beautiful, and exotic. In *our* geography the Western elite pay not to see the Other; in *their* geography, the Western elite pay for the privilege of viewing and photographing. There is a racialization at home and a primitivization over there in exotica."[38] This sensibility of pollution and place, as I will discuss further in the next chapter, may speak more accurately to the true privilege of "home," not as a material, static place, but as a position of privilege to either segregate oneself from or gain access to the Other, depending on one's desires.

In order to counter this oppressive pattern exacerbated by mass commercial tourism, the toxic tours discussed in this book highlight bodies of land within dominant tourist imaginaries that could be described accurately as "disaster" areas. No longer home to a vibrant sugar plantations industry, southern Louisiana now offers toxic tours that show how communities are resisting the pollution pervading their homes and communities from the petrochemical industry. In San Francisco, toxic tour activists invite attention away from the sea otters at Fisherman's Wharf and the sunsets at the Golden Gate Bridge toward the painful and sometimes deadly deals being made in the Financial District by polluting industries and the institutions that help maintain them. Now that goods and services are more readily traded across the borders of the United States and Mexico, toxic tours remind us how people who live on the border remain trapped in devastating living and working conditions.

Implicitly at stake in toxic tours, then, are various democratic struggles about what rights and privileges one has and should have to define and to have a voice in the fate of one's homes and one's mobility. Many of the environmental justice activists I have met during my research appear to have a strong sense of home, in terms of the "self-centeredness" that I wrote of earlier. They all continue to fight to protect the spaces they call "home," whether that is the house where they are raising their family, the water supply in their entire city, or the air blowing across the place where we all live, Earth. Yet most residents' mobility is also more limited than those of the tourists who travel through their communities. Further, without toxic tours, many tourists remain comfortably alienated from the more extreme costs of our ongoing patterns of toxification.

Acknowledging such specific historical contexts and political implications of tourist practices, as June Jordan writes, need not make our findings any more simplified than those of theorists of identity. "Race and class and gender remain as real as the weather," she states, "[b]ut what they must mean about the contact about two individuals is less obvious and, like the weather, not predictable."[39] Likewise, when a tourist leaves her or his home to visit another's, a complex set of relations through which people may interact with one another is involved. Mere physical contact does not solve all problems. Whether these tourist opportunities are used to move, silence, engage, or coerce depends on the specific circumstances of any given tour, including both the lessons taught and the lessons learned.

Educating the Tourist

Contrary to the more cynical perspectives on touring, the historical legacy of tours for educational purposes may appear more benign. Since at least the traveling Sophists of Ancient Greece, mobility and education have been articulated together. Walking was such a significant part of Aristotle's lectures that, upon graduation, his students became known as Peripatetic philosophers, or those "who walk habitually and extensively." Walking subsequently played a significant role in the thinking processes of many philosophers, including Jeremy Bentham, Thomas Hobbes, John Stuart Mill, Friedrich Nietzsche, and, of course, Henry David Thoreau.[40] Perhaps unsurprisingly, as a form of travel often involving walking, tourism has enjoyed a long history as an educational endeavor in the West.[41]

The popularity of tourism as an educational practice rose as the modern tourism industry itself grew beyond religious motivations. "Grounded in the 'grand tour' of Europe as undertaken by the rich and powerful of the late seventeenth century and popularized in the excursions of Thomas Cook in the mid-nineteenth century, moving to another place, or from place to place, for the purposes of leisure in the Aristotelian sense, an educative pursuit or for the purposes of recreation . . . is principally an issue of personal development and improvement."[42] Visiting a range of historically and geographically significant places, tourists of the time also began traveling to learn languages and the arts. "The tour," as such, "was deemed a very necessary part of the training of future political and administrative leaders, as well as patrons of the arts."[43]

Thomas Cook is credited as "the father of modern tourism," because he catalyzed this popularization of tourism as essential to experiential education. In part he did so by expanding the market for self-improvement via travel from elite men to include elite women.[44] It is telling to note, as Franklin does, that Cook himself lived during dire times of capitalistic development in England.[45] Tourism for Cook, as well as for those whom he encouraged to tour, was motivated by depressing conditions at home and elsewhere, thus providing an escape from as well as access to the atrocities of modernity.

In addition, the educational value of tours has long been connected with nationalism. Gregory Clark, for example, argues that modern, domestic tourism of picturesque landscapes in the United States offers a "public experience" through which to enact a national sense of belonging. This, in turn, often prompts "individuals to make themselves over in the image of a collective identity that they find symbolized in their national landscape."[46] In other words, by exposing tourists to a wider range of people, places, and ways of living, domestic travel promises *to teach us* who "we" have been, are, and could be. It makes the nation, an example of what Benedict Anderson calls "the imaginary community," feel more present.[47]

Given these educational processes involved in constituting the modern and national subject, MacCannell argues that we should consider the tourist both as a designation for "actual tourists" and as a model to consider modern subjectivity more generally. Mark Neumann similarly claims that, in addition to reflecting on specific tourist practices, tourism is worth appreciating as "a powerful metaphor for the broader character and conflicts of modern life. Tourism," he insists, "is a way of moving through the world."[48] Moreover, Enloe emphasizes that "[t]ourism is as much ideology as physical movement. It is a package of ideas about industrial, bureaucratic life."[49] As both a modality of political subjectivity and an expression of ideology, therefore, the pedagogical practices of tourism are influenced by and influence specific social contexts and power relations, with the potential to oppress as well as to liberate. This sense of subjectivity is not static. Tourists are always in the process of becoming, precisely through the process of learning.

Whether we are being guided through a colleague's home for the first time, "doing the town" with a friend, or reading a marker on the wall of a museum, tourist practices teach us about the value of a particular space-time and the cultural significance (or insignificance) of various structures, behaviors, and attitudes, often according to the vantage point of a tour guide.[50] In other words, as guides ourselves or as those who have been "shown the ropes" by tour guides, we choose to point out or are eager to discover what is important to us and presumably to others. "It is the 'you have got to see this,' or 'taste this,' or 'feel this' that is the originary moment in the touristic relation."[51] This pedagogical process of enunciating and sharing the "this" worth noting is not just performatively realized through stories made of words but is also constituted through gestures, turns, looks, and various other embodied expressions. As such, tourism is an inventive, embodied epistemological process of selection and deflection.

In addition to involving experiences that simply are shared, the pedagogical function of tours relies heavily on linking the places where they occur to specific educational lessons. Where tours exist and the tours themselves constitute each other dialectically. As de Certeau emphasizes, "Every description is more than 'a fixation,' it is 'a culturally creative act.' Each enunciation has distributive power and performative force (it does what it says) when an ensemble of circumstances is brought together. Then it founds spaces."[52] Involving highly descriptive and performative acts of enunciation that are both enabled by and result in the creation (or loss) of spaces, tour guides and structures (e.g., displays and placards) provide educational frames to inform us of the people, places, things, and events that are worth remembering and those that are acceptable to forget. We, in turn, tend to recall certain figures, details, and actions and to forget others.

These spatial and historical lessons, however grounded in the places of the present, are not relegated solely to contemporary ways of living. Tours of antebellum plantation homes, for example, offer a staged display of a past way of operating in everyday life.[53] Walking through houses, slave quarters, or gardens, guides claim: "This is where they lived, what they cooked, and how they worked." Such instructions perform a claim of *authenticity*: "this is a *typical* native house; this is the *very* place the leader fell; this is the *actual* pen used to sign law; this is the *original* manuscript; this is an *authentic* Tlingit fish club; this is a *real* piece of the *true* Crown of Thorns."[54] These historical lessons of the "real" or the "authentic," whether conscious or unconscious, imply the role of tourism as pedagogy.

MacCannell, however, reminds us that "the tour you get is not necessarily the tour you are given. There is always a gap. Humans interpret."[55] These varied interpretations, in turn, foster greater possibilities. "Since tourists bring with them different cultural expectations, narrative forms and meanings," as Edensor argues, "such sites are often the locus for *a proliferation of stories*."[56] Rather than completely accepting or completely rejecting these beliefs, tourists tend to negotiate both dominant and resistant beliefs framing a tour.[57] Paying attention to tourist stories may thus teach tourists and those who study tourism as much about the tourists as the toured. In addition, though there are no guarantees, like any other pedagogical or communication practice, tours can improve their probability of success based on experience, adaptability, reflexivity, and so forth.

Some criticize tours as being based on an economy or logic of consumption, a practice encouraging the subject formation of consumers and not citizens in a binary opposition. Rather than illuminating new ways of life in ways that promise to inform and to transform the tourist, this perspective emphasizes how tourism can be used as a means to objectify peoples, practices, and places by isolating, displaying, and commodifying their worth solely in terms of financial exchange. Indeed, "consumption" may connote the destructive "using up" of something, someone, or someplace. Yet, de Certeau argues that this simplified notion of consumption does not grant the consumer any agency or ability to interpret, much less to create something new from the act of consumption. Instead, he suggests that consumption might be appreciated better as a productive practice through which new possibilities may emerge. When walking in a city (as in de Certeau's famous example) or touring a particular place, the one walking or touring has choices to make and, in enunciating those choices, founds and reaffirms her or his agency.[58]

Toxic tours turn on this more nuanced conceptualization of consumption. "Although they consume time and resources," on the one hand, Giovanna Di Chiro emphasizes that, on the other hand, toxic tours denaturalize free-market individualism and teach tourists "that their consumer choices are not always based on possessing full information about the life cycle of particular products—there are very real consequences of consumer actions on the health and quality of life of other peoples and environments."[59] In other words, toxic tours attempt to highlight how consumption might "use up" time, energy, and resources in a negative sense; yet, in their own consumptive performances, they also promise the opportunity to produce something new, in this case, it is hoped, a reflexivity on the part of the tourist about her or his role in helping to produce our toxic culture.

Even for the savviest, most educated tourist, however, avoiding the unjust politics of touring is practically impossible, if for no other reason than finding a tourist destination void of bodies in pain is almost impossible. As the executive director of Amnesty International observed in 1997: "if travelers were to avoid every country that violates somebody's rights, itineraries would be remarkably short. Only one country—Iceland—has never been cited for a serious human rights abuse. And while the Blue Lagoon and Thingvellir are magnificent sites, their novelty, to say nothing of their tranquility, would quickly disappear if the world's tourists were to limit themselves to that politically pristine place."[60] Reflective of politics itself, tourism never can be politically "pure" or without compromise.[61] In effect, hating the tourist for continuing to tour given the existence of these conditions displaces claims for political accountability from the macro conditions that enable social structures of pain to the practices of individual tourists.

With all that said, seeking an educational experience might not always be what mobilizes the tourist. Consider, for example, common impulses to travel to a hotter or colder climate to feel one's body in the warmth of the sun or the crisp air of a winter sky. Even so, many tour experiences, even though not obviously educational, do suggest a pedagogy of self-improvement and becoming: "You *have* to backpack in Europe while you're young"; "You mean you've *never* taken your kids to Disney World?"; "You really *haven't lived* until you've gone to . . . " Such imperatives suggest that once you do backpack in Europe or take your kids to Disney World, and so on, you'll transform, and presumably for the better. The normative force that is foundational to touristic pedagogy is that— somewhere between the tours provided and the perspectives brought to them—new possibilities are likely to emerge.

Politicizing the Pleasurable

As noted earlier, many tourist practices continue to offer a means not only to escape temporarily from one's everyday life but also to travel to another's, thus providing what I have called a counterexperience of everyday life. A growing number of tours promise variations of this kind of counterexperience, or of "walking in someone else's shoes." Now I turn toward those instances when tours provide an opportunity to learn about how other people have lived through their most trying times. In addition to the opportunity to tour concentration camps in Poland and Germany, for example, tourists can travel to the U.S. Holocaust Memorial Museum in Washington, D.C., where they may be handed an identification card of a person who lived—and often died—during the Holocaust. The idea of the card is to offer each tourist a way to personalize the broader educational narratives displayed in the museum by identifying with individual stories. In numerous towns across the United States, from Detroit, Michigan, to Williamsburg, Virginia, tourists are also invited to participate in interactive historical reenactments of colonial slavery by imagining themselves as part of slave auctions, punishments, and escapes. Moreover, the Cherokee Trail of Tears Commemorative Park in Hopkinsville, Kentucky, located at an encampment site for Cherokees who were forcibly relocated in the 1830s, now features the burial site of two Cherokee chiefs who died during the journey, which is known as "the Trail of Tears" to most European Americans and as "The Trail Where They Cried" to most Native Americans. Tourists who plan their trips in advance can witness an annual intertribal PowWow in September. The list continues.

Like those who question if toxic tours are merely replicas of colonial zoo culture, Shohat and Stam doubt whether tours more broadly can create a pedagogical experience that initiates structural change and not merely the ethnocentric reinforcement of one's own status as somehow removed from or "above" the people and places toured: "The historical inertia of race, class, and gender stratification is not so easily erased. Nor should an antiracist pedagogy rely on empathy alone. A person might 'sample' oppression and conclude nothing more than: 'C'est la vie' or 'Thank God it wasn't me!' The point is not merely to communicate sensations but rather to advance structural understanding and promote change."[62] Similarly, Di Chiro argues that it is important for toxic tours to consider whether they are offering opportunities "to bear witness or to take action."[63] As much as they mark our fears and cynicism, these concerns belie the optimistic possibility that tours, toxic or otherwise, might enable a range of responses, including empathy, gratification, and politicization.

Touring a site of death or bodily pain particularly raises concern about the possibility of exploiting those who have suffered, not just due to the question of consent on the part of those toured, but also as a result of our cultural concerns about the relationship between pleasure and human suffering. This increasingly popular tourist trend has raised the attention of tourist scholars. Why do tourists look forward to visiting battlefields, graveyards, and the public memorials that continue to proliferate throughout our national landscape? In the nation's capital, what is the role of representing painful tragedies committed on our soil or on our bodies? Why do some tourists travel abroad to visit places where other atrocities occurred? Does this growing trend in tourism speak highly of the tourist's intentions? Or is it merely an affirmation of previous suspicions about the intentions of tourists?

Lippard recalls the term "rubbernecking" used in reference to tourists when she was a child. Instead of perceiving this term as solely negative (implying a perverse desire to relish others' tragedies), she suggests the possibility of appropriating it as a complicated set of desires that motivate a tourist "to stretch, literally, past her own experiences." Yet she calls the recent trend to tour sites where people have died "tragic tourism," presumably because they involve remembering tragedies.[64] Given her own defense of "rubbernecking," the question remains: Is the touring of these sites themselves tragic?

Alternatively, Foley and Lennon have coined the phrase "dark tourism" "to signify a fundamental shift in the way in which death, disaster, and other grotesque atrocities are being handled by those who offer associated tourism 'products,'" particularly "the commodification of anxiety and doubt."[65] Their work provides an important study of an increasing trend in commercial tourism.[66] Yet, at minimum, this characterization seems to risk placing this practice as somehow outside "pleasure," undercutting the hope expressed by those extending the invitation to learn or to become transformed by their tours.

To elaborate, "pleasure" is not a universal feeling or emotion. Planning a recent trip with two of my closest friends reminds me of this. One's ideal day includes manicures and facials; the other's involves whitewater rafting or kayaking. Further, in an undergraduate course on environmental tourism, I tested the waters early on to find out what type of tourists my students were. One of the questions I asked was, If they had to choose a vacation to Las Vegas or to the Grand Canyon, which one would they prefer? Contrary to my own desires, but unsurprising to me, the vast majority chose the currently hip, incredibly commercialized, and popularly depicted destination of Vegas.

Given these examples of various tourist desires, it seems more accurate to assume that tourists who choose to attend tours and visit tourist destinations that involve witnessing or remembering bodily pain or tragedy *gain some sense of pleasure from those visits.* Although those who choose to participate in such tours do so for a variety of reasons, this complex set of motivations exceeds "dark" or "tragic" desires, to include, at minimum, a sense of obligation, a desire to learn more, and a belief that these touring practices do make a difference. This practice might not involve the same sense of pleasure some feel when biting into a chocolate-dipped strawberry or others feel when hanging upside down on an amusement park ride; however, these later experiences are not the only forms of pleasure that exist.

Of course, sites of bodily pain can invite tourists to feel somber, heartbroken, and quite depressed. Yet what do those feelings mean in our broader lives? How do these experiences transform and interact with the subsequent acts in the social dramas of our lives? Why do we continue to educate ourselves—and others—through the seemingly complex practice of touring?

Rather than focusing on this practice as a commercial trend, this book concentrates on the types of tours that MacCannell briefly discusses in his foundational study of tourism:

> The tours of Appalachian communities and northern inner-city cores taken by politicians provide examples of *negative sightseeing*. This kind of tour is usually conducted by a local character who has connections outside of his community. The local points out and explains and complains about the rusting auto hulks, the corn that did not come up, winos and junkies on the nod, flood damage and other features of the area to the politician who expresses his concern. . . . [E]cological awareness has given rise to some imaginative variations: bus tours of "The Ten Top Polluters in Action" were available in Philadelphia during "Earth Week" in April, 1970.[67]

This last reference to bus tours is the earliest allusion to what is now referred to as "toxic tours" that I have discovered in scholarly literature on tourism.

If—in addition to writing the seminal text in tourist studies—MacCannell had been able to explore this phenomenon further at the time, however, I believe he might have attributed a name more fitting than "negative sightseeing." Yes, tours of environmental and cultural tragedies are "negative" in the sense that, at first glance, they don't seem to offer the more familiar tourist package of leisure and "escape" from responsibility and work. I would argue, however, that these tours offer the possibility to both guides and tourists of an often too rare indulgence: a sense of agency.

Many historical tours and public memorial sites, for example, share a vision of hope and, thus, a call to action. The U.S. Holocaust Memorial Museum was founded not to romanticize some lessons from history that might allow us to "understand" what happened but to "Never Again" let a Holocaust occur.[68] Similarly, the Civil Rights Memorial in Alabama was commissioned by the Southern Poverty Law Center after their initial building was firebombed by the Ku Klux Klan; it displays, among other, less conspicuous inscriptions, "UNTIL JUSTICE ROLLS DOWN LIKE WATERS AND RIGHTEOUSNESS LIKE A MIGHTY STREAM. MARTIN LUTHER KING, JR."[69] In other words, these places interpellate the tourist into the outcome of the ever-unfolding stories they begin to share. Further, from the success of Witness for Peace's journeys into politically volatile zones to the World Tourism Organization's suggestion that tourism could serve as "a great and sustaining force for peace in the world,"[70] a wide spectrum of voices has testified to the possibility that touring might promote greater understanding, sympathy, and accountability. Indeed, MacCannell's own reference to "negative sightseeing" specifically cites when such tours are provided for politicians and explores how such tours may muddle us-them binaries, challenging the "we are good—they are bad" logic that helps rationalize our alienation from each other as peoples.[71] Rather than focusing on "the negative," these invitations to agency suggest a hope that suffering need not exist, an almost utopian wish for a better world—if only people could tour the places and people where suffering has occurred and is occurring.[72]

On what I would prefer to call *advocacy tours,* guides similarly present a particular vision of their community to their visitors so that these "tourists" might be moved to do something to transform the tragic scenes they are presented. Rather than offering a staged "escape" from everyday life, as was more typical of earlier modes of mass tourism, these guides instead ask their visitors to move more closely to another experience of the everyday, toward the risks of more dramatic contamination, in the hope that they might be not only physically but also emotionally moved. For example, subsequent to a toxic tour in which I participated on the border of Texas and Mexico, my guide said: "When we come to the border, that's where we find each other. . . . Do not be indifferent." A guide who has provided several tours of the area known as "Cancer Alley," Louisiana, writes: "One of the key things that I try to impart to the persons taking the tours is that every person can make a difference if they are willing to stand up and become an activated member of the American democracy that we live in."[73] Ideally, through their interrogation of the ways in which the excesses of modernity affect their everyday lives, these tours perform a critique of the political economy as it is and, often explicitly, demand that life should be better. The guides are not reducible to locals who complain, as MacCannell's brief description might suggest. Instead, they are skillful weavers of bodies of thought, land, and people who desire to live and have the courage to risk hoping for more.

As a prevalent and potentially persuasive mode of advocacy tourism, *environmental tourism* has often invited a connection between travel and social change. Stephen T. Mather, the first director of the U.S. Park Service, wrote in 1921 of the advocacy worth of going to U.S. parks: "Our parks are not only showing places and vacation lands but also vast schoolrooms of Americanism where people are studying, enjoying, and learning to love more deeply this land where they live."[74] Of course, these lessons, when sponsored by the state or corporations, are confined by specific agendas. For example, in her study of Sea World, Susan G. Davis observes that "pollution and extinction and endangerment are only obliquely mentioned; when they are, they come up as problems that more research will solve. They have no discernible social locations or causes. Nature itself is remote and decontextualized. It is simply an object for pity and consumption."[75] As such, both progressive and conservative impulses have framed environmental tourism throughout history.[76]

A more specialized market within environmental tourism, *ecotourism* has come to distinguish not only those tours that focus on the pleasure of visiting picturesque environmental sites but also those that include an overtly political agenda on the tour itinerary. Although definitions vary, ecotourism tends to indicate "travel to fragile, pristine, and usually protected areas that strives to be low impact and (usually) small scale. It helps educate the traveler; provides funds for conservation; directly benefits the economic development and political empowerment of local communities; and fosters respect for different cultures and for human rights."[77] The popularity of this type of tour is grounded not only in aesthetic and educational pleasures but also in the optimistic belief that touring changes the world for the better.

Di Chiro argues that toxic tours are a form of ecotourism because both focus on environmental and social problems; both believe that firsthand experience may result in action, thus challenging the remoteness of the "tourist gaze"; and both claim to present an "authentic" experience.[78] She emphasizes that the ecotourist is a "primarily Western, middle- to upper-middle-class tourist not interested simply in gawking . . . but in asking questions and finding answers—how did we get ourselves into this ecological conundrum, and how can we unite with others to create solutions?"[79] I would add that the smaller scale of ecotourism within the broader category of environmental tourism also tends to resonate with the size of toxic tours.

Contextualized within broader histories of social change, however, toxic tourism need not fall under the rubric of the more popular, commercial counterpart of ecotourism. Although toxic tours might share characteristics and a timeline with the more recent boom in commercial ecotourism, it also seems worth considering toxic tourism as part of the longer history of what I am calling "advocacy tourism" within the U.S. environmental movement. That is to say, toxic tourism is part of a broader, historical, and grassroots effort through which various rhetorical tactics have been chosen to attempt to explain the worth of a place and its inhabitants—particularly when such places and inhabitants have appeared threatened by human activities.

In addition to writing, speaking, painting, photographing, and protesting as modes of environmental communication, environmentalists have invited people to travel with them on guided journeys as a compelling mode of social critique since at least the late nineteenth century. Significant instances of what I prefer to call "environmental advocacy touring" in the United States occurred at least as early as the early 1900s in the camping trips of the Sempervirens Club, which were organized to "save the Redwoods," and continued to involve historic events, such as David Brouwer's Colorado River rafting trips to preserve the Grand Canyon from being flooded. One of the most famous examples of environmental advocacy tourism was recorded by U.S. President Theodore Roosevelt in his autobiographical account of being guided by John Muir on a three-day trip in Yosemite Valley. Muir himself, of course, was an avid traveler and tourist. As founder of the oldest environmental organization in the nation, the Sierra Club, Muir often brought people on environmental advocacy tours, claiming the pleasure of the experience could transform cultural attitudes toward nature. "If people in general could be got into the woods, even for once, to hear the trees speak for themselves, all difficulties in the way of forest preservation would vanish," he wrote.[80]

Although employing tours as an environmental advocacy tactic began as a means of protecting more traditional environmental areas such as mountains and forests, the scope of tour topics has expanded as grassroots communities and social movements have broadened our appreciation of what the "environment" itself is. More recently, examples include Witness for Peace excursions into farms to highlight the environmentally unjust working conditions of migrant farmworkers, and environmental education schools that offer survival and skills courses designed to foster and to implement environmental ethics.[81]

With the rise of grassroots environmental activism against toxic pollution, therefore, it is not surprising that tours have been used as a form of anti-pollution advocacy since at least the late 1960s.[82] Newspapers provide written evidence of naming this practice as "toxic tours" since at least the late 1980s.[83] Today you can find out about or see an example of a toxic tour on the internet at well over a dozen sites, generally sponsored by communities and organizations fighting for environmental justice.[84] Beyond the warmth of camaraderie and laughter that is often shared on toxic tours, the subsequent chapters aim to illustrate the pleasurable sense of agency motivating those who host toxic tours. I hope their sense of hope, despite all odds, will be infectious.

Toxic Tours as Public Participation

This chapter has aimed to complicate criticisms of tourists and characteristics of tourist practices. Although the exploitative possibilities of tourism remain important to consider, tourism also suggests opportunities for embodied engagement, counterexperiences of everyday life, education, interpretation, and advocacy. Our cynicism about tourism may be understandable within particular contexts, but we would do well to interrogate those feelings by delving more deeply into the sources of our fears and desires about tourism more specifically and cultural politics more broadly, including differentiation, consumption, modernity, nationalism, and human agency for social and environmental change.

Rather than assuming that toxic tours embody yet another superficial mode of exploitation, we can appreciate them in more optimistic terms— as an innovative, relatively affordable, embodied grassroots intervention into redefining public participation in environmental decision making. Although the national government has increased efforts to incorporate public participation, many shortcomings remain. Stephen P. Depoe and John W. Delicath, for example, note the tendency to operate on technocratic models of rationality, the late incorporation of the public, adversarial perceptions of public activism (leading to "decide-announce-defend" patterns), a lack of adequate means for informed dialogue, and the failure to actually empower grassroots voices to have an impact on the environmental decisions that influence their lives most directly.[85]

Placing practices of toxic tourism into dialogue with tourism more broadly, therefore, involves more than merely identifying a gap in existing literature or collecting examples of a relatively emergent and oft-ignored practice. Rather, it requires that we reimagine our current performances and beliefs about public participation itself. By highlighting these four characteristics of tourism outlined in this chapter and how they are negotiated by toxic tourism, we have laid the grounds from which to reassess our assumptions about civic life and how various perspectives might become able to gain traction in the negotiation of power.

Tourism's long relationship with democracy is predicated on access and interaction. The environmental justice movement's efforts to articulate chains of equivalence among a plurality of publics to resist toxic assault pivot on the *reappropriation* of democracy. As Ernesto Laclau and Chantal Mouffe note, "The task of the Left therefore cannot be to renounce liberal-democratic ideology, but on the contrary, to deepen and expand it in the direction of a radical and plural democracy."[86] It is perhaps fitting that toxic tours not only reclaim democracy for grassroots communities but also reappropriate tourist discourse as an inventional and palpable cultural resource for dissent.

2

Toxic Baggage

During a toxic tour in Cincinnati, Ohio, in 2001, I snapped a photograph (see figure 1). The charter bus that appears on the left side of the picture brought the tourists (in this case, a gathering of environmental communication scholars) to an area of the city called Lower Price Hill, which is disproportionately burdened by waste, industry, and toxic production. Our guide, a local environmental justice community activist and resident named Linda Briscoe, asked for the bus to stop at this point in the tour so that we could see the landfill across the way.

When I look at this image, two observations immediately occur to me. First, why are we looking? The rolling hill in the center of the image—that is, the landfill—does not appear to be an eyesore or a sign of something dangerous. If I had not been told what it was, I could have easily mistaken the hill as a welcoming "green space" in a city that is full of pavement and buildings. Viewing this landscape provides me with no empirical evidence that this hill is full of waste or that it is a problem for the local community. In short: at first glance, what I see does not look like a site worth photographing.

This leads me to my second reaction to this image: this scene is quite banal. This street does not have any markers that make it distinctly "Cincinnati." The size of the cars perhaps indicates that this place is in the United States; but, without knowing where it was located, I am not even sure I would be able to guess that this is a location in a city, let alone one of the most industrialized areas of that city. Even the weather seems banal.

Figure 1. Toxic tour stop in Cincinnati, Ohio. Author photo.

There are no clouds in the sky or bright sun. The leaves on the trees suggest it is summer, but there are no signs of heat or cool breezes. There are no people or dogs or birds to create a sense of motion or activity. Without a guide to frame this landscape for me, it looks like an unremarkable place.

I have dwelled on this image because it is indicative of stops provided on many toxic tours. As such a commonplace example, this photograph invites us to consider the role of two important characteristics addressed on toxic tours: visibility and banality. In the previous chapter I addressed the theme of the visual when I discussed the politics of tours as a mode of operating more broadly. This picture further emphasizes the limits of the visual on a toxic tour. The banal is another important theme to which I now turn. More specifically, this chapter examines the role of toxic pollution in relation to banality's counterpart, the extraordinary, and then it returns to the ways that toxic pollution is also culturally imagined as a banal part of everyday life. I establish these patterns by focusing on the ways that various popular media sources, such as women's magazines and comic books, have articulated the toxic since the second half of the twentieth century. These popular literatures bring perspectives to bear on our perceptions of toxins that exceed my own participant observation of toxic tours and more official reports from newspapers, scientific magazines, chemical industry journals, and academic literatures.

In addition to the constraints that toxins themselves impose (e.g., invisibility, scale, and danger), toxically assaulted communities face the challenge of having to speak publicly about bodies in pain. The second half of this chapter, therefore, focuses on the ongoing conversations in academic literature about how we can talk in productive ways about bodies and pain. This overview illustrates how discourses of sexism, racism, classism, and ableism that are inscribed on the body, along with the ways in which the physical and emotional pain that is manifested in the body tests the limits of language.

Overall, the context provided in this chapter seems a necessary precursor to discussing toxic tours, as it helps to make sense of the larger political and cultural terrain they inhabit. By taking seriously popular cultural depictions in the same breath as more sanctioned and official resources, this chapter engages stories and perceptions that too often are excluded from official conversations about toxic pollution and the pain it causes. Put differently, the historical articulations and structures of feeling that are enabled by the connections mapped in the following pages offer a broader cultural context for the baggage that travels with us on toxic tours.

The Extraordinary

As it does with most things that are bad for us, our cultural imaginary persistently perpetuates a love-hate relationship with toxins, both metaphorically and literally. As U.S. pop singer Britney Spears reminds us in the chorus of her 2004 international chart-topping hit, "Toxic," we both romanticize and demonize the toxic.[1] We feel "addicted" to or dependent on it, as if we cannot live without it, and yet, when pushed, we reluctantly admit that its effects are deadly. In order to better understand our inability thus far to resist its alluring "ride" and walk away, I believe it is worth spending the time to identify what "it" is that we are talking about and how "it" has been constructed culturally as both extraordinary and banal. To

begin, let us consider the ways toxic chemicals have captured our imagination and hearts to spark a desire for romanticizing the toxic.

If our production levels are any indicator, we cannot seem to stop ourselves from making toxins. According to the Toxics Release Inventory
(TRI) 2001 Executive Summary Report, there are approximately 650
toxic chemicals and chemical compounds that facilities currently must
report to the Environmental Protection Agency (EPA). That number
represents less than 1 percent of the approximately 75,000 chemicals
manufactured in the United States. From this same data, the government
admits that more than 5.5 billion pounds of toxic chemicals enter into
the national environment annually, including 75 million pounds that are
recognized carcinogens and released by no less than 20,000 industrial
facilities. In addition to producing a massive amount of toxins, we produce a wide variety. From Abamectin to Zineb, the 2001 U.S. EPA TRI
chemical list includes everything from familiar names such as lead, mer-
cury, ozone, and vinyl chloride to the less familiar (e.g., polychlorinated
biphenyls, PCBs) and to the practically unpronounceable (e.g., 2, 2, 4-
trimethylhexamethylene diisocyanate). Annually, mining industries domi-
nate the list of the worst toxic chemical polluters.[2]

Toxic chemicals, of course, are only a portion of the chemicals in the
world, because not all chemicals are toxic. Chemicals, as we are taught
early on in our science classes, are the building blocks of life itself. Following the turn of the twentieth century, however, "breakthroughs" in scientific studies of and experiments with chemicals, particularly human-
produced organic chemicals, catalyzed "a chemical revolution that rivals
the industrial revolution in its historical importance."[3] Of course, these
two movements, industrial and chemical, were linked historically. The Industrial Revolution involved the use of power-driven machinery, the
migration of people from rural to urban areas, a transfer of production
from homes to factories, and the creation of a new working class.[4] These
changes in the practices and structures of everyday life transformed what
was—and what was thought to be—possible. Likewise, in a sense, toxins have made our wildest dreams come true. They are as integral to our
economy as money or natural resources. Since the inception of the chemical revolution, human-made chemicals have become used in almost every
facet of our lives, including pharmaceuticals, solvents, adhesives, dyes,

paints, preservatives, plastics, electronics, and aerospace industries.[5] It is not an exaggeration to say that over the past one hundred years the nation has fallen in love with chemicals, making chemistry with chemistry.

Chemical industries continue to earn astounding economic profits.[6] Unsurprisingly, and for a wide variety of reasons, many consider the overall U.S. chemical industry to be a "success story."[7] Exemplary stars in this romance are often singled out for their ability to excel. According to the *Washington Post,* for instance, BASF is "the world's largest producer of chemicals and related products, with sales of approximately $34 billion and over 90,000 employees . . . BASF Corporation (the U.S. affiliate of the German-based BASF AG) had sales of $7.9 billion in 2000."[8] Corporations that create chemicals are quick to promote their own stories of success. In 2002, for example, DuPont celebrated its two hundredth anniversary in Taiwan with a self-congratulatory photo exhibit titled "Epitome of Science and Civilization."[9] Having fallen in love so quickly and intensely, we seem to have held back little praise over the years.

Yet, while many romanticize the benefits brought to us by chemical-producing industries, other public discourses suggest that we have begun to wonder if this intoxicating feeling is too good to be true. A love affair gone wrong. For at least the past forty years, whether toxins conjure memories of the sinister abuse of human-made chemicals documented in Rachel Carson's *Silent Spring* or vague images of unidentified people in white space suits walking through sludge taking samples of unknown substances, toxic chemicals and the places we associate with them (e.g., Love Canal, Times Beach, Three Mile Island, and Chernobyl) have become just as likely to invoke nightmarish images of science out of control, progress gone awry, and technological disaster.

Sometimes, citations of the mere scale of chemical production—toxic or not—can overwhelm us, like a horrifying, amorphous monster that seems too large to tackle or even to comprehend. Consider the following descriptions drawn from writings on toxic pollution since 1993:

> Underground chemical and petroleum storage tanks scattered throughout cities, suburbs, and rural America number between three and five million; 30 percent already leak. Pesticides have con-

taminated water supplies in 23 states, leaching into aquifers and washing into streams and rivers where they end up in the water we drink and the fish we eat.[10]

The Conservation Foundation reports that every year the United States generates approximately 50,000 pounds of air, water, and solid wastes *per each of the existing 240 million U.S. residents.* . . . Spills and other releases of hazardous materials occur in U.S. communities almost 500 times per week, or 25,000 times per year.[11]

Synthetic organic chemical production in the United States . . . reached 30 billion pounds by 1950, and 300 billion pounds by 1976. Today [in 2000] there are more than 5 million chemicals known to humankind, 65,000 of them in commercial use, with more than 10,000 of these produced at greater than a million pounds per year.[12]

These estimates, from national to individual impacts, pervading our communities down to their underground aquifers, are enormous in scale. Trying to imagine such quantities, let alone how to assess their impact, appears epic in proportion and, thus, despite their clear numerical categorization, to most of us, what is happening annually to our bodies and to the body of land surrounding us remains inconceivable.

In addition to the monumental magnitude of chemical production, the nature of toxic chemicals themselves challenges our ability to detect and trace these substances. As noted previously, Michael Reich observes that any attempt to construct a counterdiscourse to toxic production faces constraints predicated upon physical attributes, such as the invisibility of the toxic agent, difficulties of identification, and nonspecificity of toxic symptoms.[13] Moreover, toxins sometimes have latent effects. Although they accumulate in our bodies, the signs of their impact may remain dormant in the short term, their horrors apparent only in the long term.

Furthermore, despite their "toxic" label, the extent of the damage caused to the human body and the Earth by toxic substances remains uncertain. Regarding the government's ability to measure toxic chemical exposure in humans at the turn of the millennium, the Government Accounting Office (GAO) reports that

(1) federal and state efforts to collect human exposure data are limited, despite some recent expansions; (2) HHS [the Department of Health and Human Services] and EPA have been able to take advantage of improved technology to measure exposures for more people and for a broader range of chemicals; (3) still, with existing resources, HHS and EPA surveys together measure in the general population only about 6 percent of the more than 1,400 toxic chemicals in GAO's review; (4) for those toxic chemicals that GAO reviewed, the portion measured ranged from 2 percent of chemicals prioritized for safety testing to about 23 percent of those chemicals most often found at Superfund sites and considered to pose a significant threat to human health; (5) even for those chemicals that are measured, information is often insufficient to identify smaller population groups at high risk, such as children in inner cities and people living in polluted locations who may have particularly high exposures.[14]

To reiterate: our knowledge about chemicals and their toxicity to human health is "limited," and that limited knowledge itself is "insufficient," particularly for children and adults living in toxically assaulted communities.[15] The GAO reiterated this uncertainty in 2005, noting that it remained "unclear" whether the EPA has sufficient funds and information "to determine chemicals' risks to human health and the environment."[16] In this sense, I refer to "toxin" and "chemical" interchangeably in my own writing at times, not only because the sources of each are often interrelated but also because of the sometimes blurry epistemological and cultural boundaries between the toxic and the chemical.

To emphasize what might be their most obvious characteristic, "toxins" or "toxics," *by definition,* refer to those substances that pose environmental and human health hazards.[17] Although they might be produced during the process of making goods to improve our lives, toxins destroy life itself. Toxins have been linked to a range of devastating diseases and defects, such as lung/respiratory disorders, central nervous system anomalies (e.g., mental retardation, cerebral palsy, spina bifida), depression, heart defects, asthma, skin disorders, memory loss, immune system suppression, and cancer (e.g., lung, ovarian, testicular, breast, brain, stomach).[18] With regard to cancer, Richard N. L. Andrews argues: "Fear of chemical hazards [is] not new, but it grew into a major public concern *as it was linked to the fear of cancer.*" The specter of anxiety that chemicals invoke, therefore, is linked historically to the diseases associated with them—particularly cancer, one of the leading causes of death in the United States.[19] Given their association with disease and morbidity, toxins are articulated to the truly grotesque elements in our public culture.

Furthermore, toxins do not merely induce illness and death; they can also prevent birth and the conception of life itself. The rise of infertility and of fertility-inducing practices in the United States is linked to toxic pollution. In the best-selling book *Our Stolen Future,* scientists estimate that as a result of toxic pollution, "the thirty-year-old man in 2005, who was born in 1975, would have a sperm count of . . . about one-fourth the count of the average male born in 1925."[20] Even if conception does occur, spontaneous abortions and reproductive disorders may occur. As one of the authors emphasized in an interview, moreover, the global fertility rate dropped to about half starting in 1970, "about the time that the first set of individuals exposed in the womb were reaching reproductive age."[21]

Those children who are lucky enough to be born healthy remain susceptible to toxic pollution. In fact, since their bodies are smaller and less developed than those of adults, children are more vulnerable to chemical contamination. The especially precarious effects of toxic chemicals on children's health have raised the chemical industry's awareness of their responsibility to youth. In *Chemical and Engineering News,* for example, a guest editorial attempts to articulate a "middle ground" in the name of children: "We all acknowledge that chemicals have enhanced the quality of children's lives in countless ways and have contributed to reductions in childhood mortality and to increased life expectancy. But still we have a responsibility to determine what adverse effects synthetic chemicals might have on the health of children, and we share a responsibility to take intelligent action to protect them."[22] And yet, a disclaimer at the end of this seemingly innocuous proposal underscores and reminds us of the constraints faced by those who aim to address the health concerns posed by toxic chemicals, even in children: "Views expressed on this page are those of the authors and not necessarily those of ACS [American Chemical Society]." Seemingly, the ACS finds a potential transformation of the chemical industry more horrifying than the potential deaths of children.[23]

Largely due to their excessive scale, obscurity, and overall danger, toxins often appear surreal for those of us who do not live, work, or play in or near toxic facilities or dumps on a daily basis. Precisely because they promise us both dreams (of science, technology, and upward mobility) and nightmares (of insignificance, fallibility, and illness), toxins appear as the *extra*ordinary, as that which exceeds our everyday understandings, in the national imaginary. Perhaps unsurprisingly, this double-edged projection of toxins as the epitome of the extremely good and the purely evil has provided suggestive fodder for fantasy, particularly in popular media. Comic books are one of the most illustrative examples of this perception. The Teenage Mutant Ninja Turtles, for example, were four "ordinary" turtles who were mutated by a toxic slime that had fallen off the back of a truck and, hence, became superheroes. Their toxic encounter enabled them to use their mutant characteristics toward good, against evil.[24]

Still, this narrative about the important role of toxins in the world of comics is not all that rare or new. Many comic book characters are the accidental by-products of toxic chemicals, especially if we include stories about nuclear radiation.[25] Particularly notable are two stories from Marvel Comics that have recently been brought to the silver screen. Introduced in 1963, a year after the release of *Silent Spring,* both the X-Men and Spiderman embody our torn relationship with toxic chemicals. "The last one hundred years," we are told, "have brought extraordinary social and technological changes. In the world of the X-Men, they have also brought the evolution of the human race to a crossroads . . . people born genetically different."[26] The motto of Spiderman, who is also a product of atomic radiation, albeit through the bite of a spider, reminds us of what these consequences mean: "with great power there also comes great responsibility."[27] Not only are both the X-Men and Spiderman physically abnormal products of the changing times, but they also are portrayed as heroes who are misunderstood, liminal, and often suspected of wrongdoing by the public at large.

Beyond these examples, many more superheroes and supervillains reflect our fantastic relationship with the abnormal effects of toxic chemicals, including figures such as Spiderwoman (a woman exposed to radiation and injected with spider serum), the Joker (an everyday bad guy who became a supervillain once he fell into a vat of toxic chemicals), Doctor Octopus (described as an arrogant nuclear researcher who is transformed by a laboratory accident), the Lizard (a geneticist gone bad), Morbus (a Nobel Prize–winning scientist who attempted to create a cure for his rare disease), the Green Goblin (another scientist who tried a bizarre chemical formula that made him become evil), the Scorpion and the Rhino (scientific experiments), and a series of figures whose power is the result of gamma radiation (e.g., the Hulk, Gargoyle, Ant-Man, Giant-Man, the Abomination, Dr. Samson, Sasquatch, and She-Hulk).

Our love-hate feelings about the toxic chemical industry are reflected by and negotiated through these fantasy characters. First, toxins in the world of comics often symbolize humanity out of control. Superheroes frequently fight the aberrant forces that have mutated their bodies in order to save "ordinary" humans and the planet from the more commonly understood effect of toxic waste: mass destruction. Conversely, toxins also serve in these narratives as the catalyst for moving the world beyond our current limitations as humans so that we may imagine flying, predicting the future ("spidersense"), performing feats of remarkable strength, having telepathic and telekinetic abilities, healing at super-fast speeds, and so on.

More recently, this comic book narrative of a larger-than-life superhero swooping into a toxic area despite all potential personal costs has reverberated in the Hollywood tales of *A Civil Action* (starring John Travolta) and *Erin Brockovich* (starring Julia Roberts). Although these are based on "true life," of all the stories regarding toxic waste, it is not surprising to discover which ones have captured the popular imagination. These are not the countless stories of everyday grassroots communities working together to resist the industries killing them; rather, with varying degrees of success, *A Civil Action* and *Erin Brockovich* focus on exceptional superhero-like outsiders swooping in and trying to save "the locals" from threatening toxic industries. Both films clearly could have been more representative in their depictions of the environmental justice movement, and, tellingly, they perpetuate the ideology that individual efforts—particularly those of lawyers—will make the difference.[28]

Given the national collective fantasies and horrors that are projected onto and inspired by the toxic, it is not fair or accurate to say that an *unquestioned* love affair remains with toxic chemicals; yet we—meaning those who are invested in U.S. culture and life—currently face a dilemma. Although we may no longer share a naive love, many of us still are alienated from the social, political, economic, and environmental costs of our ongoing amorous affair with broader chemical-producing industries. Therefore, our own sense of agency or our ability to feel we are able to intervene and make a difference is seriously limited. In other words, we may have declared our breakup with *toxic* chemicals, but we have yet to move on or to reexamine our relationship with industrialization as a whole. In a sense, we have yet to unpack our toxic baggage. We will ask incredulously, "Who is *for* toxic pollution?"[29] Yet not only are toxic chemicals still produced and distributed on a daily basis in the United States, but some of us continue to call the broader chemical industry a "success" without noting its relationship with toxins (e.g., the same companies often produce both). Why? What makes so many of us skim the high statistics of toxic chemical production and the long words of the toxic chemical substances that are being produced? How can we know, somewhere in the back of our minds, that toxic chemicals are polluting our environments and our bodies every day and still feel unmoved to do anything about it? Why are we unconvinced of the need to resist the chemical industry's relationship with toxic chemicals? This apparent contradiction is central to the struggle of those who offer toxic tours.

The Banal

Far from fantasy, toxins in our everyday lives matter. "Whether it's the risk from breathing polluted air or from the consumption of contaminated fish, abstract risk manifests itself in real harm to real persons in particular places," Roger C. Field reminds us.[30] For those exposed to toxins, the privilege and fantasy of feeling overwhelmed or waiting around to be "saved" simply does not exist. Identifying, tracing, and naming specific toxic chemicals in a manner that makes them appear present to those who are not dying from them is a necessary survival skill. It is true that no community can detoxify itself without outside financial, legal, or technological help; yet this is different from saying that a superhero or superstar will "save" them. The price of the nation's affair with chemical-producing industries must be raised in public discussions and environmental decision making in a way that illustrates the complexity of not only the chemicals involved but also of the various people and institutions affected by them.

Ironically, the recurring narrative of the costs of toxic chemicals has created its own challenge: when it is not fodder for fantasy, the toxic appears so incredibly banal that avoiding harm seems utterly impossible. Rather than extraordinary, toxins sometimes seem all too ordinary. In addition to providing the basis for exceptional stories of superheroes and villains, "toxic" is used to name a wide range of everyday events and items, from pop songs to candy and hot sauce. Because the label appears almost everywhere, it becomes difficult to discern when calling something or someone "toxic" is worth our attention and concern. Communities resisting toxic pollution, therefore, are faced with a balancing act of sorts: how do they avoid becoming pigeonholed as fanatics who cannot discern "fantasy" from "fact," on the one hand, or, on the other, as alarmist Chicken Littles who keep shouting that the sky is falling?

To explore this second, more banal role of discourses about the toxic, I examined women's magazines listed in the *Reader's Guide to Periodical Literature* since the late 1950s, the same time period in U.S. industrial history that gave birth to the worries of Rachel Carson and the extraordinary discourses found in comic books. Whereas comic books have historically been read more by young boys, women's magazines target an adult female audience. Comparing their representations of the toxic is important, then, for illustrating the pervasive role of public discourses about toxins in the nation's broader imaginary. In addition, women's magazines are known for focusing on practices considered essential to everyday life, such as cooking, cleaning, child rearing, and romance. As such, they are a useful resource for exploring how toxins or the toxic have figured into everyday cultural perceptions.[31]

The term "toxic" begins to appear with some regularity in women's magazines in 1970, a year that many identify as the beginning of the "environmental era": President Nixon signed the National Environmental Protection Act (NEPA) on New Year's Day; the first Earth Day was celebrated on April 22; the EPA was founded; and environmental issues came onto the radar of the mainstream media.[32] Since then, the related articles can be categorized roughly into two major trends: the rise of "toxic" awareness due to the popularity of the environmental movement, and, accordingly, the call for increased surveillance of toxins in our everyday lives.

Calling for us to remember that our world "is a home," Margaret Mead writes in a 1970 issue of *Redbook* that women would do well to recall the historical traits of "responsible and devoted caretaking" as we try to improve our ability to "encourage all men [*sic*] to become the vigilant conservators of their inheritance of earth and air . . . and all the life of the world."[33] This appeal to rearticulate women's traditional roles as mothers and wives to acting as caretakers of the Earth manifests itself in articles encompassing a range of themes, including children's environmental education opportunities, female environmental activists and scientists as "America's unsung heroines," and more famous leaders who have made headline news.[34] In addition, coverage of toxic disasters from Tom's River, New Jersey, to Cameroon in west Africa received increased attention.[35] By 1985, *Glamour* magazine stated that 88 percent of the readers who participated in a poll about chemicals "fear a chemical disaster," and 94 percent believed there should be "criminal penalties for executives who deliberately conceal a known or potential industrial hazard."[36]

This rise in the coverage of toxic pollution issues reflects the broader, growing popularity of the environmental movement since the 1960s. By most estimates, the environmental movement is considered a "success."[37] Polls consistently suggest that the majority of people in the United States consider themselves environmentalists.[38] By its twentieth anniversary, Earth Day grew from approximately 20 million participants in the United States in 1970 to more than 200 million in 141 countries in 1990.[39] Green advertising has become one of the fastest-growing markets targeted by advertising industries.[40] Nature programs can now be found all day long on television.[41] And almost four decades after *Silent Spring,* there is a World Wrestling Federation (WWF) move named the "DDT" for its supposedly parallel effects upon the body.[42] Some even estimate that "more Americans now recycle than vote for president."[43]

In women's magazines since 1970, the rise of concern about toxic pollution and disasters is often translated into an invitation to transform oneself into a toxic-savvy individual, one who detects, avoids, and responds to toxins in her everyday life with increased vigilance and shrewd crisis management skills.[44] Articles provide women with advice on how to adapt to chemical exposure through personal habits in the workplace and at home, including frequently published lists of "What to Do If Your Child Swallows Poison."[45] Of these, only one article I found, titled "Do You Jog beside a Freeway? Staying Healthy in a Toxic World," suggests that in addition to regular exercise, weight loss, and changing the location where one works out, we should also ask questions about where we live to see if there is a local pollution problem that warrants further concern. Unsurprisingly, the author is environmental justice activist Lois Gibbs.[46]

The trouble with the advice to respond to negative chemical exposures solely by changing personal habits is twofold. First, it deflects attention away from broader systemic causes that are the source of these pollutants. In her study of the privatization of public space at Sea World, for example, Susan Davis notes, "Human relations to the biological world are reduced to individual relations. . . . This is the generic 'Don't Pollute' injunction familiar throughout schools, but it tells children nothing about the real problems of pollution, the reasons for the massive waste stream American industry generates, or the relationships between the production of plastics, solid wastes, and toxics, for example. . . . Real environmental problems . . . involve conflicts of interest over the gross exploitation of the earth and its resources."[47] According to Davis, we are taught stories that focus on our individual responsibility to the environment rather than on pursuing more collective structural critiques. Similarly, Lawrence Grossberg argues, "the very empowerment which struggles within everyday life make available can be articulated into larger structures of disempowerment which continue to subordinate people by erasing the possibility of political struggles in another space."[48] When the monitoring of our personal everyday waste is put forth as the solitary means of achieving tangible environmental improvements, the waste of larger entities such as the state and corporations can be ignored.

The specific environmental crime in this deflection of reality is not so much the telling of stories about individual responsibility but rather the claiming that lessons directed toward individuals are the only ones that matter. As Richard Hofrichter asks, "how do corporations create acceptance of the idea that we are all responsible for the environmental crisis, when the source of most environmental degradation derives from corporate and military decision making?"[49] It is not that we are not all responsible; rather, our responsibilities need to be weighed in the light of our impacts. Although I am a vegetarian who drives a relatively fuel-efficient Hyundai and uses cloth bags at the grocery store, for example, these choices cannot compare to the environmental impact one corporation such as General Electric could have if it reduced its toxic output even by 5 percent, or that the U.S. government could have if it stopped using depleted uranium in its military operations. Does this mean it is futile to bring my own bags when I go shopping? No. Certainly, a town of people who did so would, at minimum, use less landfill space in a year. Yet it does mean that my choice to bypass the "paper or plastic" question should not stop Congress from passing and enforcing a stricter Clean Air Act.

Scientists and policymakers have known for decades that automobiles are a primary source of air, water, and land pollution. Despite the supposed popularity of "environmentalism," however, the nation's desire to consume gasoline in order to drive massive vehicles with poor fuel economy only has increased during that same period of time. Likewise, we know which chemicals we should be tracking as "toxic," yet we continue to allow industries and the government to produce them.[50] Yes, starting with the reduced amount of toxins released into the environment every year, the state of the environment has improved over the past three decades; however, this does not mean that people no longer are suffering from environmental pollution.

Indeed, the ongoing presence of bodies suffering in various kinds of pain—pain that has not yet brought polluting practices to a halt—has been driving increasing numbers of communities to host toxic tours. Before turning to three examples of specific toxic tours, therefore, I want to engage some ongoing theoretical conversations about bodies and pain. Part of what I want to emphasize in the final two sections of this chapter is that the "toxic baggage" we carry with us is not limited to items directly related to toxins. Rather, our "baggage" about whom we believe we are as people and how we have or have not related to others is a result of both literal toxic pollution and metaphorical public discourses about the toxicity of cultural pollution.

The Corporeal

Mary Douglas's cross-cultural study of "pollution ideas" indicates that various communities use the term "pollution" both to influence behaviors and to express "a general view of the social order."[51] Labeling certain practices or systems as "polluting," therefore, exceeds scientific discourses and includes the categorization of acts ranging from menstruation to adultery and from caste systems to diet regimens. All of these examples also highlight the importance of the body in understanding cultural perceptions of pollution.

We cannot take it for granted that people know what we mean when we talk about "the body." For some, the body evokes experiences of illness, pain, or shame. For others, the body seduces us to indulge in fantasies about desire, love, or pleasure. For most, the body moves us in different ways depending on the context and the manner in which it is presented, challenged, and/or celebrated. Bodies—our bodies, the bodies that surround us, the bodies that haunt us, the bodies that inspire us—are both banal and extraordinary, part of our everyday lives and part of spectacular events, instrumental and poetic. Bodies enable and limit action. Bodies carry weight.

Conversations about the body seem to warrant an engagement with specific human bodies and, yet, necessarily exceed those bodies as well. Our illnesses, pains, shames, desires, loves, and pleasures all locate themselves *within our bodies* ("that tumor"; "those flushed red cheeks"; "his smell"; etc.) and *outside our bodies* ("according to the medical report"; "induced by glancing at a single snapshot"; "after hiking through the forest"; etc.). In a dialectic that appears inherent to the human condition, bodies act on the world as the world acts on bodies.

Given the simultaneous ambiguity and necessity of the body, it is perhaps unsurprising that corporeality (that which involves bodies, carnal life, and physical matters) is a topic that is gaining increased attention across many disciplines in the academy. Apropos of this growing scholarly interest in bodies, let me return to a quotation from the introduction. Caren Kaplan astutely notes the interconnected ethic warranted by politically invested and academically informed corporeal research: "Bodies of knowledge, physical bodies, and bodies of land coexist as subjects of feminist inquiry into the social construction of raced, gendered, sexed, and classed material life."[52] Kaplan's statement suggests that when one is attentive to the coexistence of bodies that are both purposely and broadly defined, writings about the body raise questions concerning the relationship between social construction and materiality: how do physical bodies become inscribed by oppressive, socially constructed discourses, such as racism, sexism, homophobia, ableism, and classism? Conversely, how do bodies serve as evidence that such discourses are limiting, inaccurate, and demeaning? How do we mobilize our bodies to resist hegemonic epistemologies about who we are and what we are worth? What do we gain when we refer to knowledge and land as bodies? When we expand our notion of bodies to include knowledge and land, how do we account for *their* corporeal nature?

For some feminists, the move to raise questions regarding "bodies that matter"[53] reflects a specific desire to dispute patriarchal assumptions about sex and gender. Elizabeth Grosz summarizes the relevance of this project in terms of the historical articulation of women to corporeality and men to disembodiment:

> Patriarchal oppression . . . justifies itself, at least in part, by connecting women much more closely than men to the body and, through this identification, restricting women's social and economic roles to (pseudo) biological terms. Relying on essentialism, naturalism, and biologism, misogynist thought confines women to the biological requirements of reproduction on the assumption that because of particular biological, physiological, and endocrinological transformations, women are somehow *more* biological, *more* corporeal, *more* natural than men. The coding of femininity with corporeality in effect leaves men free to inhabit what they (falsely) believe is a purely conceptual order while at the same time enabling them to satisfy their (sometimes disavowed) need for corporeal contact through their access to women's bodies and services.[54]

This conception of the female body as excessive indicates how perceiving specific practices *as particularly grotesque or disgusting pollutants* enables the categorization of entire populations, such as women, as potentially contaminating to the larger social body.[55]

In response to technical, political, and popular discourses that have relegated women to bodies in a derogatory sense (as excessively nonintellectual, utilitarian extensions of heterosexual men's desires and reproductive needs), feminists have begun to talk about the body as a means of retheorizing and challenging a range of oppressive practices, for example, thinking that reifies a mind/body split,[56] suppression or denial of female agency, and spatial politics of gendered labor. *Resisting* such patterns further fosters conversations about reimagining these dynamics, such as exploring the performativity of gender, reexamining holistic approaches to medicine, and challenging spatial boundaries that limit female mobility.

Noting the second-wave feminist stance of connecting the personal and the political, Sharon Crowley argues that "[n]egatively charged cultural constructions of women's bodies as both dangerous and fragile have forced women to become highly conscious of their bodies—the space they occupy in a room, on the street, in a crowd."[57] Not based on an essentialist view of women, Crowley's argument is that the lived experience of most women lends itself to a certain level of self-reflexivity and self-consciousness about bodies.[58]

In addition to feminist writings about the body, scholarship regarding cultural, economic, and political patterns of racial oppression similarly has argued for the pivotal role of corporeality in addressing both domination and resistance. For instance, as Douglas has observed, constructing "whiteness" as clean and pure invites practices that distance white bodies from the bodies of racial Others. As a result, several cultures have articulated—or linked—uncleanness and nonwhite bodies together as symbols of chaos, or dis-order, which must be resolved or erased from white spaces.[59] In these cultures, exposure of "whites" to people of color is seen in many cases as working like a contagious and debilitating disease, one that attacks the "white" body, thus leading to stigmatization and systematic discrimination for those who risk association across racial boundaries.[60]

This desire to identify people of color with pollution creates a pattern that Robert R. Higgins theorizes as a rationale for "appropriately polluted space." "[W]hen environmental pollution is relegated to such appropriate socially polluted spaces," Higgins observes, "the environmental pollution is really 'in its place,' and therefore is not as noticeable as an anomaly or as an aberrant thing: it is relatively invisible in its physical and cultural separation from predominantly white, elite centers of power."[61] In these instances, both waste and people of color are considered undesirable, unnecessary, and contaminating. As a result, the racial Other and the waste have historically been isolated in "separate areas of existence," essentially outside elite white space.[62] In other words, efforts to keep the racial Other from one's (white) body and to keep one's (white) body from resembling that of the racial Other have influenced not only *who* some whites have wanted to be but also *where* some whites want to be: away from the polluting "disposable" and "unclean" racial Other. This pattern of distancing and degrading people of color *as pollution* is also evident in persistent patterns of residential segregation in the United States and what popular contemporary media call "white flight," in which white bodies flee from exposure to the bodies of racial Others.

Within our current cultural and political terrain, the act of avoiding the bodies of people of color can be read as an act of avoiding the body itself. Like sexist fantasies of masculinity, the racist dream of white space might be best understood as a fantasy of disembodiment, a longing to live where one is no longer confined to one's earthly form. In his writings about whiteness, Richard Dyer argues that the way in which "whiteness aspires to dis-embodiedness" is foundational to the definition of "whiteness": "To be seen as white is to have one's corporeality registered, yet true whiteness resides in the noncorporeal."[63] Likewise, as Charles W. Mills observes, despite racial segregation, the black body has historically been hypervisible in U.S. culture insofar as it has been articulated to evil, sex, shit, savagery, and the subproletarian. Mills argues that the term "white trash," for example, has traction within U.S. culture because it is an articulation of what is perceived as two distinct elements ("white" and "trash"), whereas the absence of the term "black trash" indicates an implicit cultural belief in its redundancy.[64]

Mills's argument about racial "trash" reminds us that, in addition to gender, sex, and race, the body has also been inscribed by class politics.

Evidence of economic patterns of separation and objectification is re-vealed in what Peter Stallybrass and Allon White call "the 'body' of the city: through the separations and interpenetrations of the suburb and the slum, of grand buildings and the sewer, of the respectable classes and the lumpenproletariat (what Marx called 'the whole indefinite disinte-grated mass thrown hither and thither')."[65] That is, the physical and cul-tural geographies where our bodies dwell reflect the economic stratifica-tion of "the body politic" itself. What we do for a living even becomes articulated to parts of the body. For example, white-collar work is asso-ciated with the mind, whereas blue-collar work is associated with the neck down and, perhaps most explicitly, with the hands—as if the labor of the first could be achieved without a body, or that of the second, without a mind.

Similar to the symbolic economy of racism, classism also constructs a stigma in which people who are poor are perceived *as symbolic pollutants themselves.* Hence, when Mikhail Bakhtin writes about the medieval Rus-sian folk practice of "carnivalesque," he notes how transgressive prac-tices such as laughter, jokes, and bestial costumes were perceived as gro-tesque.[66] Likewise, in a study of disgust in contemporary Western culture, William Ian Miller notes the linkage between class and the grotesque: "ideas of pollution, contagion, and contamination are not constrainable to the body; stenches arise from sinful deeds and also from lowly positions in the hierarchy."[67] Socially, residentially, and politically, therefore, gener-ally the wealthy elite actively attempt to distance themselves from those who are poor.

In addition to perceptions of social pollution imposed on specific popu-lations, being ill or unhealthy—as many people are in toxically assaulted communities—further exacerbates polluting metaphors. Perhaps it is un-surprising that survivors of toxic disasters often experience reactions and costs similar to those of people with AIDS, including stigma, fear, and expense.[68] "Illnesses," Susan Sontag reminds us, "have always been used as metaphors to enliven charges that a society was corrupt or unjust . . . an infection in the 'body politic.'"[69] For those suffering from illnesses brought on by environmental conditions, there is a vicious cycle in which people who are toxically polluted become ill and, in turn, as ill people, come to be perceived as a source of pollution themselves. They are the trouble-makers, the contagions. From this perspective, the safest thing for every-one else to do is to keep their distance.

Regrettably, the list of people associated with pollution metaphors could go on. I highlight women, people of color, lower-income commu-nities, and people living with illnesses because these are the populations who tend to host toxic tours. My point is that the "toxic baggage" the nation carries exceeds the material impact of toxins and public discourses about them. It includes our cultural perceptions of our bodies and the bodies of "polluted" and "polluting" Others.

Despite the current trend in scholarship to return to valuing all bodies and challenging the patterns of oppression enabled by the Cartesian split, there remains another constraint that compounds the enormity of revers-ing these cultural patterns of subordination: the inexpressibility of bodily pain. For people whose bodies are literally dying *from* pollution and are marginalized *as* pollution, toxic tours present a viable means of addressing these challenges.

The Painful

Despite the prevalence of "the toxic" in extraordinary and banal dis-courses, and despite persistent cultural legacies of social pollution, the ability to name, discuss, or imagine the pain that toxins can create remains remarkably absent in public life. As I have suggested, this challenge is in part a reflection of our conflicted cultural imaginary about "the toxic." Our toxic baggage is, however, inextricably interlinked to cultural atti-tudes about pain and, more specifically, to the dilemma that pain itself creates for communication.

In her landmark text *The Body in Pain,* Elaine Scarry posits that three interrelated subjects should inform our understanding of pain: first, that pain is difficult to express; second, that there are myriad "political and perceptual complications that arise as a result of that difficulty"; and third, that the desire to express pain "eventually opens into the wider frame of invention." Thus, she argues: "To have pain is to have *certainty;* to hear about pain is to have *doubt.*" When we feel intense pain, we tend not to question its existence; pain feels real, immediate, and present. In fact,

Scarry suggests that "the most crucial fact about pain is *its presentness*."[70] As much as some of us would like to ignore mundane physical pain in our everyday lives, such as arthritis or headaches, pain—all too often—is persistent. Similarly, as much as those who have survived torture or more extreme circumstances of pain would like to forget the physical pain that one has felt, pain—all too often—is both physically and psychologically tenacious. Conversely, Scarry contends, when we hear about someone else's pain, their pain is difficult to imagine; pain fosters mistrust, suspicion, or at least uncertainty. Because we do not feel the pain ourselves, we are challenged to confirm its existence. Searching for a way to assess the alleged pain, we ask: "What do you mean your stomach *hurts?*" "*Where* does it hurt?" "What do you think *caused* that pain?" "*Could* there be another explanation?" "Is it *really* that bad?" "On a scale from one to ten, how does it rate?"

Given pain's dual relationship with certainty and doubt, for Scarry the political consequences of pain require that we focus on improving our capacity to communicate it: "The failure to express pain . . . will always work to allow its appropriation and conflation with debased forms of power; conversely, the successful expression of pain will always work to expose and make impossible that appropriation and conflation." Critical to addressing and remedying various kinds of corporeal pain, then, is our ability (or inability) to express that pain to others. If we do not find more satisfying modes by which to convey pain, we will continue to be less equipped as a people to reduce the amount of pain collectively felt in the world. The inexpressibility of pain—the difficulties we face when presented with the task of telling another of our pain and of appreciating physical pain that is not our own—is, in part, what increases the power of pain's impact on our bodies and lives. Thus, for those who have been in pain and for "those who speak *on behalf* of those in pain," the capacity to exert power is predicated upon one's ability to share or to communicate.[71]

This process of communication, more specifically, is a rhetorical act of *invention*. As Scarry concludes: "In the long run, we will see that the story of *physical pain* becomes as well a story about the expansive nature of human *sentience*, the felt-fact of aliveness that is often sheerly happy, just as the story of *expressing* physical pain eventually opens into the wider frame of *invention*. The elemental 'as if' of the person in pain ('It feels as if,' 'It is as though') will lead out into the array of counterfactual revisions entailed in making."[72] Despite the futility of striving for complete communicative transparency, this fumbling for words, for language to express what we are feeling, offers hope. It is an act whose purpose is to bring two or more people closer to appreciating each other's perspective.[73]

Of course, cynicism about the utility of "walking a mile in someone else's shoes" as a means to know, learn, and decide about environmental and human pain clearly remains. As Sontag suggests in *Regarding the Pain of Others,* "Citizens of modernity, consumers of violence as spectacle, adepts of proximity without risk, are schooled to be cynical about the possibility of sincerity. Some people will do anything to keep themselves from being moved." People's entrenched cynicism—or at the very least skepticism—about the pain of others requires more than merely going someplace to affect people in a way that will be persuasive. Responding to people's reactions to mediated images of war, Sontag writes:

> That we are not totally transformed, that we can turn away, turn the page, switch the channel, does not impugn the ethical value of an assault by images. It is not a defect that we are not seared, that we do not suffer *enough,* when we see these images. Neither is the photograph supposed to repair our ignorance about the history and causes of the suffering it picks out and frames. Such images cannot be more than an invitation to pay attention, to reflect, to learn, to examine the rationalizations for mass suffering offered by established powers. . . . Images have been reproached for being a way of watching suffering at a distance, as if there were some other way of watching. But watching up close—without the mediation of an image—is still just watching.[74]

In acknowledging the cynicism of many in response to our reactions to war images, Sontag proposes that proximity to and mediations of pain both risk similar choices: either to do something about what we are witnessing or not. Going to the places where pain has been inflicted, she suggests, offers no more (or less) of a guarantee of social change than a mediated image.

I will delve further into the recalcitrant debate over whether or not a hierarchy of communication media exists in chapter 5. For now, I want to wrap up this chapter by exploring the overlap of Scarry's and Sontag's projects. Namely, physical pain itself must be communicated to some degree in order to reduce pain itself. To be clear: the goal is not complete communicative transparency or coherence, as if one could finally and definitely "know" or "experience" another's pain. Neither Scarry nor Sontag imagines some ideal type of "pure" communication. Both even insist on the impossibility of this proposition. Sontag concludes her argument by stating: " 'We'—this 'we' is everyone who has never experienced anything like what they went through—don't understand. We don't get it. We truly can't imagine what it was like. We can't imagine how dreadful, how terrifying war is; and how normal it becomes. Can't understand, can't imagine. That's what every soldier, every journalist and aid worker and independent observer who has put in time under fire, and had the luck to elude the death that struck down others nearby, stubbornly feels. And they are right."[75] In this sense, no tour of a rain forest or a park or a community will enable a visitor to truly know what it feels like to be a resident.

Yet the limits of our ability to understand the pain of other people—and, I would add, that of the Earth and all its inhabitants—does not mean that it is futile to strive for a closer understanding. If we give up on improving our ability to communicate with each other at all simply because communication is necessarily imperfect and incomplete, then we give up completely, because there is no resistance without communication. Social change cannot occur without communication. Scarry suggests that the flaws inherent in communication are precisely what make it such a powerful facet of our lives: "Whatever pain achieves, it achieves in part through its *unsharability*."[76] By not sharing, by not communicating, by not fumbling with language, our only option is to remain instruments for and objects of those who continue to create pain in the world.

This is why tourism becomes important once again, for as Dean Mac-Cannell writes, "The term 'touristic' should have been restricted to refer to the circulation of the gift of shared notice."[77] At its most fundamental level, MacCannell argues, tourism is an opportunity for a person or community to share, or to communicate, with another person or community about what is sacred, worthwhile, pleasurable, or meaningful. In a sense, tourism provides the possibility for us to unpack the baggage—the extraordinary and the banal, the good and the bad, the pleasure and the pain—that we as people, cultures, and inhabitants of the Earth carry with us. To expand on what such a perspective of tourism might mean within the context of material and symbolic toxic pollution, I will now turn to specific practices of toxic tourism.

3

Sites and Sacralization

The moment I stepped off the bus (I have allergies) I was hit with a migraine headache and shortness of breath and in real distress. I just started crying for the people that call the community home and must be breathing that toxic air all the time. . . . I think the tours are a great idea, even though it made me sick to go on the tour. If the people in power or decision makers would go on a toxic tour I believe they would smell the light as well as see it.

—Catherine Murray, 2002, personal correspondence with author subsequent to a toxic tour in "Cancer Alley," Louisiana

Louisiana—particularly New Orleans—attracts tourists.[1] From Mardi Gras parties and Cajun restaurants to jazz funerals and plantation homes, the area is admired for its promises of fun, culturally diverse experiences, and engaging historical sites. In addition, the region's proximity to several waterways, such as the Mississippi River and the Gulf of Mexico, is inviting to outdoor enthusiasts interested in everything from fishing to swamp boat tours. Central to Louisiana's appeal to most tourists, at least in part, is its rich multi-racial and multi-ethnic history. As I was told on a commercial cemetery tour in New Orleans, for example, among the area's many claims to fame is its role as the grounds for *Plessy v. Ferguson*. Although stories about the impetus for this legal case vary, most accounts generally describe how Homer Plessy, an African American, "passed" as "white" when boarding a train and, after the ride began, stood up to announce his race. Subsequently, Plessy was arrested, and the U.S. Supreme Court issued its infamous "separate but equal" ruling.[2] Cultural performances in Louisiana of "slave auctions, Mardi Gras parades, Wild West Shows, and the staging of the Plessy case," Joseph Roach argues, provide opportunities either to accept the historic rationalizations provided for "the bloody frontier of conquest and forced assimilation" of Native Americans and African Americans or, alternatively, to embrace the historical possibilities of "another version of 'Life in Louisiana.'"[3]

Louisiana—particularly the body of land along the Mississippi River from New Orleans to Baton Rouge—has also attracted petrochemical industries due to its cheap, accessible, and welcoming reputation since "the collapse of the sugar plantation system after World War II." Today this area "accounts for nearly one-fourth of the nation's petrochemical production. Some 125 companies in this corridor manufacture a range of products including fertilizers, gasoline, paints, and plastics." As a result, residents "have also described their environment as a toxic gumbo."[4] Just as Louisiana's multicultural history and convenient geographical location for water transportation are inviting to tourists, many argue that these features also are central to attracting polluting industries. In addition to the practical asset of water routes, petrochemical industries would not have arrived or begun operating as they have if they had not first identified areas where the local population was predominantly Native American and African American. To expose this exploitative relationship between waste and race, which activists refer to as "environmental racism,"[5] local residents have renamed this "industrial corridor" "Cancer Alley" (and more recently as "Cancer Death Alley"). In a similarly provocative vein, they have begun to bring together the two businesses for which the area has become so well known—tourism and the petrochemical industry—by organizing toxic tours.

By combining the more traditional categories of nature and culture tourism, toxic tours attempt to persuade tourists (or outsiders) to help mobilize further democratic action for environmental justice—or as Catherine Murray describes in the above epigraph, to encourage people to "smell the light as well as see it." Since juxtaposing the celebrated with the reviled is a fundamental facet of a toxic tour, it is perhaps unsurprising that toxic tours are often—though not always—organized in areas that are popular for commercial tourism. In places where the tourist industry is popular, tourism serves as a cultural resource for both hegemonic and counterhegemonic discourses.

To illustrate how the rhetorical and cultural force of toxic tours is constituted through their performance, this chapter provides an in-depth example of one "typical" toxic tour.[6] In other words, the tour follows the format of guiding visitors through an area where residents live, work, play, and pray, providing stops along the way to highlight particular concerns, such as pollution sources, peoples' physical ailments, and related environmental and social problems. As a cultural performance, this and other examples of toxic tours throughout the book should make apparent that toxic tours are not "pure efficacy or pure entertainment."[7] That is to say, all toxic tours reflexively negotiate power through the inextricably interlinked practices of play and politics.

One of the primary ways in which tours in general provide a means of negotiating power is through the process of "sight sacralization," or the articulation of sociosymbolic meanings to specific places. Dean MacCannell outlines sight sacralization as a five-stage process involving naming, framing/elevation, enshrinement, mechanical reproduction, and social reproduction.[8] In this chapter I illustrate how toxic tours tactically resist hegemonic perceptions of bodies of land, people, and thought by appropriating the conventional tour process of sight sacralization to counter accepted notions of the sacred and the profane. To do so, I particularly focus on the tour guide's role in framing the tour.[9] Since this toxic tour was provided for the Sierra Club, however, I first want to elaborate on the relationship between the environmental movement and the environmental justice movement.

Political Foes or Allies?

Upon receiving the Goldman Prize in 2004 for her leadership in southern Louisiana as a grassroots environmental justice activist, Margie Eugene-Richard recalled: "There were times I thought it was an impossible task. I remember standing in my yard thinking, 'Lord, will there ever be hope?' But a little voice within me kept saying, 'If we don't tell them, how will they know?'"[10]

Indeed, Eugene-Richard and many others from southern Louisiana have shared their struggles, stories, and hopes with numerous people.[11] Two years earlier their efforts had achieved an important milestone. After more than a decade of grassroots activism, the first community relocation environmental justice victory in the Deep South was achieved. The multinational Shell Oil Company agreed to move residents of one community and to reduce their emissions at the neighboring plant. When the community held a meeting to celebrate the settlement, they thanked a long list of people and organizations, many of which had participated in toxic tours of the region. Among them were more established environmental organizations such as Greenpeace and the Sierra Club. Understanding the significance of this acknowledgment warrants an appreciation for the difficulties that have arisen in past attempts for such alliance building.

Decades of tension between these two movements exploded into the public sphere in 1990. In January of that year, the Gulf Coast Tenant Leadership Development Project sent a letter to the "Group of Ten"[12] national environmental organizations. Two months later, another letter followed from the Southwest Organizing Project, which included 103 signatories and solidified a broader level of support for the first letter. They claimed: "There is a clear lack of accountability by the Group of Ten environmental organizations towards Third World communities in the Southwest, in the United States as a whole, and internationally."[13] The list of grievances included environmental organizations supporting legislation that chose preserving the land over people (especially people of color), endorsing policies that do not account for cultural heritage as a factor in environmental decision making, lacking employees or volunteers who are people of color, and working with corporations that oppress people of color.

Subsequently, a flood of criticism for the more established environmental movement appeared in public discourse. For example, the *New York Times* headlined: "Environmental Groups Told They Are Racist in Hiring."[14] Although some overlapping interests had existed historically between the environmental and environmental justice groups, numerous books, chapters, and articles published in the 1990s increasingly testified to the historical and ongoing frustrations of people of color and low-income communities toward the insularity of the more established and privileged environmental movement.[15]

More than a year after the letters were written, from October 24 to 27, 1991, environmental justice activists gathered in Washington, D.C. for the First National People of Color Environmental Leadership Summit.

Convened by the Commission for Racial Justice of the United Church of Christ, the Summit brought together more than six hundred people from around the world. Throughout the Summit, delegates such as Pat Bryant, Executive Director of the Gulf Tenants Organization, expressed feelings of frustration that echoed those of the environmental justice movement's initial letters: "We knew we needed allies, but when we reached out to the Sierra Club, we found that only one Sierra Club member could understand us. . . . Somehow, racism has made itself palatable to the intellectuals and to the environmentalists."[16]

On the third day of the Summit, a session entitled "Our Vision of the Future: A Redefinition of Environmentalism" invited statements from the Executive Director of the Natural Resources Defense Council (NRDC), John H. Adams, and the Executive Director of the Sierra Club, Michael Fischer, with a response by Dana Alston, Panos Institute official and member of the Summit Planning Committee. This discussion proposed continuing the spirit of dialogue between environmental justice and environmental groups and leaders in an open forum.

Perhaps unsurprisingly, responses from environmental groups to environmental justice gestures ranged from defensiveness to a willingness to change. Many environmentalists responded by emphasizing the work that they had been doing for decades, though without the vocabulary of "environmental justice." Fischer, for example, noted: "The Sierra Club works a lot on rocks and trees and mountains and scenic beauty. But that is not all we do. It is most important to know that, particularly in the last 10 to 15 years, much more of our energy has gone into a very broad mission . . . [i.e.,] toxics." Adams similarly stated: "For 20 years, NRDC has relentlessly confronted the massive problems associated with air, water, food and toxics. These issues form the core of NRDC's agenda, a public-health agenda."[17]

Despite their resistance to being pigeonholed or stereotyped as solely tree-hugging, whale-saving preservationists, both directors recognized a need for change. "We know we have been conspicuously missing from the battles for environmental justice all too often, and we regret that fact sincerely," Adams stated. "I believe that this historic conference is a turning point, however, and while we can still say the *mea culpas* from time to time, this is a charge to all of us to work and look into the future, rather than to beat our breasts about the past. . . . We national environmental organizations are not the enemy. The divide-and-conquer approach is one that the Reagan and Bush administrations have used all too successfully for all too long." Fischer concluded by urging: "Let us pledge to each other that we will make it so."[18]

Rather than recognizing the environmental movement's past efforts to achieve what was now being labeled "environmental justice" or immediately embracing Adams's and Fischer's calls for change, Alston emphasized the basis for building a political alliance between the two movements: "The real basis of the challenge is how some of the actions and the policies of environmental organizations have a drastic impact on the economic, social and political life of our communities." Insisting that she could not "leave this room without telling some truths," Alston concluded: "So gentlemen . . . the only thing I have to say is, it is up to you who have come here today and laid out your understanding, to challenge your brothers and sisters on this. It cannot continue to be our role alone to keep raising this issue. . . . We will continue our challenge from the outside."[19]

Since these and other initial conversations occurred in the 1990s, little has been written in a positive or encouraging tone about the efforts of environmentalists to meet these challenges.[20] For the most part, if any notice has been made, attempts have been criticized, if not ridiculed. In one example from the early 1990s, a *Wall Street Journal* reporter attended a toxic tour with the Sierra Club and a local environmental justice group, Jesus People Against Pollution (JPAP), in Columbia, Mississippi, and concluded with the following description of tension and miscommunication:

> Early in the evening, the Sierrans gather around a table with the Jesus People to discuss what the Sierra Club might provide in the way of money. "How much you talking about?" asks Nick Aumen of Sierra Club's Golf Coast Regional Conservation Committee.
>
> "Let's start with a zillion dollars," shouts back Deeohn Ferris, an attorney with the Lawyers Committee for Civil Rights Under Law, flown down by the Sierra Club to assist Jesus People.
>
> The Sierra Club tour group answers that while the club could help JPAP apply for money from foundations or hit up the Mississippi congressional delegation for funds to relocate families, it can

provide little in terms of financial assistance. "We're not a golden cow ready to throw money on the table," says Mr. Kulik of the Mississippi chapter. "We understand you don't have a golden *calf*," answers JPAP president Charlotte Keys, correcting Mr. Kulik's biblical reference.[21]

If one had read only this article, one might be led to believe that no common ground was found and that the toxic tour was a "freak show" at best.

I turn to this article not only because it illustrates the intertwined nature of toxic tours and the environmental justice movement's relationship with environmental organizations, but also because both Sierra Club and JPAP volunteers have reminded me of this article when I have asked about toxic tours more broadly.[22] For example, JPAP Executive Director Charlotte Keys, an African American environmental justice activist who has hosted toxic tours for more than a decade, and I had the following conversation during an interview. In order to avoid accusations of convenient editing given my own subject position as a Sierra Club volunteer at the time, I quote this interview at length.

Pezzullo: Have you had negative reactions on your tours?
Keys: Yes, we have. We've had people—it was when the Sierra Club was in here—
Pezzullo: Ahhhh—
Keys: —at one point. I think they brought in someone from *Wall Street.*
Pezzullo: Oh! Yeah, yeah—
Keys: Yeah, that article. . . . And that was very negative—
Pezzullo: The article itself?
Keys: . . . The article itself. And the guy's heart was not in the right place.
Pezzullo: Mmmm—
Keys: It was more geared towards what industry wanted. . . . No one wants their community trashed. No one wants to live in a dirty environment. Everyone wants to be in a clean, healthy, safe environment—whether that's dealing with the workplace, where the children attend school and pray or you know, just living. And

given that such an article was written, that just shows you the kind of mind-set that certain people have about the underserved population and how folks actually don't realize that human beings that is living under these types of constraints don't want to live in a dirty environment . . . because of the lack of education and resources, these are the populations that are targeted for the unwanted by-products of, you know, rich, powerful folks that is in positions to help them improve or do better.

Pezzullo: . . . I thought his article—now, I'm trying to remember—I thought his article, though, was supportive of your community and was sort of insulting the Sierra Club saying they were, that it was sort of ridiculous for them to come to your community and that the Sierra Club was sort of silly in that scenario. . . . I'm trying to think of his words; but, I thought he was sort of saying that your community had a point, but the Sierra Club coming in was just, you know, mostly—I think he had a picture of John McCown—but, beyond that, mostly white liberals coming in to your community like it was like a zoo, sort of—

Keys: Yeah.

Pezzullo: And that he kind of felt like: "How is the Sierra Club really helping you by coming on the tour?"—

Keys: —when communities is not organized, and empowered in such a way that folks understand that organizing is a business. To organize your community and set it up with some kind of structural format that can help communities, be organized enough to receive the resources that is needed or to help change things in that community. Sierra Club and different organizations—they call them the Big Ten—they're in a position, more than not, to help bring resources on the ground to direct problems. And also even when you have communities up against industry and you have very few folk that is supporting basically the way you approach or deal with industry in a sense where you're trying to get folks to sometimes mediate a situation rather than go into the litigation process. Different organizations can play a key role in assisting certain things that they have been formed and they're out there.

Pezzullo: Right—

Keys: So, you shouldn't basically put down on different ones that are trying in some way to assist—one of the things, too, that happens is communities look for these tours to be a tool that would actually, as I stated before, cause folks to have some compassion in their hearts to want to help them change and turn things around that things work—[23]

This exchange surprised me because I did not expect Keys to associate the newspaper article with industry interests. As a Sierra Club activist, I had heard of the article as yet another example of how a "mainstream" environmental group was "bashed" publicly for its (failed?) attempt to work with an environmental justice group. Keys, on the other hand, already had assumed the newspaper reporter was aligned with industry interests, because the reporter focuses the article on criticizing the Sierra Club rather than on the environmental conditions in which she lives. When I finally fumbled through the words to explain what I perceived as the difference between the two perspectives, Keys clarified why she saw the "divide-and-conquer" approach to be aligned with industry interests rather than her own community's.

I do not mean to suggest that either Charlotte Keys or I would argue that the environmental movement has resolved all of its racial and economic biases. Yet I also believe that the above conversation is illustrative of an exasperation that at least some environmental justice activists feel toward those who attempt to divide them from the environmental movement. Rather than poking fun at efforts to create partnerships or political alliances, Keys suggests that it is more useful to continue to find ways to work together. John McCown, an African American Sierra Club environmental justice organizer hired less than a year after the Summit, agrees: "I strongly believe we are being tested here. For so long we have allowed industry to divide us on the basis of race and class. We're going to have to come together as brothers and sisters—as human beings—to stop this problem of environmental injustice. As John Muir said, there's a connectedness between all things. If people in Columbia, Mississippi, are suffering, then something is ailing European Americans from North Carolina to California as well."[24]

Yet this work of building an alliance is not straightforward. At the 2002 Second National People of Color Environmental Leadership Summit in Washington, D.C., I was one of a small group of people who attempted to craft Principles for Collaboration between the two movements. Since then, neither grassroots environmental justice leaders nor scholars have mentioned it with any recognition close to that of the Principles that grew out of the first Summit.[25]

This continued tension between the two movements is important to note for at least three reasons. Most obviously, it serves as a synecdoche for the historical relationship between these two environmental movements. It also highlights the liminal space that I occupy as a participant observer and that many toxic tourists occupy as "outsiders." And, as a result of both of those contexts, it provides a reminder that we should not take interactions such as those enabled by the subsequent toxic tour—and others like it—for granted.

"A Toxic Tour Is Not Just about the Chemical Plant"

This chapter focuses on a toxic tour held on May 12, 2001, in southern Louisiana, one year prior to the relocation victory previously mentioned and one decade after the Summit. The primary audience was a group of Sierra Club volunteers, Sierra Club staff organizers, and environmental justice activists from across the United States who had been working with the Sierra Club.[26] As one Sierra Club publication noted when describing the gathering: "Sammy James, a Navajo medicine man, prayed aloud in his native tongue, weeping through his words at times. Elaine Purkie strummed her guitar and sang a from-the-gut Appalachian fight song about coal mining and union might. Balinda Moore, an African-American pastor from Tennessee, shared . . . [a] story of [racism]. . . . This was a Sierra Club Meeting."[27] Politically, it is important to recognize the diversity of this constituency and the Sierra Club's own belief that this diversity is "newsworthy," because it symbolizes a shift—or, at minimum, a perception of a shift—in the work of a more traditional environmental organization such as the Sierra Club in relation to the relatively younger environmental justice movement. That this diversity is not taken for granted also reminds us of the previously mentioned work involved in building community across cultures and geographical regions for the environmental justice movement, which ideally aims to expand both its sense of community and the issues that warrant attention from that community.

The toxic tour began approximately at 12:45 P.M. in uptown New Orleans at the conference center where the participants were staying, and it concluded around 9:00 P.M.. For obvious reasons, I cannot provide a complete description of the entire tour; rather, I will try to convey a sense of its overall significance and function by considering, in chronological order, the beginning, the three primary stops, and the end of the tour. The primary tour guide's verbal performance appeared nonlinear insofar as he spoke about issues and places as they occurred to him or as they arose geographically. I intend to illustrate how the guide's ongoing verbal performance and the stops on the tour—while lacking a single climax—served rhetorical and cultural purposes that both contested and reinvented the area's value as a sacralized sight.

Since the tour began when the bus pulled up and people boarded, it is important to consider the space in which most of the tour took place. Buses themselves served repeatedly as focal points for the U.S. Civil Rights Movement. Recall the bus boycotts in cities such as Montgomery and Tallahassee during the late 1950s, the 1956 U.S. Supreme Court ruling on bus desegregation, and the Freedom Rides in the summer of 1961. These struggles have been memorialized repeatedly in popular culture, and even the most traditional history books today remember Rosa Parks.[28] Buses, in these moments, represent public spaces in which people can come together to engage each other. As such, they aid us in traveling not only physical but also cultural distances and, therefore, offer a public space in which cultural obstacles can be negotiated and transformed.

Robin Kelley suggests that further exploration of public forums such as buses may help to open up our assumptions about what black working-class struggles have been and to be more inclusive than traditional civil rights histories of resistance. Kelley thus argues for the usefulness of imagining the spaces within buses and other forms of public transportation as public arenas for negotiating power, control, and community: "In some ways, the design and function of the busses and streetcars rendered them unique sites of contestation. An especially apt metaphor for understanding the character of domination and resistance on public transportation might be to view the interior spaces as '*moving theaters.*'"[29]

When provided on a bus, of course, toxic tours are intended to be a different kind of theater, at least in part, because they are not used for public transportation. The toxic tour bus is privately chartered and, therefore, purposefully predetermines who enters the bus and where the bus stops. Further, as a cliché of mass commercial tourism, the chartered bus marks participants as visitors in a way that can physically exaggerate the distance between the tourists and the toured. Yet, in both instances, the bus is transformed into a "moving theater" or space for revitalizing connections between people and places. The bus, in these instances, takes us places and is a place, or destination, itself.

Departures

Rather than being a one-dimensional actor, a tour guide is charged with coordinating a complicated series of interactive performance events both backstage and onstage, usually with the added responsibility of attempting to make this complex of performances appear effortless or "natural."[30] Standing at the front of the inside of the bus with a microphone in hand, our guide, Darryl Malek-Wiley, was a middle-age man of European descent with a big, white, wiry beard. When he began speaking, his voice was deep yet playful (see figure 2).

> Malek-Wiley: Do you know the person you're sitting next to?
> Tourists: Yes.
> Malek-Wiley: Do you know them well?
> Tourists: Yesss—
> Malek-Wiley: [*Disapprovingly, he shakes his head back and forth.*] If you know somebody you've met before, you're supposed to sit next to somebody you've never met before—you're supposed to sit next to somebody else. The idea of this tour is to meet new people. Larry and Sheila know each other, I think. [*The crowd laughs, because Larry and Sheila are married.*] But, the idea is that every time we get off the bus or get back on the bus, you sit down beside somebody different. That's part of the idea. [*He pauses as*

Figure 2. Darryl Malek-Wiley, toxic tour guide in New Orleans, Louisiana. Videotape still recorded by author.

some people on the bus begin switching seats.] Rule Two: Anybody got a cell phone? Turn it off. We're not listening to nobody outside the bus until we get to where we're going. So— [*He briefly pauses again, looking around the bus.*] My name is Darryl Malek-Wiley. I'm the Group Chair of the New Orleans Group. I've been involved with the Sierra Club since 1972 and have been doing toxic tours here in Louisiana since about 1983. So, we're going to take a road up the river and we're going to see things and talk about the whole concept of toxic tours and how they can be used in your community. And my view is: a toxic tour is not just about the chemical plant, it's about the history, the culture, everything that goes on . . .

Malek-Wiley's introduction immediately marks off the space of the bus as a theater that is both material and symbolic: we are instructed to be engaged with each other, attentive to him, and open to what we are about to witness. This introduction also establishes Malek-Wiley's credibility as a guide by highlighting his experience in providing toxic tours and his involvement in local environmental activism.

As is often the case in social movements, I had heard of Malek-Wiley before I met him. A carpenter by trade, he has been involved in environmental, labor, and social justice activism since the early 1970s. His is the type of story that is often lost in official versions of history, the Left, and even in environmental justice literature. It speaks to diverse coalitions and to his personal dedication to the interconnected struggles of environmental, racial, and economic justice. I believe it is important that the tour begins with and continues to highlight his story, not because it is necessarily typical or completely unique, but because it is an exemplary story, one "*worth* saving, *worth* repeating."[31]

As the following excerpt illustrates, Malek-Wiley persists in weaving his performance of self with narratives about the history of the area.

Malek-Wiley: The real levee system got started in the 1930s and '40s. But, we have to think about New Orleans going back before that, before the levees, before the Europeans got here, and back to the Native culture that was very active in this area. [*Brief pause to offer driver some directions.*] We have to understand some things that we were taught in history are not necessarily true. I don't know if that'll shock anybody here—

Voice from Bus: Get outta here!—

Malek-Wiley: —Yeah, I know, it's hard to believe that. But, I learned early. My family traveled. I learned history in Ohio, U.S. history. Then, we moved to West Virginia, and I learned U.S. history in West Virginia. Then, we moved to North Carolina, where I learned about the *real* U.S. history. [*He smiles.*] So, it's different. But, all of those places didn't talk about the *vast* cultures of Native Americans that was here. There's a whole vast culture of Native people throughout the Mississippi-Ohio river system for hundreds of thousands of years before the Europeans came. . . . They estimate that there were 9 billion Native Americans throughout the United States—about 3 billion in the Mississippi-Ohio region. *What happened?* . . . Being an environmentalist, I like to ask questions. That's what I do.

Remembering history with such broad brushstrokes is an explicit theme of Malek-Wiley's performance. Rather than being caught up in details, his performance challenges any commonsense understanding of a singular "true" version of history and illustrates how history shifts depending on one's perspective, just as our perspectives promised to shift as we searched for and found different seats on the bus between stops. At this point in the tour, therefore, what is most important is the invitation to become open to alternative perspectives.

What I find most interesting in this excerpt is the emphasis of the last three sentences: "What happened? . . . Being an environmentalist, I like to ask questions. That's what I do." In these initial moments and throughout the tour, Malek-Wiley builds his ethos as an environmentalist among environmentalists. In many ways, he looks like a stereotypical environmental movement leader: European American, male, and bearded. The social memories of his political credentials not only build his credibility as an expert on Cancer Alley but also offer a role model for the rest of the participants on the tour, all activists invested in the difficult work of building democratic political alliances among environmentalists, labor advocates, and civil rights activists.[32] Malek-Wiley's assertion invites all on the bus to do the same as he: ask questions. This ethic of critical inquiry, when applied to environmentalism, opens the possibility for political dialogue in which a variety of voices are encouraged to speak but in which judgments are still made.

First Stop: Norco

After sharing a series of stories about the history of Cancer Alley, approximately two hours into the tour, Malek-Wiley directs the bus driver to turn into a predominantly African American town of St. Charles Parish called Norco, which he explains claims roots that extend much farther back than the arrival of the surrounding chemical industries.[33] There, the bus driver parks, and Malek-Wiley invites us to step out. The paved road we walk down is lined with residential properties on one side and a chain-link metal fence on the other, officially marking off the property of a Shell Company chemical plant. Toward the end of the road, we meet a group of people.

One person we encounter is a well-known African American environmental justice organizer who worked for Greenpeace at the time, Damu Smith. He spontaneously begins providing a brief history of the community and notes that we just have missed a community meeting discussing the advantages and disadvantages of having Shell pay for relocation of local residents. Smith also passes out fliers for a toxic tour he is organizing for the following month.[34] Then, to his credit, Smith gives the floor to Margaret Evans, a local African American community member. This gesture exemplifies how both national environmental groups and local environmental justice groups can speak and work together toward a common goal without the larger institutions smothering the smaller ones. It also enables those of us on the tour to hear a remarkable impromptu speech.

> Also, what I wanted to say is what Shell has done: they've wanted to be clever. What they have done is that they're saying when the people here move out, they're going to have a nice *green* area for a walkway. . . . Also, saying in a subtle way: "There's nothing wrong with living here." They're saying they're having a "voluntary move." And they're not saying it's a buffer zone; they're saying "a *green* belt." And my mother's tree is dying—there's nothing green about that beltway! So, their terminology and their *wording* is *saying:* "There's nothing wrong." And I tell you: if they want to volunteer, they can buy *your* property—*if* they want to "volunteer" that's the word or terminology they use for *not* showing responsibility. They're saying that they're willing to work with anybody who wants to sell their property: "They're welcome to come." They're not taking actual responsibility, saying: "*Yes,* we have done wrong to you. *Yes,* we have hurt you. *Yes,* we have damaged everything and we're going to buy you out." *No.* They are saying: "vol-un-tary programs." So, that shows the cutoff of the word "responsibility."

Evans's speech critically interrupts Shell's discourse in powerful ways.[35] More specifically, Evans evidences the performative power of language.[36]

It is not merely that Shell uses language she would not choose; her point is that by choosing particular words, Shell articulates specific behaviors and (un)ethics that harm her community. Put differently, Shell's discourse performs a lack of responsibility and accountability, disavowing the connection between itself and the toxification of local bodies of people and land. Evans contests Shell's official framing of her community and environment as disconnected from what happens on the other side of the fence. By denying their actions and claiming instead that the potential relocation of the Norco community is "voluntary," Shell is transforming the situation into one of choice and consent instead of one that honestly admits abuse and coercion, argues Evans. Shell does "buy people's houses, with a going rate about $10,000 to $15,000 for a trailer and $45,000 for brick homes," but it claims that "these purchases have nothing to do with dangers from the plant, but are to help it build a 'green belt.'"[37] By reclaiming the language used to describe the situation, Evans's words contest Shell's power to name and frame the community's conditions.

Evans also questions the "clever" privileging of corporations and capitalism over people and community. By using the term "voluntary programs," she argues that Shell cuts off the recognition that they "have done wrong," "hurt," and "damaged everything." In other words, there is no acknowledgment that her community is worthy of being preserved. There is a lack, in a sense, of what MacCannell identifies as the first stage of sight sacralization, the process of naming "when the sight is marked off from similar objects as worthy of preservation."[38] Put differently, throughout this toxic tour, the logic of what or who has been considered expendable is subverted insofar as the tour both marks what or who is traditionally preserved in a culture *and* contests the choice to continue preserving those traditions over others.

Subsequently, Evans lists the illnesses that threaten the preservation of the people in her neighborhood, including respiratory problems, cancer, and learning disabilities. In order to track the toxic air contaminants that she and others say are responsible for these maladies, she informs us, the community had become part of what is called the Bucket Brigade. In brief, the Bucket Brigade offers a means by which people without formal technical education can test their air by collecting samples and sending them off to an EPA-approved laboratory for results. Prior to and after the tour, the Sierra Club donated money to the community to help them have access to this expensive process, which costs approximately five hundred dollars a sample. A community member provides a demonstration of how a sample is collected for those of us on the tour with an unspoken acknowledgment of who sometimes paid the bill. Such gestures can have cyclical effects. For example, Sue Williams, a Sierra Club volunteer, shares: "The information about the bucket brigade which was presented at the church on the tour I took has stayed with me. . . . That was the first time I'd heard about it and I realized how badly we need it in Memphis."[39] Williams's words are interesting because they remind us that even though a Sierra Club group or Program is sponsoring bucket brigades in one location, it does not necessarily follow that another Sierra Club group or Program would know, since there is a vast scope of issues, people, and places that are involved in and with the organization. By offering an occasion for activists to exchange ideas and practices that help achieve common or, at least, related goals, toxic tours help forge a political alliance. In this sense, the toxic tour provides opportunities to learn not just about the people and places toured but also about those doing the touring.[40]

When we were heading back to the bus, the following exchange occurred between me and another tour participant:

> [She] asked: "Do you smell that?" Feeling a bit guilty for not having smelled anything noticeable—after all, I was on a mission to record everything—I replied, "No—but, I think some people are naturally more sensitive to smells—just like some people are more apt to have cancer." She looked me directly in the eyes and said: "Well, I can smell it and feel it—my eyes are irritated and, earlier, I felt my throat tighten up. That's why I've got to get back on the bus. I'm finding it hard to breathe." She paused and then, added: "But, I also have cancer—" and launched into her own community's struggle against toxic pollution. (field notes)

Again, the space of the toxic tour provides opportunities for connection between those being toured and between those on the tour itself. Spontaneous conversations such as this one are constitutive of the tour's value. They illustrate the possibility for moments of solidarity among those facing common struggles as well as the ways in which a toxic tour is a multisensory, embodied experience for those touring. Spontaneous conversations also suggest the opportunity to create further distinctions, such as those who can or cannot appreciate a particular facet of the tour and those who do or do not belong to a particular identity (e.g., people with cancer). This marking of difference highlights the heterogeneity inherent in any community.

Second Stop: Holy Rosary Cemetery

After we have gathered on the bus, Malek-Wiley begins to describe the landscape we are moving through, his finger pointing around all sides of the bus.

> Malek-Wiley: So, we're now on top of the levee. And you can see
> Shell behind us, Union Carbide over here, you go up beyond
> Union Carbide, it's Occidental Chemical. Next to them it's
> Becker. And in this dome right in front of us is a nuclear power
> plant. And beyond the nuclear power plant, those are two gas-
> fired energy plants on that side of the river. And two gas-fired
> plants on this side of the river. . . . This plant moved in on top
> of this community. And this happens time and time again. And
> people ask: why did this happen? . . . Why are they here? . . . It
> goes back to French Louisiana . . . What happened after the U.S.
> Civil War changed that system somewhat. After the Civil War, all
> of the African Americans who had lived on plantations were given
> land. Now, it wasn't forty acres and a mule. They didn't get that.
> They got a small plot of land, and most of that was immediately
> adjacent to the plantation land.

Moving figuratively between the present and the past, Malek-Wiley's performance pushes the audience to remember the relationships between cause and effect, past and present, and to question the establishment of official boundaries that supposedly "protect" the communities in this area from the abundance of industries we saw. Just as former slaves lived on small plots of land adjacent to the sources of their oppression, so, too, do their descendants live on land connected to the industries that both demean the value of their lives and jeopardize their survival.

Figure 3. Toxic tour vista of Holy Rosary Cemetery in Louisiana. Author photo.

The next stop after Norco is a place called the Holy Rosary Cemetery. The church previously adjacent to the cemetery was bought and moved by Union Carbide. Noting the symbolic visual value of this place, Malek-Wiley stops the bus at the environmental justice equivalent of the more traditional scenic vista. According to the dictionary, a *vista* is "(1) a view or prospect . . . ; (2) such an avenue or passage, esp. when formally planned; and (3) a far-reaching mental view: *vistas of the future*."[41] Since the towers of the industrial building in the background are so clearly mirrored in the religious icons of the graveyard that are positioned in the foreground, this tour stop represents a symbolic elevation of environmental injustice by juxtaposing the sacred and the profane, the "progress" promised by corporate development and the incommensurable vulnerability of human bodies. A vista such as Holy Rosary Cemetery provides a striking articulation of the environmental and human costs incurred by toxic pollution. The power of this vista's forecast is not lost on the tour group, and many of us walk out of the bus to take photographs (see figure 3).

Existing in the space of both politics and play, tourist performances such as this often attempt to re-present evidence of what has and has not been, what could and could not be. As Stuart Hall writes, "Positively marked terms 'signify' because of their position in relation to what is absent, unmarked, the unspoken, the unsayable. Meaning is relational within an ideological system of presences and absences."[42] Presence and absence thus dance dialectically between the gained and the lost, the marked and the unmarked, the spoken and the unspoken. Any discussion of one necessarily implicates the other. Raymie McKerrow observes: "*Absence* is as important as *presence* in understanding and evaluating symbolic action."[43]

After we leave the cemetery, Malek-Wiley recalls how the area became known as "Cancer Alley":

> Malek-Wiley: This idea of "Cancer Alley"—that you're in now—that *term* was created by a gentleman by the name of Richard Miller[44] and myself. . . . And we just started putting our press releases out. This is when we were involved in the BASF fight.[45] . . . We termed it "Cancer Alley" and started sending our press releases out: "From Cancer Alley"; "From Cancer Alley"; "From Cancer Alley." You know, and all of a sudden, it caught on. And the media caught on. The *term* set the terms of the debate. The debate was: "Is this a Cancer Alley? Is it not a Cancer Alley? If so, why?" If, you know, it wasn't an "industrial corridor," like the industry likes to talk about it, it was a Cancer Alley. And the latest data that came out from the Tumor Registry . . . last year said that we don't live in Cancer Alley, meaning we don't have a higher cancer incidence rate than the rest of the country, "statistically speaking," quote unquote. But, we do have a higher cancer death rate than the rest of the country. So, I've updated my schpiel. We don't live in Cancer Alley anymore. We live in Cancer Death Alley. So, you know, when you tell people—you weren't in Cancer Alley—you were in Cancer Death Alley.

Understood as what MacCannell describes as the first stage of sight sacralization, "the naming phase" involves a "great deal of work into the authentication of the candidate for sacralization."[46] By setting the terms of the debate in the region, the name "Cancer Alley" has provoked at least one study to assess this claim. Ironically, as Malek-Wiley points out, the "more accurate" description of the area sounds even more frightening: "Cancer Death Alley."[47] Clearly, naming the region has become a powerful tactic for environmental justice activists. This tactic has helped them to reframe public debate by foregrounding the deadly health effects produced by what industrial officials would otherwise describe innocuously as an "industrial corridor."

Third Stop: The Ashland Estate

Bringing the writings of Erving Goffman to bear on tourist practices, MacCannell argues: "The touristic way of getting in with the natives is to enter into a quest for authentic experiences, perceptions and insights. The quest for authenticity is marked off in stages in the passages from front to back. Movement from stage to stage corresponds to growing touristic understanding." Reflecting this pattern, the third stop on the tour provides, I would argue, a backstage look at the front stage. It enables tour participants to see how far we have come on our journey by visiting a more traditional tourist sightseeing location: the historic preservation of a plantation. It both elevates and frames the ideology embedded in the region, or, as MacCannell puts it, "the putting on of display of an object . . . [and] the placement of an official boundary around the object."[48] The following description of this part of the tour is excerpted from my field notes:

> About two and a half hours into the tour, Darryl began saying: "For people who remember *Gone With the Wind:* Tara. We're going to go by it. It's now owned by Shell Chemical. This is the plantation that was used. . . . " And I lost track of his voice. I was engrossed with the signs that stood below me on the ground:

> (FIRST SIGN) Ashland, built in 1841. Welcome to Ashland, which is being preserved by Shell Chemical Company. Although it is closed, please enjoy the view of the home and grounds. For information or if you have comments, please phone (225) 201-0550.

> (SECOND SIGN) The 2001 Ascension Parish Pilgrimage has been cancelled by the Ascension Parish Tourist Commission. For information please call 675-6550.

(THIRD SIGN) Private Property Shell Chemical Company No Trespassing.

A car was parked in front of the signs and estate gates with the driver sitting inside—a tourist of another kind. . . . I began registering Darryl's voice again . . .

Malek-Wiley: Shell has done some exterior renovations. . . . So, it's plantation culture that has continued on from the slave days now to the chemical plantations, who are the masters. And I mean that in a political sense also, because they are the major donors to all the campaigns around here. . . .

Pezzullo: What a trip—that Shell is preserving that. I can't believe they're preserving that.

Van Dam: Shell is preserving that whole plantation way of life. Just expanding [the] base of the servitude.

Shirley Van Dam recently had boarded the bus. She is a local labor organizer. Her reference to servitude resounded with me. Of course, I was wondering if this was another "Yankee moment," as my University of North Carolina students sometimes call it. Perhaps I was not supposed to believe that Shell's preservation of a plantation home was ironic, a bad public relations move that too easily led critics to the same conclusions we seemed to be making on the bus. Perhaps I was supposed to appreciate historical preservation in much the same way that I often support environmental preservation.[49] But, to be honest, I was simply horrified. . . . (field notes, supplemented by direct quotes from videotaping)

My subsequent research on Ashland uncovered a newspaper article that describes the estate as follows: "The fact that Ashland-Belle Home Plantation is standing is a little miracle. . . . The home, one of the grandest and largest plantation homes ever built in the state, was purchased by Shell Chemical Co. in 1992. 'It was in terrible condition,' said Winnic Byrd, a preservationist. . . . 'When Shell expressed an interest in acquiring the property for their operations and indicated they would take over stewardship, it was looked to by preservationists *as a lifesaver.*'"[50]

By leaving this stop for the latter half of the tour and, thus, offering a chance to witness the quality of life experienced next to Shell's plant, the toxic tour inverts this sociosymbolic "lifesaver." Marking the choice to establish this commercial tourist site as sacred, the toxic tour invites us to consider an interpretation of this "authentic" historical marker of heritage from the perhaps more "authentic" backstage. In a sense, contesting this official tourist site ironically marks what MacCannell calls the stage of "enshrinement" in sight sacralization, insofar as Speer and Fine note, "enshrinement is as much a movement through verbal doorways as physical ones."[51] Rather than passing by local communities to stop at this tourist site, we visit surrounding local communities along the way so that we might appreciate how the historical enshrinement of this more traditional tourist site is sustained performatively.[52]

From this alternative perspective, environmental justice activists argue that, in addition to polluting the environment where people live, the industries in the area practice "economic blackmail" where people work. Bullard explains how economic blackmail haunts the region: "The plantation owner in the rural parishes was replaced by the petrochemical industry executive as the new 'master' and 'overseer.' Petrochemical colonialism mirrors the system of domination typical of the Old South. In addition to poisoning the people, this new master is robbing many of the local residents (many of whom are descendants of slaves) of their ancestral homes. Environmental racism is now turning century-old African-American communities into ghost towns." In short, corporations keep racism alive by asserting: "you can get a job, but only if you are willing to do work that will harm you, your families, and your neighbors."[53]

As quoted above, a local labor organizer implies that by simultaneously polluting the area and preserving the Ashland estate Shell is "just expanding the base of servitude," both physically and ideologically. In addition to increasing the number of people exploited, MacCannell writes, the broader practice of placing a people and their culture on tour may also expand the number of people capable of acting as exploiters: "As the rhetoric of hostility toward minorities is replaced with a rhetoric of appreciation, the circle of their potential exploiters is dramatically expanded."[54] Of course, as Michael Bowman reminds us in his study of antebellum home tour guide performances, "tourism also permits the possibility of rejecting what is seen; it includes moments of skeptical assessment as well as wide-eyed wonder."[55] Thus, while the toxic tour tactically invites what MacCannell calls "the rhetoric of moral superiority," through which is expressed, ironically, how "tourists dislike tourists,"[56] it seems more useful to recognize this moment as an opportunity to mark tourist conventions as such and to explore what democratic alternatives might be realized through this process of destabilization.

The End of the Tour

After leaving Ashland, we stop for dinner at a locally owned restaurant. There, local environmental justice activist Juanita Stewart briefly speaks to us about her community's struggles, during which time we have more time to socialize in our newly constituted "backstage." When we return to the bus, the sky is dark. Malek-Wiley concludes by offering an upbeat speech about the range of more traditional political opportunities that are available to us, including reading political books, buying T-shirts satirizing the state of politics, writing letters to the editor, and getting involved in local and national political elections and legislation. To conclude, he states: "But, what the environmental community has got to do is get outside ourselves and into the communities more and really build our coalition with labor. . . . In the seventies, we got involved in labor, in the eighties, race. But, right now, we're losing the war on the environment. . . . It's time to get up and get moving. And it's tough." Here again, Malek-Wiley reiterates his desire for our response to the tour: a sense of increased personal empowerment and motivation for democratic, grassroots alliance building across environmental and environmental justice agendas.

Before allowing us simply to talk among ourselves (or rest) for the remaining bus ride back to New Orleans, Malek-Wiley ends his role as a tour guide by introducing and playing a forty-seven minute-film directed by Laura Dunn, *Green: A Film about Environmental Injustice.*[57] The video, interestingly, is a documentary version of a toxic tour of Cancer Alley. We are seeing the tour again, in a sense, from another perspective. In the process of tourist sight sacralization, sharing such a film resonates with what MacCannell calls the stage of "mechanical reproduction," when the tourist is set "in motion on [her or] his journey to find the true object. And [she or] he is not disappointed. Alongside the copies of it, it has to be The

Real Thing."[58] On this toxic tour of the region, the videotape provides a map of the area we have visited, interviews with people affirming the stories we have been told, and visual depictions of the places where we have been. Shown once the sun has gone down, these confirmations of our experience that day enshrine the tour as something worth documenting and worth remembering. Furthermore, it portrays stops we had not visited, people we had not met, and sites we did not see. In other words, the film performs as a reminder that our journey, though valuable, had been incomplete. As we are being transported out of the area, back toward the front stage of New Orleans, we are encouraged to remember that we only have experienced a glimpse of this "Life in Louisiana."

Conclusions

In this chapter I have illustrated how, along the Mississippi River, on the roads between Baton Rouge and New Orleans known to many as Cancer Alley or Cancer Death Alley, toxic tours illuminate the exigence of environmental justice struggles and invite new political alliances. By remembering histories along with Malek-Wiley, listening to Evans's analysis of corporate discourse, smelling the air, visiting the Holy Rosary Cemetery and the Ashland estate, watching *Green,* and interacting among ourselves, the specter of environmental racism's historical and contemporary effects is made more present and, thus, significant through the tour. These cultural memories, voices, and material sites perform as affective reminders of the grotesque ugliness, wastefulness, and painful violence that continues to happen in our racist, classist, and environmentally unjust world. They invite an embodied sense of presence *among* people, places, and concepts that formerly appeared more abstract to those less familiar with a grassroots perspective on "Life in Louisiana."

Although it is grounded within a specific cultural space, this chapter has illustrated two facets indicative of toxic tours as a democratic tactic of resistance. First, it provides us an opportunity to revisit the tensions between the environmental movement and the environmental justice movement. Second, it offers an example of how the conventional tourist practice of "sight sacralization" is appropriated by grassroots activists. Both have relevance to the broader themes of this book.

This tour and my interview with Charlotte Keys about toxic tours suggest that environmental justice criticisms have mattered to some environmentalists, at least to some degree. For example, Malek-Wiley drew
upon his tour guide role as an occasion to recall memories that may have
been forgotten both as a locus for constructing a collective identity between the two movements and as a rupture of persistent oppressive practices of material and symbolic toxification. Further, Keys was interested
in noting the importance of long-term environmental movement support
of environmental justice struggles; but, she was not willing to be caught
up in a divide-and-conquer rhetoric grounded in the cultural differences
of the two movements. Although toxic tours do not necessarily resolve
the questions that trouble what work needs to be done, by whom, when,
where, and how, toxic tours do tend to literally bring activists closer together, signaling the potential for future collaborations. "The challenge to
the new [and, I would add, the older] movement remains," as Jim Schwab
explains, because they both have "a chance to contribute a perspective
both new and very old that the world, in its current environmental crisis,
sorely needs. If we listen to each other, we may once again learn to listen
to the earth."[59] On this toxic tour, listening to each other and the Earth
illustrated the interrelated effects of toxic pollution on people, land, and
the ways we perceive the world. As such, they reinforce the relevance of
calls from the environmental justice movement to broaden our definition
of "environment" to include people and the places where people live,
work, play, and bury the dead.

The bus itself shaped the type of tour that was provided. Through the
performance of the tour, the bus became a theater to negotiate public
culture. As such, the toxic tour functioned as a means to bring together
and constitute political alliances and to rehearse new discourses.

In addition to emphasizing how a toxic tour can provide a forum within
which to negotiate potential alliances between environmental and environmental justice movement activists, therefore, this chapter has focused
on how toxic tours appropriate discourses of tourism as inventional resources for resistance. Considering particular populations, practices, and
places profane (disgusting, grotesque, and polluting) has enabled the per-
sistence of patterns of oppression. By appropriating the epistemological
framework or body of thought called "sight sacralization," this toxic tour

illustrates the possibility of a more democratic world by denaturalizing previously established labels of the "sacred" and resacralizing the bodies of people and land in pain that previously were considered profane.

This chapter's analysis has focused, therefore, on how a toxic tour can both contest official tourist discourses of the sacred and resacralize its own perspective. Although the tour itself minimally cited examples of social reproduction (when we were informed of previous and subsequent toxic tours in the region), it extensively reflected the remaining four stages of sight sacralization outlined by MacCannell and extended by Fine and Speer. Naming—of the region (from "industrial corridor" to "Cancer Alley" to "Cancer Death Alley"), of Shell's relationship to Norco and, of what was worth preserving—was repeatedly highlighted on the tour. Framing and elevation—of the Norco community, of the lives of those who have passed, of the importance of toxic touring itself—was negotiated explicitly and implicitly as a vital means of contesting worth, what is sacred, and which histories should be told. The process of enshrinement on a toxic tour, as I have illustrated with the example of the Ashland estate, is transformed into an occasion to question authenticity, particularly of common-sense assumptions about tourist value itself. Finally, the photographs taken by participants during the tour, the film played at the end of the tour, and even this chapter suggest at least some of the forms of mechanical reproduction that reify the value of the tour experience.

By appropriating this normative model of conventional tourism, this toxic tour and others like it also challenge cynical perceptions of tourism itself. Rather than further exoticizing or exploiting the people and the land visited, it promises the possibility of bringing diverse peoples and places together in ways that counter alienating and undemocratic patterns of alienation and oppression.

As illustrated in this chapter, the narratives shared on toxic tours both draw from and struggle to rearticulate cultural memories by contesting conventional representations, showing *the presence*—namely, the evidence—of injustice, and highlighting *the absence* of accountability or justice. Performing memory, in this sense, indicates a longing for social change, particularly in terms of strengthening alliances between communities. "For cultural memory," as J. Robert Cox notes, "may be both a locus of the public's identity (where we 'belong') and also a source of rupture, a critique of things as they are. . . . [It] assumes that history is open; that aspects of our heritage that have been forgotten can be retrieved; that standing in those places, we rediscover principles for judgment; and that, thus, we also keep alive the promise of what is 'not yet.'"[60]

Through critiquing the effects of toxic pollution, appropriating tourism's ability to sacralize, and invoking memory as the grounds for judgment, this toxic tour poignantly invites a reevaluation of historical *accountability* within southern Louisiana and beyond. " 'Accountability,' " as Wright, Bryant, and Bullard argue, "has to become a key word in the environmental justice movement."[61] Yet, as Vivian M. Patraka notes: "Accountability is not the same as reverentiality: accountability leaves room for critical inquiry, for debate, and risks being more invitational."[62] We must persist, therefore, in critically asking who is responsible for this ongoing toxic pollution and who is willing to challenge these institutions. We must continue to question dominant culture's reasons for labeling certain people and places sacred and other people and places profane. After participating in a toxic tour of Cancer Alley in May 2001, poet Haki Madabuti reiterated the need to carry on the critique of the toxic tour after it is over: "I look upon this as a mission. We need to be the drum. There's going to be a drumbeat that resounds throughout this nation."[63] This chapter, therefore, is just one beat of the growing drumroll, one more movement in anticipation of what is still to come.

4

Cancer and Co-optation

There must be some way to integrate death into living, neither ignoring
it nor giving in to it.

—Audre Lorde, *The Cancer Journals*

After I began my research on toxic tours, one of my cousins was diagnosed
with cancer. Her doctor told her that she was "the healthiest person with
cancer" that he had ever met. It wasn't much consolation. She was thirty-
two. She also was pregnant. Within two years, she gave birth to a healthy
baby girl, and she died. Trying to find a way to deal with her death and
what it meant to my life, I searched online for toxic tours addressing cancer. Knowing about the linkages between cancer and toxic pollution, I
assumed that such a tour must exist. Given how radical it remains to talk
about the relationship between the two, it did not surprise me to discover
one in San Francisco, California.

Situated between the Pacific Ocean and the San Francisco Bay, San
Francisco is a popular tourist destination for many reasons. Amid its steep
hills and temperate weather, San Francisco tourist icons include Alcatraz
Island, the cable car, and the Golden Gate Bridge, to name just a few.
Tourist "must-have" food lists often include everything from the "tourist
traps" of Fisherman's Wharf (like Boudin Bakery's sourdough bread and
Ghirardelli chocolates) to the numerous culturally diverse and distinct
neighborhood restaurants serving a range of global cuisines, including, of
course, "Californian." Located in what is called "the Bay Area," the city
also promises close proximity to the environmental and cultural sites of
Marin County, Oakland, San Jose, Palo Alto, and San Mateo—with "the
wine country" of Napa and Sonoma not far away. I have lived in more rural
areas since 1996, and when I visit my friends in the Bay Area, I am regularly
struck by the wonderful bookstores, the proliferation of "dot com" billboard advertisements, and how much it costs to live in such small places.

Despite—or, perhaps, partially as a result of—the high standard of living, one of the main attractions to San Francisco, at least for me, is the city's long history of progressive political activism.

The toxic tour that I want to explore in this chapter inverts the rhetorical performance of site sacralization more commonly practiced on toxic tours, such as the one illustrated in chapter 3 (i.e., when environmental justice advocates travel to and through communities that have been toxically-assaulted). Instead, this toxic tour challenges cultural perceptions of the sacred and the profane by taking grassroots grievances to the doorsteps of the institutions that activists believe are responsible for producing and enabling toxic pollution. By marking what is usually ignored by or lurking in the background of mainstream tourist routes, this toxic tour focuses on the institutions that are sacralized in U.S. culture with the hopes of desacralizing them and, thus, opening their practices up for debate.

The tour is held every October during National Breast Cancer Awareness Month (NBCAM). Epitomized by the pink ribbon, NBCAM is a monthlong, multi-pronged public health campaign that provides opportunity for numerous organizations and individuals to raise awareness about breast cancer detection, legislation, and experiences. Given that opposition to NBCAM is rarely heard, the discourse promoted by NBCAM arguably has become institutionalized as a hegemonic "common sense" and, thus, sacralized in the current approach to breast cancer in the United States.[1]

In this chapter I examine how one coalition of activists is attempting to reveal the gap between *the appearance of* and *the practices enabled by* NBCAM, or, in the words of one advocate, "to rip off the mask of polluter-sponsored Breast Cancer Awareness Month." Specifically, I analyze the San Francisco–based Toxic Links Coalition's (TLC) annual "Stop Cancer Where It Starts Tour." Over the years, TLC has developed its tour to target corporations, nonprofits, government agencies, and public relations firms, all of which arguably are powerful actors that frame dominant public opinion and discourse about breast cancer and toxic pollution.

Listening to the cues of these activists, this chapter examines how a toxic tour can provide a productive tactic of resistance for social movements attempting to challenge the corporate co-optation of their struggle.

Exceeding its scheduled stops, this toxic tour helps illustrate the vital roles played by spontaneity and creativity. Further, the embodied rhetorics of resistance enacted become all the more salient when anti-toxic activists mobilize around the pain caused by cancer.

Although cancer is currently a popular cause in the United States, the risks of such a tour remain high, for as Mary Douglas and Aaron Wildavsky have argued, "more is at stake in the debate on the causes of cancer than mere hypotheses. Whole empires of industry and of government depend on the answers."[2] To enhance our appreciation of at least some of what is invested in this dispute, I now turn to the institutional justifications for establishing NBCAM and then for creating TLC. This brief history aims to enable a more informed assessment of NBCAM and TLC as rhetorical interventions into public life as I then turn to one of TLC's toxic tours.

National Breast Cancer Awareness Month

A good number of us have known someone with cancer or have survived cancer ourselves. For approximately every citizen alive in the United States, one in three will contract cancer and one in five will die as a result of cancer.[3] For women in the United States, breast cancer is the most frequently diagnosed form of cancer,[4] accounting for approximately one-third of all new cancer cases in women.[5] In addition to the more than two million current breast cancer survivors nationally, the Y-ME National Breast Cancer Organization claims that every year, "breast cancer will be newly diagnosed every three minutes, and a woman will die from breast cancer every 13 minutes."[6]

October was designated National Breast Cancer Awareness Month in 1984 by Zeneca, a subsidiary of Imperial Chemical Industries Ltd. Zeneca is an international pharmaceutical company that has merged and "demerged" since 1912 with various chemical corporations, including Du-Pont, Imperial Chemical Industries Ltd., Merck, and Astra.[7] Now called AstraZeneca, it is one of the world's top three pharmaceutical companies.[8] One journalist characterizes the scope of the company as opportunistically touristic: "It's a case of have passport, will travel. AstraZeneca is quoted on the UK, US and Swedish stock exchanges. Its global corporate headquarters are in London. Group R&D [Research and Development] is directed from Sodertajle in Sweden and it has a strong presence in the all-important US market. Plus sales and marketing operations in more than 100 countries; manufacturing facilities in 19 countries and six major research centres."[9] Given the company's global reach, it is not surprising that AstraZeneca's profits are in the billions.

AstraZeneca explains its motivation for marketing breast cancer detection in the following description on the NBCAM website:

> Prior to their merger with Astra in June 1999, Zeneca, Inc. conducted an in-house breast cancer screening program, beginning in 1989. . . . In 1996, the company analyzed the total direct healthcare and lost productivity costs of screening, referrals, and initial management of malignancies. The total cost of implementing the in-house screening program was $400,000. Without the program, total direct costs would have been almost $1.5 million (if the cancers were discovered at later, more advanced stages). Therefore, the calculated savings with the program were $1.1 million. AstraZeneca has published the Breast Cancer HealthSite Guide to assist other companies—large and small—in developing a workplace screening program.[10]

AstraZeneca's initial justification for NBCAM was not based in any critique of how women's health care has been assessed or implemented or in a desire to prevent women from developing breast cancer; rather, it was one of basic accounting: it was cost-effective for a company to detect cancer in its employees during the disease's earlier stages. Hence, in NBCAM's message—"Early detection is your best protection"—the "you" was and continues to be not necessarily the broad public of "women" but rather female employees of self-interested companies. "*Your* best protection," in other words, could easily be interpreted as an attempt to constitute a public in response to employers' interest in profit and productivity.

Since its original screening program, AstraZeneca has added that the health of women is a motivating factor. A 2001 company press release quoted David Brennan, President and Chief Executive Officer, Astra-Zeneca L.P., U.S., as saying: "The most important advantage of worksite programs is their ability to save lives."[11] Indeed, the medical community generally has agreed that early cancer detection in adults over fifty increases a person's chances of survival compared to those of a person who does not discover that she or he has cancer at an early stage.[12]

Although AstraZeneca remains the principal sponsor of NBCAM, the board of sponsors has grown to involve a range of organizational institutions, including nonprofits, government agencies, and health professionals. In 2005 this list is composed of the American Cancer Society, the American College of Obstetricians and Gynecologists, the American College of Radiology, the American Medical Women's Association, the American Society of Clinical Oncology, AstraZeneca, the Breast Cancer Resource Committee, CancerCare, the Cancer Research and Prevention Foundation, the Centers for Disease Control and Prevention, the Centers for Medicare and Medicaid Services, Men Against Breast Cancer, the National Cancer Institute, the National Medical Association, the Oncology Nursing Society, and the Y-ME National Breast Cancer Organization.[13] Presumably, this large and well-established sponsor list suggests the popularity of AstraZeneca's stance on breast cancer, a combination of the "cost-effectiveness" for corporations to provide breast cancer screening and the medical fact that early detection increases the chances that a person living with cancer will survive for a longer period of time.

Although neither of these factors directly reflects feminist critiques of patriarchy, one end result of NBCAM could be saving women's lives—a goal that would qualify as a feminist value without question. Further, the diversity of groups on this list suggests that the activities involved in NBCAM offer possibilities for a wider range of purposes and agendas than mammograms. In addition, as NBCAM has grown exponentially, more people than ever before have begun to talk about breast cancer, a feminist accomplishment in itself.

Again, increased awareness motivates a greater number of women to be screened for cancer (which, in turn, may save lives) and helps those with cancer feel less isolated. These positive effects of NBCAM are a good reason for the symbolic pink ribbon of breast cancer awareness to resurface every October in countless venues, from television commercials and award ceremonies of the stars to U.S. Postal Service stamps and everyday attire such as pins and bracelets. In this sense, NBCAM creates and sustains a counterhegemonic public discourse in relation to previous silence on the subject.

Besides, every step matters, right? Who cares if "Checks for the Cure" donates only 5 percent of each purchase to breast cancer research? Or if KitchenAid only donates $50 for each *pink* stand mixer sold in the month of October? Or if it costs more money to mail a NBCAM Yoplait yogurt lid in to the company than they will donate (ten cents/lid)? These charity practices are not unique to NBCAM, and corporations are not going to abandon their desire to earn profits. If they are driven by their bottom line, isn't some percentage of the profits, however small, the most for which we can ask? With so many corporations involved, these incremental steps seem to add up. Although cause-related marketing is "used to consolidate existing markets, capture new ones, and increase corporate profit," as Samantha King argues in her study of breast cancer corporate philanthropy, it also may be "posited, in part, as a response to the consumer's desire for an ethical, meaningful, community-oriented life."[14]

Thus the question remains: why would anyone want to resist NBCAM? Without belittling the life-altering possibilities enabled by early detection, the Toxic Links Coalition offers an answer that "counters" the common sense of sacralizing NBCAM's own discourse by asking why we have not done more to stop the *sources* of environmentally linked cancers, particularly breast cancer. To appreciate more fully the politics that inform such a stance, I now turn to the origins of TLC.

The Toxic Links Coalition

In response to the breast cancer epidemic, activism has increased rapidly since the mid-1980s to form the breast cancer movement.[15] Amid the growing publicity, research funds, and attention given to breast cancer, identifying the causes of breast cancer remains one of the movement's top priorities. Some activists and institutions prefer to focus on genetics; others hone in on "lifestyle" choices, such as whether or not a woman gives birth to children, uses birth control, or is overweight.[16]

Although much of our knowledge about breast cancer and cancer more generally is fraught with uncertainty, it is generally accepted that at least *some* people have developed cancers as a consequence of toxic pollution.[17] Assuming for the sake of argument that the skeptical estimate of "two percent put forth by those who dismiss environmental carcinogens" is minimally accurate, Sandra Steingraber notes:

> Two percent means that 10,940 people in the United States die each year from environmentally caused cancers. This is more than the number of women who die each year from hereditary breast cancer—an issue that has launched multi-million dollar research initiatives.[18] This is more than the number of children and teenagers killed each year by firearms—an issue that is considered a matter of national shame. It is more than three times the number of nonsmokers estimated to die each year of lung cancer caused by exposure to secondhand smoke—a problem so serious it warranted sweeping changes in laws governing air quality in public spaces. It is the annual equivalent of wiping out a small city. It is thirty funerals every day.

Further, Steingraber emphasizes, "none of these 10,940 Americans will die quick painless deaths. They will be amputated, irradiated, and dosed with chemotherapy."[19] Despite the staggering number of deaths and lives represented, grassroots efforts to address cancer continue to encounter significant obstacles when attempting to bring the truly disgusting effects of toxic pollution into the foreground of public dialogue about cancer.

One of the primary roadblocks in this effort is the co-optation of social movements. The environmental movement calls it "greenwashing" when the appearances of products and commodity consumption are linked to their movement, particularly when such acts make no attempt to address the company's wider deliberate disavowal of environmental impacts. "In a cultural climate characterized by a growing awareness of environmental hazards," Robert Goldman and Stephen Papson explain, "the problem of corporate public relations is to reposition commodities whose production and consumption may be damaging to the physical environment as 'earth-friendly.' By placing the green consumer and the environmentally concerned corporation together on the same high moral ground, green marketing seeks to legitimate commodity consumption."[20] Many environmentalists argue, thus, that a gap is growing between talk about being "green" and action taken to stop environmentally destructive practices.

Discourses about *breast* cancer warrant a closer examination of greenwashing and also illustrate the ways that dominant institutions and figures engage in what might appropriately be called "pinkwashing," by which I mean talk about women that does not necessarily correlate with empowering women. Karen Fitts, for example, argues that although "physicians often presume cosmetic concerns are primary to newly diagnosed women, many patients look instead to high rates of incidence (one in eight women), the ordeal of treatment (slash, burn, and poison), and the fact that the number of breast cancer deaths per year (50,000) has not diminished in fifty years." In other words, Fitts claims that cultural and medical discourses often promote the business of "saving breasts, not lives."[21] Indeed, although questions of cosmetics are important to many women, how one looks is usually relatively unimportant compared to reducing the lethal effects of cancer and the debilitating ordeal of medical treatment. As in arguments regarding greenwashing, a tension exists between *appearances of caring for women* and *practices that improve women's lives.*

Recognizing social movement discourses as a cultural resource to mobilize people is a logical move for corporations. At times, it may even be an admirable endeavor. Yet, for social movements, responding to the co-optation of their struggles remains a challenging dilemma.

The San Francisco Bay Area of California has the highest rate of breast cancer of any area in a Western country.[22] For women under forty, a predominantly African American community in the Bay Area, Bayview/Hunters Point, has the highest breast cancer rate in the country.[23] Partly in response to these findings and to concern over the co-optation of the breast cancer movement, the Toxic Links Coalition was founded in the Bay Area in 1994 by representatives of groups such as Breast Cancer Action, Greenpeace, the West County Toxics Coalition, and the Women's Cancer Resource Center.[24] TLC describes itself as "a growing alliance of community groups, women with cancer and cancer survivors, health care and environmental justice organizations, silicone survivors, women with endometriosis, and other reproductive disorders, and concerned individuals working together to educate our communities about the links between environmental toxins and the decline in public health."[25]

TLC's primary campaign has been to reclaim the breast cancer debate from corporations such as AstraZeneca. In other words, TLC is attempting to recast NBCAM as the prevailing, sacralized public response to breast cancer and to challenge that unquestioned dominance by desacralizing NBCAM and creating an alternative counterdiscourse. The objection to NBCAM is at least twofold. First, TLC disapproves of the initial sponsor of NBCAM. AstraZeneca, TLC argues, "profits by first producing many of the toxins implicated in the breast cancer epidemic and then by selling the drugs used to treat the disease."[26] In addition to sponsoring NBCAM, AstraZeneca is "the manufacturer of the world's best selling cancer drug (Nolvadex, or tamoxifen citrate, with sales of $470 million per year) and does a $300 million annual business in the carcinogenic herbicide actochlor."[27] At one point, the corporation was the third-largest producer of pesticides in the United States.[28] AstraZeneca thus profits from the entire cancer cycle, from cause to detection to treatment.[29] Although the latter two activities might individually appear to have positive implications for women, TLC argues, combining the three agendas warrants a closer examination of AstraZeneca's intentions.

Second, TLC wants to shift public discourse about breast cancer from promoting mammograms to "what might be causing breast cancer"[30] or to "the environmental causes of cancer."[31] In other words, TLC objects to framing cancer discourse within the singular focus of *detection* and, instead, wants to foreground the question of *prevention*. TLC emphasizes the necessity of bringing an end to the production of carcinogenic toxins.

To do this, TLC has renamed the month of October "Cancer Industry Awareness Month" (instead of NBCAM) and sponsors annual "Stop Cancer Industry Tours," one-hour walking "toxic tours" to protest the institutions that have contributed to environmentally caused cancers by producing dangerous chemicals or by covering up hazardous chemical exposures to the public.[32] Since 1994 the size of the tour has ranged from approximately one hundred to four hundred participants.[33] Although a predominantly European American group tends to participate, the speakers represent a range of ethnic backgrounds, including African American and Asian American activists. Both women and men are scheduled as speakers and attend as participants. Logistically, Di Chiro notes "[t]he tour is always held on a workday during lunch time for maximum visibility and to accommodate working people willing to relinquish their lunch hour."[34] This time of the day enables a broad audience, from the increased foot traffic on the sidewalks to the congested and, therefore, slowed vehicle traffic on the roads.

While TLC remains a marginalized perspective nationally, evidence that its discourse about environmental links to breast cancer is beginning to reach a wider audience may be found on the local television news, in newspaper coverage, and in a mural that has been exhibited nationally as a public art advocacy piece.[35] Additionally, in 2000, TLC "persuaded the cities of San Francisco and Berkeley, as well as the County of Marin, to pass resolutions naming October 'Stop Cancer Where It Starts Month.'"[36] However, articles and television news clips of TLC's tours provide only brief glimpses of this emerging campaign. To examine the discursive and nondiscursive activities involved, I attended one of their tours as a participant observer and interviewed tour organizers.[37]

"Stop Cancer Where It Starts"

On October 3, 2001, approximately one hundred people traveled to downtown San Francisco's Financial District to participate in TLC's toxic tour.[38] In addition to the initial welcome, there were four scheduled "stops": Pacific Gas and Electric (PG&E) (for running a polluting power plant in Hunters Point and refusing to clean up the toxins or compensate for residents' health problems at Daly City's Midway Village), Bechtel (for engineering and building nuclear power plants and raising the price of water in San Francisco), Chevron (for operating an oil refinery in Richmond, California, that pollutes local communities with toxins and for their international environmentally racist practices), and Solem and Associates (for providing public relations services to the aforementioned businesses). Each stop included one to four speakers from the coalition groups, with eleven speakers overall. These voices included women and men of varied age, race, ethnicity, class, and "health" (i.e., some were people who had survived cancer, and some had not been diagnosed with cancer).

As the tour moves from business to business, stopping traffic, tour participants walk across streets and through several blocks, encountering crowds of people who are on sidewalks and in cars as part of their everyday routine. Although one presumably could follow this route on any given day, TLC's tour creates an inventive, spontaneous, persuasive, and risky mobile theater for cultural performance by communicating physically, visually, emotionally, corporeally, and aurally.

Visually, numerous signs on wooden sticks display campaign messages such as: "TOXINS in our world = CANCER in our bodies"; "HEALTH BEFORE CORPORATE WEALTH"; "STOP CANCER WHERE IT STARTS"; "ENVIRONMENTAL JUSTICE NOW." In addition, there are signs designed specifically for each site that often target specific green- and pinkwashing campaigns (e.g., "$OLEM & A$$OC.: *LIARS* FOR HIRE"). We walk behind a large banner held by two to four people that displays the TLC logo (a hand with the following design in its palm: a circle and slash, symbolizing "no," over a barrel with a skull and crossbones label, spilling liquid) and states: "TOXIC LINKS COALITION: UNITED FOR HEALTH AND ENVIRONMENTAL JUSTICE."

Among the various signs and banners, tour participants are asked for a one-dollar donation in return for a pin that displays the iconic "Breast Cancer Awareness" pink ribbon looping downward into a rope that reflects an upside down, yet symmetrical, shape of a noose and the words: "fight the CANCER INDUSTRY; TOXIC LINKS COALITION." Choosing to link the popular symbol of the increasingly institutionalized pink ribbon with the insidious image of a noose performs a powerful rhetorical juxtaposition: silky ribbons transform into knotted ropes, implying that women are not just dying but being purposefully killed. This image signifies the "wash" of a public health campaign gone awry. In other words, the symbol articulates NBCAM, the campaign that purports to be doing something to end breast cancer, to death. The linkage is provocative, at minimum, prompting the question, "Is it true?" Perhaps NBCAM isn't perfect, but is it *killing* women just as publicly and certainly as a hanging would?

The performative power of eye-catching signs and costumes is constitutive of and vital to TLC's attempts to critically interrupt taken-for-granted practices on the day of their tours. Several participants dramatically embody the tour's message by creatively performing alternative personae. For example, two participants, calling themselves the Queen and King of Cancer, wear torn costume ball outfits with crowns (declaring their titles) attached to their wigs. To add to their deadly looks, their faces are painted white with large black circles surrounding their eyes and dark lipstick on their mouths. The King's facial "skin" is peeling off his face, contributing to his aura of deterioration. Another participant struts about on stilts. With a flowing white outfit, she moves high above us, like a haunting ghost. One woman, with the assistance of two others who help her carry the weight, steps into a papier-mâché puppet costume, approximately ten feet tall and twenty feet wide, of a purple woman with an exposed mastectomy scar on the left side of her chest and two large hands that display the TLC logo in their palms (see figure 4). Although these individuals do not officially speak with words on the tour, their dramatic personae invite spontaneous rhetorical engagements that enact TLC's message, particularly on the walks between stops.[39] Constructing such visual displays, as Kevin Michael DeLuca argues in regard to U.S. environmental and environmental justice movements, provides powerful opportunities to "both deconstruct and articulate identities, ideologies, consciousnesses, communities, publics, and cultures in our modern industrial civilization" and to enact "critique through spectacle."[40]

In addition to physically, visually, and emotionally performing TLC's message, the tour also aurally turns public places into spatial theaters of political dissent and social critique. Most speakers use a microphone to amplify their voices. Participants blow whistles, clap, hiss, laugh, shout, and repeatedly chant TLC's message, "STOP CANCER WHERE IT STARTS." Walking amid the skyscrapers and traffic of downtown San Francisco, those of us on the tour frequently see people peering down at us from their office windows to find out what all the noise is about.

Detours: "Sister, You Are So Brave"

Unlike a casual walk alone in the city, a toxic tour is limited in its paths and choices. Yet the possibilities for social change exceed those of the scheduled tour itself. "Walking through heterogeneous tourist space permits the invocation of involuntary memory through sensual immersion," Tim Edensor reminds us. "The sensual and often undefinable recollections of childhood, and the furtive memories of stories and fantasies can be involuntarily resurrected in the welter of movement, sights, sounds, and

Figure 4. Toxic Links Coalition papier mâché puppet in San Francisco, California. Author photo.

smells."[41] Likewise, Dipesh Chakrabarty suggests: "The bazaar or the street expresses through its own theatre the juxtaposition of pleasure and danger that constitutes the 'outside' or the open, unenclosed space. The street is where one has interesting, and sometimes marvellous, encounters. They do not always eventuate but the place is pregnant with possibility."[42] With this open-ended, embodied interpretation of a tour, and at the risk of not spending more time on the tour itself, I occasionally wander off the route in order to emphasize how the possibilities enabled by toxic tours exceed the scheduled "stops" and synergistically interact with the planned tour itself. In other words, the verbal and nonverbal performances on the tour—planned and spontaneous—should not be positioned as opposed to each other, because the rhetorical force of the tour lies in the synergy created by all of its parts. In fact, the next scene begins just before the tour officially starts; yet the tour would not have been the same otherwise.

While looking around at the people gathering for the tour, I notice a shiny black sport utility vehicle pull up to the sidewalk. Some of us begin to move, attempting to obey the police order to allow people to walk into the PG&E building if they want, when the passenger and driver emerge. Immediately, my attention is drawn to the driver, who is wearing a wide-brimmed red hat with a black flower and a matching red dress. I then look at the passenger. To my confusion, she is placing a gas mask on her face. The driver then walks in front of the police line, proceeds to unbutton her dress, pulls out her right arm, and exposes her mastectomy scar. As the tour crowd cheers, the two begin posing for photographs. The police, of course, cannot stop or detain the woman in red for indecent exposure, because although it is illegal to bare a woman's breast in public, she has exposed no breast.

RavenLight, as I later learned is the driver's name, explains to me that although she is not part of TLC, she participates in every TLC tour in order to lend her body to such events. She also notes that she consistently stands a bit apart in order to attract attention and to allow the groups who plan these events their space, in case they are not "comfortable" with her exposed mastectomy scar.[43] Indeed, my observations of how drivers and pedestrians react to the tour is that those who catch sight of RavenLight's exposed body typically stare and sometimes quickly look back once or twice before moving away. Not having time to question them, I cannot know what these observers feel: disgust? intrigue? shock? admiration? Clearly, however, they find the image of RavenLight, a survivor of breast cancer, difficult to ignore and perhaps even more difficult to forget.[44]

During the tour, we are led up one of those steep streets for which San Francisco is known, and RavenLight turns to look for oncoming traffic. A young woman steps in between RavenLight and myself. When she sees RavenLight's chest, she gasps. We stop. RavenLight glances back in the woman's direction. The young woman then reaches one hand out in the direction of RavenLight's exposed scar as she brings her other hand to her own chest, which is covered with a T-shirt that sinks to her touch. Her eyes well up with tears and she says, "Sister, you are so brave." RavenLight smiles, and they hug. In that moment, all three of us—the woman in red who risks contact, the younger woman who risks reaching out to communicate, and the observer who risks sharing that intimate exchange—appear *present.*

What is productive about these feelings of presence is that RavenLight evokes strong and sensual reactions from others. Her body's performance of an alternative discourse suggests that if we wish to transform politics, we need to expose our physical, emotional, and political scars. We also need to reflect on why we feel compelled to look and to look away. In terms of TLC's campaign, we need to consider the costs of our ongoing patterns of toxification. And we need to examine the reasons that a breast cannot be present in our body politic until it is made absent. By extension, we need to ask, what is the place of women in our body politic? RavenLight's body speaks alternative possibilities about women, cancer, and "progress."[45] This is an example, as noted in Chapter Two, of how the lived experiences of many women arguably lead to a certain level of self-reflexivity and self-consciousness about corporeality. It testifies to how some activists, as DeLuca observes, "have challenged and changed the meanings of the world not through good reasons but through vulnerable bodies, not through rational arguments but through bodies at risk."[46] By exposing her scar, RavenLight performs an embodied rhetoric, both playful and defiant, that goads witnesses to confront that which is dangerous to and fragile within our body politic.

Welcome: "Why I Hope You're Here"

Barbara Brenner, the Executive Director of Breast Cancer Action (BCA), stands in front of the first stop, PG&E, to offer a welcome speech: "I want to tell you why I'm here and why I hope you're here. I'm here because a woman is diagnosed with breast cancer every three minutes in this country. I'm here because thirty years ago a woman's risk of breast cancer was one in twenty—and today it's one in eight. I'm here because this year in the United States alone, 238,000 women will hear the words: 'You have breast cancer.' And I'm here because just continuing to diagnose ever-increasing cases of breast cancer is simply unacceptable. What we need, what we demand, and what we will not rest until we get is true cancer prevention." Beginning with statistics that affirm the increasingly larger number of women who are diagnosed with breast cancer every year, Brenner establishes the exigence for her and for this tour: a lack of "true cancer prevention" in the ongoing public dialogue about breast cancer. She also reinforces the goal of the tour: shifting from the discourse of "awareness" promoted by NBCAM to one of "prevention" that addresses environmental causes. As she puts it, "we will not rest" until prevention becomes the goal.

Brenner then articulates what TLC believes is necessary in order to address prevention:

> I'm here because it's time, it's way past time for people concerned about cancer to start making connections. Connections between increasing incidents of many kinds of cancer—including my own kind of cancer, breast cancer, and equally scary, childhood cancers—and what we as a society do to our air, our water, and our food supplies. Connections between what PG&E does to our poorest communities like Hunters Point and Midway Village while claiming to look out for our interests in this so-called power crisis. Connections between the pharmaceutical companies that make millions on breast cancer drugs and the message you hear every October that mammograms are the answer to the cancer problem.

Making the personal political, as the feminist adage goes, Brenner uses her own body and lived experience with breast cancer to identify with others' political struggles with childhood cancers, poverty, racial injustice (the references to Hunters Point and Midway Village), and corporate profits. This connection is reinforced by the T-shirt that she is wearing with an "X" over one side of her chest, touting a nickname of her organization: "the Bad Girls of Breast Cancer."[47]

In focusing on the theme of "connections," Brenner highlights the "wash" of NBCAM's discourse by articulating the inconsistencies between what we are told and the costs of such discourses. The appearance of NBCAM as a relatively popular discourse about breast cancer, her words suggest, may serve to obfuscate continued environmental degradation that causes breast cancer. This tactic of "making connections" is further evident in TLC's name, the Toxic *Links* Coalition. By linking or articulating experiences of environmental injustice with the profits and images of public institutions that support NBCAM, Brenner and TLC are able to suggest a critique of the discourse promoted by NBCAM as a strategy of green- and pinkwashing. Throughout the tour, TLC's message about NBCAM's reactive focus toward cancer and its refusal to address toxic pollution is repeated. In these public performances, the interconnectedness of domination—environmental, gendered, racial, and economic—is articulated as the motivation for TLC's anti-NBCAM campaign.

Brenner concludes her speech by defining the tour as an act of resistance and issuing a call to action: "The pressure for that type of prevention starts here, in the streets, in front of PG&E and Bechtel and Chevron and the American Cancer Society and Solem and Associates, their PR firm. And we're having a huge impact. A few years ago, Chevron began sponsoring the Race for the Cure. When are we going to see the Race for the Cause? So, take this tour today with hope in your hearts, with the knowledge that you are making a huge difference, and with a commitment to staying involved after it's over. Stop Cancer Where It Starts. Thank you." Brenner's dynamic address characterizes the tour as the starting place for "pressure," the opportunity to make "a huge impact," and a promise to build a growing community with a future "commitment to staying involved." She encourages other people to join her—to invoke a familiar cultural cliché—not just in talking the talk, but in walking the walk, even after the tour itself ends. She reiterates that the goal of the tour is not for corporations to promote a "Cure," but instead for all involved to begin to interrogate the "Cause."

Concretizing the messages of the tour through signs, costumes, chants, and speeches continues throughout the day. As the signs protestors are holding visually represent both general TLC messages and specific slogans targeted at particular institutions on the tour, the themes Brenner addresses are also repeated in subsequent speeches to the specifics prompted by each stop. Before we leave PG&E, two other speakers again link the need for the tour with their exasperation of how PG&E "had one hundred years to tell us they care about clean energy" and their anger with the company for their its practices, which is why the people of "Bayview/ Hunters Point blame PG&E" for polluting their bodies and neighborhoods.[48] In front of the second stop, Bechtel, Danny Kennedy of Greenpeace's "Clean Energy Now" campaign connects the themes of the tour with Bechtel's role in everything from domestic uranium mines and nuclear power plants to roads built for the U.S. military from Kuwait to Iraq. "Bechtel is there wherever you have problems in the energy industry," he explains. In other words, it quickly becomes clear on the tour that "stopping cancer where it starts" requires accountability of specific institutions for their actions implicated in the otherwise seemingly decentralized and globalized terrain of breast cancer industries, marketing, and advocacy.

Walking . . .

As I noted regarding the bus used on the toxic tour in chapter 3, transportation choices have cultural histories and political consequences. On this tour, we walk between stops. Although walking is a practical choice for traveling during a busy time in a busy part of the city, it also has effects on the toxic tour itself. In the case of TLC's toxic tour, political arguments are constituted, at least in part, through the practice of walking, as we physically link the individual industries on the tour with our footsteps.

"Walking is an activity central to tourism," Edensor argues.[49] Unfortunately, it also tends to be taken for granted, often considered an unremarkable and solely instrumental form of mobility. Meanwhile, tourist studies tend to focus upon tourists' "confinement in the 'environmental bubble,'[50] the mobile enclave in which they travel that enables confrontation with the other from a safe distance. . . . [c]nvironmentally isolated from noise and smells and cut off from interaction with locals."[51] In doing so, theorists are inclined to an even greater degree to believe in the sensual primacy of vision to tourist practices. Yet, Rebecca Solnit contrasts the desire to avoid contact in everyday life with the connectedness that she feels *walking* itself incurs: "Many people nowadays live in a series of interiors—home, car, gym, office, shops—disconnected from each other. On foot everything stays connected, for while walking one occupies the spaces between those interiors in the same way one occupies those interiors. One lives in the whole world rather than in interiors built up against it."[52] Imagined in this sense, through the proximity of our bodies as we travel, the act of walking promises the possibility of exposing us to a counter-perspective toward "the whole world." In this way, walking may serve as a rhetorical argument unto itself, an embodied act that holds out the possibility for feeling present.

Michel de Certeau similarly suggests, "the act of walking is to the urban system what the speech act is to language or to the statements uttered. . . . Considered from this angle, the pedestrian speech act has three characteristics that distinguish it at the outset from the spatial system: the present, the discrete, and the 'phatic.'" Clarifying "the present," de Certeau writes that "if it is true that a spatial order organizes an ensemble of possibilities . . . and interdictions, . . . then the walker actualizes some of these possibilities. In that way [she or] he makes them exist as well as emerge. But [she or] he also moves them about and [she or] he invents others, since the crossing, drifting away, or improvisation of walking privilege[s], transform[s] or abandon[s] spatial elements."[53] Walking thus suggests the possibility of transformation—one of the primary promises of tours, as I have argued. The act of walking implicates tourists in a series of inventive selections about where to move, how, and why. It encourages tourists to connect what they are hearing with the ways their bodies are moving: from place to place, in public, and with conviction.

"More Than Just Talk"

Standing in front of the third stop, Chevron, Henry Clark from the West County Toxics Coalition reiterates the lack of corporate accountability for causing health complications in his community (see figure 5):

> Although to this very day, Chevron denies any type of responsibility at all for any of the health problems in our community ["Boos" from the crowd], we know that's a lie. They will want to blame people's lifestyles; they want to blame every other reason but those tons and tons of chemical poisons that are being spewed into our community like daily dioxins or methylene chloride or the 127,000 tons of chemicals that were being spewed from their hazardous waste incinerator there at the Chevron-Arco Chemical Company in our community before we got it shut down and got it dismantled a few years ago. [Audience cheers.]

Figure 5. Henry Clark at toxic tour stop in San Francisco, California. Author photo.

Just as Brenner used the tactic of "making connections," Clark links corporate pollution with public health problems. Despite Chevron's denial of accountability, Clark suggests that his community was not fooled by this "lie." According to Michael Reich's study of chemical disasters, it is common for corporations to deny responsibility and for communities to resist this response: "Private companies use administrative action to avoid or delay litigation, reduce negative publicity, and minimize the company's overall liability."[54] Industry attempts to contain and privatize the conflict, in other words, while communities such as Clark's hope to do just the opposite by expanding and socializing the conflict.

Appropriately, Clark subsequently links his local struggle to a global one:

Chevron said that they wanted to be a "good neighbor," and we're going to hold them accountable to being a good neighbor; but, being a good neighbor is more than just talk. Being a good neighbor is taking some action and listening to the community's concerns and demands and reducing those chemicals that are being released into our community and investing some of those profits into pollution prevention and compensating people for the health damages and the destruction that has occurred in our community over the years. That would be the test of a real good neighbor. [Audience cheers.] And not only being a good neighbor to us in Richmond—because we're going to hold them accountable—but, to being a good neighbor to our brothers and sisters internationally where Chevron has their operations at—be that in Ecuador or be that in South Africa or wherever it's at. The bottom line, Chevron, is this here: is that you can't give no lip service to us in Richmond—talking about being a good neighbor and you're poisoning and polluting our brothers and sisters in other parts of the world—because this is one struggle, this is one fight, and we're going to hold you accountable wherever you are.

Drawing on the corporate appropriation of the phrase "good neighbor," Clark reappropriates the language by defining what such a role would entail ("taking some action"). Similarly, at the end of his speech he directly addresses the corporation ("you"), appropriates the corporate term usually reserved for evaluating economic gains ("the bottom line"), and redefines the grounds for assessing the "bottom line" as accountability. Additionally, like other arguments we hear during the tour, his argument makes connections. It brings the tour's struggle to an international scale insofar as the neighborhood TLC is defending is every neighborhood. The line TLC questions is the one straddling capitalistic profits and human health not just where we are standing in San Francisco, but everywhere on Earth.

Moments of Disgust

The toxic tour crosses paths with the most people not directly involved in the tour when we are in front of the Chevron building. In many ways, this was logistical: the sidewalk seems widest at that point, and the building stands in the middle of a block on Market Street, the main street of the Financial District, where the subway stops are. Although some people passing by take fliers and a few actually stop to listen and to look, most people rush past us wearing office attire, presumably trying to catch a quick bite to eat before returning to work. Some people, however, actually bring their shoulders in and duck their heads, as if standing upright while walking past might make them more susceptible—"to what?" I wonder.

Later on, at the public relations firm stop, two women who come out of the building remind me of a photo I had recently seen on the news about bombings in the Middle East. That's how scared they look: scurrying away, hunched over, peering at the crowd out of the corner of their eyes. These uncomfortable, visceral responses to the toxic tour raise an opportunity to address how disgust plays another role in struggles against toxic pollution. More specifically, I believe that part of the contemporary challenge anti-toxic activists face is an all too common cultural *disgust* of engaging others. By "disgust," I mean the sense that William Miller describes as "a complex sentiment . . . declaring things or actions to be repulsive, revolting, or giving rise to reactions described as revulsion and abhorrence. . . . Disgust . . . conveys a strong sense of aversion to something perceived as dangerous because of its powers to contaminate, infect, or pollute by proximity, contact or ingestion. All suggest the appropriateness, but not the necessity, of accompanying nausea or queasiness, or of an urge to recoil and shudder from creepiness."[55] Disgust is not merely visually or psychologically experienced. When we feel disgust we simultaneously categorize, label, and react emotionally, conceptually, and physically. Disgust, at minimum, is a sensual structure of feeling that evokes strong reactions. It is reasonable to argue, therefore, that whenever we feel disgust, we feel presence (though not necessarily vice versa). Disgust is absorbing.

Disgust, it seems to me, also doubles itself. When we are absorbed we feel both the urge to distance ourselves and the urge to recapture the disgusting—by looking back again or smelling one more time, for example. Disgust averts and attracts attention. There is a potential hybridity, therefore, to the disgusting. It signals our presence in a heterogeneous space where the unpredictable demands a response.

Political arguments are particularly susceptible to feelings of disgust, for as Aristotle notes, "political speaking urges us either to do or not to do something."[56] In other words, the risk of contact with political arguments often appears greater due to the stakes. Not only are political judgments based upon uncertain knowledge, but they also entail choices, which often have effects—uncertain effects. This possibility makes addressing politics itself disgusting to some. Although the desire to distance oneself physically and psychologically from contact with political arguments is far from new, many have argued that it is a defining characteristic of our time.[57]

In presuming that disgust *may* be mobilized for political ends, some advocacy groups appear to draw upon emotional appeals to the disgusting implicitly or explicitly as an integral component of their political tactics. Consider posters of aborted fetuses displayed prominently for anti-choice/pro-life groups or red paint thrown on fur coats to symbolize the "blood" of the animals that died in the name of "fashion" for anti-fur/animal rights activists. Such practices, despite the intentions of their perpetrators, might not lead to a favorable political reaction. Miller, for instance, suggests that when we are disgusted, we often feel the desire to "recoil" or distance ourselves from that which made us feel disgusted. Anti-choice and anti-fur activism, in fact, has been questioned for its choice of disgusting tactics, given the high risk of repelling "persuadables" while not necessarily gaining political efficacy.[58] Breast cancer activism faces similar dilemmas of trying to expose the disgusting industries that perpetrate this disease without becoming linked or articulated to the disgusting themselves.

Likewise, the structure of feeling disgust both motivates and repels potential tourists. As I illustrated in chapter 3, toxic tours provide a mode for challenging site sacralization, including significations of both the sacred and the profane. More specifically, Dean MacCannell argues that feelings of disgust help ground the moral order of "modern touristic consciousness": "A touristic attitude of respectful admiration is called forth by the finer attractions, the monuments, and a no less important attitude of disgust attaches itself to the uncontrolled garbage heaps, muggings, abandoned and torn down buildings, polluted rivers and the like. Disgust over these items is the negative pole of respect for the monuments."[59] In a sense, then, toxic tours compel us to reflect on why and to what ends we have attached feelings of disgust to certain bodies and feelings of respectful admiration to others.

"Dirty Power"

On the way to our final scheduled stop, one activist convinces the group to stop in front of an institution that has been highlighted on previous tours: the American Cancer Society (ACS). Many people seem not to hear this speaker, since the action is not organized ahead of time and tour participants are caught off guard. The reason for stopping momentarily, she quickly reminds us from the sidewalk, is for ACS's role in downplaying environmental causes of cancer, not taking a stance on any environmental legislation (such as the precautionary principle), and not using their influence with polluting corporations that fund their research and serve on their board. The ACS, she points out, "is a dirty power of a different kind." Again, even though this stop is not planned, linking toxic pollution with the cause of cancer and the cancer industry's complicity with polluting corporations are the main themes. Although more structured than other spontaneous interactions, this self-inspired speech indicates the generative democratic possibilities of a toxic tour.

"Why We're Here"

The role of the public relations industry in promoting green- and pink-washing was emphasized most explicitly at the last tour stop. Standing in front of the PR firm of Solem and Associates, Judith Brady, one of the founders of TLC, talks about the ways that PR fosters a corporate-dominated discourse about breast cancer.[60]

> Brady: Maybe you're wondering why we're here in front of this innocuous-looking office building—
> Anonymous voice: Tell us why we're here!!
> Brady: We're here in front of the offices of a public relations agency by the name of Solem and Associates—
> Audience: Boo!!! Hsssssssssss . . .
> Brady: So, let me tell you what their job is. Their job is to make sure that you think in such a way that other companies such as Chevron

can profit. It's kind of a no-brainer. If people really knew what Chevron did, would they support it?

Audience: No!

Brady: If people really knew how PG&E was ripping us off, would they support it?

Audience: No!

Brady: If people really knew how dangerous nuclear power is, would Bechtel still exist?

Audience: No!

Brady: You know how come they still exist? Because of people like Solem and Associates. This PR agency has among its clients PG&E, Bechtel, and Chevron. One of their favorite gimmicks is to create what we call an astroturf organization. They create phony grassroots groups, and it is through those phony groups that they give their live voice to the public. They've done it many times. In terms of PG&E, these folks here, Solem and Associates, have a very unsavory history. In 1994 they created a phony group called "Citizens for Economic Security" in Alameda, across the Bay, when Alameda was trying to municipalize its own gas lines. Watch for it. You can bet they will do it here. And they also have knee-jerk names with words like "Freedom" and "Security" and stuff like that. You can imagine we're going to find groups like "San Franciscans for Utility Freedom" or "Californians for Dependable Power" or "Citizens for Free Enterprise"—something like that. And through that, through those groups, they will tell their lies.

The theme of deception runs throughout Brady's interactive speech. Environmentalists such as Brady have taken to calling PR front groups "astroturf" (in contrast to "grassroots") to symbolize their fake appearances and rootless public support base. As Brady's speech and other facets of the tour point out, greenwashing strategies provide "the *appearance* of public support and citizen advocacy" while making no attempt to engage people in dialogue that will foster just change.[61]

As we remain in front of Solem and Associates, Bradley Angel, one of the founders of TLC, delivers the last scheduled speech.[62] He decides to conclude the tour by acknowledging the attack on the United States that occurred just three weeks prior to the tour, on September 11, 2001, and linking it to the tour that day. To avoid having his words taken out of context, because I believe they might be particularly susceptible to that, I will quote him at length:

You know in the last three weeks, the papers have been covered— and justifiably so—with news about the victims of terrorism. And we should all constantly reflect about that terrorism. But, as we're here today on what polluters call Breast Cancer Awareness Month, what we call Stop Cancer Industry and Stop Cancer Where It Starts Month, we also need to be reflecting [on]—and I wish we were seeing story after story in the paper about—the other victims of terrorism. In this case, corporate terrorism with names like Chevron and PG&E and Bechtel that are not only poisoning our communities, but are directly guilty of causing death and injury to people here in the Bay Area, around the United States, and in the world. And, as much as we need to mourn and remember the innocent victims of the terrorist attacks three weeks ago, as we speak here today, people in Midway Village and Daly City are living and dying on top of PG&E's toxic waste and they are terrorized by PG&E and government criminal activities. In Richmond, as we speak, deadly chemicals are being emitted into the lower-income community of color in Richmond, a community that is constantly and repeatedly terrorized by Chevron and other corporations there. Bechtel does the same with their nuclear power plants that they're involved in. So, I think that when we're in front of PR firms, they don't want those stories to be in the paper, and it's up to all of us to be sure that the truth is going to be told. Because if we collectively don't do it, I think we know that nobody else is going to. [*Crowd cheers.*] And I guess the last thing that I want to say is that the innocent civilians who are dying every day from cancer from pollution unfortunately are every bit as dead and every bit as innocent as those people who were killed a few weeks ago. And, with that in mind, that should be a rallying cry for all of us. To not only keep up the fight, but increase the fight. . . . Please, get involved . . . get involved even more than you have done. I know it's been really hard to focus lately with the tragedy that happened a few weeks ago. But, we can't take even a step back, we need to take a step forward. So, if you're not already involved in the Toxic Links Coalition, there's meetings every month—please, get involved. If you're not involved in community struggles in Richmond against Chevron, get involved. Support the people in Midway Village and Bayview/Hunters Point and communities all over the San Francisco Area that are fighting cancer where it starts. . . . Let us continue to rip off the mask of polluter-sponsored Breast Cancer Awareness Month and let's fight for every single life, because that's what's going on and it's as real as it gets. Thanks for coming.

Although he is not the first speaker during the tour to address the terrorist attacks, Angel offers the most direct, in-depth rearticulation of the 9/11 tragedy that had begun to transform U.S. public culture.

For those invested in political campaigns unrelated to 9/11, there are mainly four choices after the events of that day: (1) drop what you are doing and focus on those events and the Bush administration's response to them; (2) drop what you are doing period; (3) link your campaign or cause to 9/11; or (4) ignore the fact that 9/11 ever happened. The last option, for most of us, is impossible. The first two options leave us in a political culture where nothing else can matter beyond 9/11, and although these choices may appear feasible to some, Angel asks us to consider another option: rearticulate 9/11 to TLC's campaign.

The common factor between the two, he argues, is the tragic death of innocent civilians. Civilians were killed on 9/11, and civilians are killed every day by polluters. Drawing this parallel is a risky but powerful rhetorical trope with which to end the tour. As soon as the first airplane flew into the first building, the nation was riveted by 9/11 and what we should do in response. Given the immediate sacralization of the people who were killed during the attack, Angel draws on the inventional resources that 9/11 brought about arguably because *nothing else felt more present to us at the time.* If the exigence of TLC's campaign could be articulated to the exigence felt as a result of 9/11, we could not forget TLC's campaign when we walk away from the tour. TLC and the communities it represents would become present or, as Angel suggests, "as real as it gets."[63]

Appropriating the discourse of "terrorism," however, is more than an opportunistic or simply timely way to frame the pain of those affected by breast cancer. Given the nation's current obsession with terrorist discourses, many critiques of the "War on Terror" have involved a similar line of argument. In 2003, even the pop music group Black Eyed Peas' number one international hit "Where Is the Love?" asked why "terrorism" is limited to people outside the United States.[64] Thus, years after the events of 9/11, what it means to identify a "terrorist" or be "terrorized" remains ambiguous and contested. As anti-toxic environmental justice activists such as Bradley Angel point out, toxic pollution does violence to people. Toxins terrorize our bodies and transform lives forever. Although that violence may not appear to be politically motivated, the outcome is the same and is very much predicated on a particular political worldview that fanatically pursues its mission (corporate profits) with the belief that those who are killed as a result of their zealousness are insignificant. In response, TLC's toxic tour invites us to reconsider whether or not the lives of those affected by breast cancer are worth defending.

Conclusions

Breast cancer is an epidemic that currently risks the lives of too many women, and NBCAM does bring public attention to this issue annually. Although NBCAM may have initially been inspired by profits, it has exceeded AstraZeneca's original intentions. NBCAM has raised public awareness of breast cancer. It is no small accomplishment to find people in the United States talking about "cancer" and "breasts" in public forums without constantly facing silence or snickering. These cultural shifts in opinion and discourse can be attributed, at least in part, to NBCAM. NBCAM has fostered a public dialogue that runs counter to the hegemonic frame that marginalizes the significance of breast cancer by critiquing previous silences and inactions that characterized public attitudes and by empowering women through offering an alternative perspective on the inevitable impact of the disease on their lives.

Yet identifying the counterhegemonic potential of NBCAM as a part of the breast cancer movement does not preclude the possibility of reading TLC's toxic tour as a counterhegemonic response to the unquestioned sacralization of NBCAM. Like most social movements, breast cancer activism is constituted by multiple critiques and actions. By linking toxins and cancer, health and wealth, environmental justice and feminism, TLC has offered a potentially persuasive counterdiscourse to NBCAM's position as the predominant response to the breast cancer epidemic in the United States. Prior to finding out about TLC's campaign, I never questioned National Breast Cancer Awareness Month. Having heard responses about this tour from students, colleagues, and friends, I know I am not alone. TLC's cultural performance of a toxic tour goads people to consider more closely the causes of breast cancer and to ask, at minimum, what else a month dedicated to fighting breast cancer could become.

As rhetoricians have long known, no communicative act is universal; each context is contingent and poses particular constraints. The context in which TLC's toxic tour has performed an "emergent" discourse is one where dominant society often green- and pinkwashes public discourse, commodifying environmental and feminist causes without necessarily enacting change in the best interests of the environment or women. NBCAM was initiated by AstraZeneca, a corporation that has profited from the entire cancer cycle, producing carcinogens, mammogram machines, and drugs that treat people living with cancer. This context clearly creates constraints for any counterdiscourse. It has limited TLC because NBCAM slogans such as "detection is your best protection" have enjoyed a hegemonic status. In addition, if you are a breast cancer activist, it has become common sense to highlight or initiate one's public health campaigns in the month of October. Although NBCAM has opened up possibilities for TLC by making breast cancer activism more "newsworthy," TLC has seized this opportunity to stress the detrimental effects of the commodification that may occur when activists partner with polluting corporations.

TLC, which lacks the funds of corporate sponsorship, has been challenged to find creative ways to perform both appeals to those who are already sympathetic toward the breast cancer movement and demands of the institutions that perpetuate the cancer cycle. The toxic tour serves as a tactic to interpellate public support in ways that are physical, visual, emotional, corporeal, and aural. The signs, costumes, shouts, speeches, and movements of TLC's tour all constitute a cultural performance of resistance. It is a risky performance insofar as it creates a mobile theater for enacting an oft-ignored discourse; it addresses environmental causes of breast cancer and the role of corporations in the co-optation of the breast cancer movement in a cultural context where such a discourse is considered marginal, when considered at all.

By literally walking up to the front door of these traditionally more sacred institutions during lunch hour in the Financial District of San Francisco, this chapter illustrates how TLC's tour both appeals to those who are already sympathetic toward breast cancer struggles and demands public disclosure of the practices that perpetuate the cancer cycle. TLC's walking, therefore, constitutes an inventive effort to create a greater sense of *communitas* and serves as an act of mobility that attempts to negotiate social critique.[65]

Walking, of course, also is pedestrian in every sense of the term. Following the lead of de Certeau and Solnit, however, this banal act of everyday life might communicate more than we realize. Rather than taking walking for granted or considering it a passive activity, this toxic tour further illustrates how the act of walking implicates a series of choices about where to move, how, and why. It opens and closes possibilities for contact, which limits and enables the occasion for presence in political arguments. It reminds us that the tourist privilege of returning home with a "c'est la vie" attitude is challenged by advocacy tours. On this tour, walking is integral to the political efficacy of the tour itself, providing moments between tourists and between the tourists and those surrounding the tour. These present, discrete, and phatic moments all mattered.

It also was apparent to me as a participant observer of TLC's tour that the productive role of the body should not be ignored in a dialogue about how we should respond to cancer caused by environmental injustices. The rhetorical force of RavenLight's exposing "the scar" of breast cancer is a powerful public act of confrontation. Recognizing the personal and political symbolism of this act served as a poignant reminder that the bodies of women with breast cancer have largely been excluded from our discussions of the disease. Since women have historically been articulated as somehow *more* corporeal than men, the disconnection between discourse about breast cancer and the bodies of women (who have survived, who continue to fight, and who have lost the battle against breast cancer) has been all the more ironic. By choosing to enact this disconnect through a toxic tour, TLC participants placed their bodies on the line to convey their message. Attempting to influence public opinion and discourse beyond what words alone might portray opened rhetorically inventional spaces.

Clearly, some will find TLC's toxic tour disgusting—for acting too passionately, for sounding too loud, for asking too much. Some may remember RavenLight or the pink ribbon turning into a noose or the references to 9/11 and feel a desire to recoil, to further distance themselves from those people, that image, and their words. Who wants to be surrounded by scars, symbols of violence, or to talk about corporate terrorism perpetrated by people within the United States? Certainly, not everyone. Considering how some might find these facets of the toxic tour "disgusting," therefore, reminds us that although these tourist practices may still feel present with us, they need not necessarily motivate social action.

I believe it is critical to note, however, that what we do once we have felt disgusted is a choice. The structure of feeling disgust does not preclude political action; rather, for some of us, it indicates an occasion *for politics*. When TLC risks contact with those who might feel disgusted in order to link people, paths, and points closer together, they open up pathways for a shift in public culture. By creating a heterogeneous space of performance "to integrate death into living,"[66] they challenge everyone they encounter to become more aware of the choice to become more involved. Rather than indicating an end to politics, therefore, TLC's toxic tour suggests the very possibility of politics.

A vital part of the toxic tour's embodied rhetorics of resistance were the guides' speeches. Providing tourists and passersby with the verbal tools to question NBCAM's hegemonic discourse, the guides identified the links they had made as activists exploring the links between breast cancer and toxic pollution. Embodying a range of political perspectives and surrounded by people in costumes, banners, and signs, guides at each stop shared how their personal experiences were connected to the politics embodied on the tour that day. They emphasized the important connections among various individual corporations, the public relations firm that represented them, the governmental policies that enabled their polluting practices to continue without accountability, and cancer advocacy institutions that refused to challenge these hegemonic relations. They linked local struggles with global ones. They reminded us that the collection of institutions sponsoring NBCAM—despite its overwhelming popularity—has not succeeded in reducing the number of deaths caused by breast cancer or the number of women terrorized every day.

In this chapter I have illustrated how TLC's toxic tour performs an acrobatic flip of hegemonic attitudes about disgust and breast cancer: from their own direction (as activists criticizing a public education campaign as revered and institutionalized as NBCAM) toward NBCAM itself and institutions that mismanage toxic waste or enable these practices. Instead of asking why anyone would want to resist NBCAM, TLC asks why anyone would not. Instead of romanticizing detection, TLC reminds us how horrifying the moment is when someone hears those three words, "You have cancer." Instead of focusing on what people cannot change (e.g., heredity), TLC asks, what can we change?

Although their campaign is not always received with open arms, TLC is raising the profile of the controversy about environmentally linked causes of breast cancer despite the "wash" of corporate-sponsored discourses. More than a merely visual argument, TLC's toxic tour is an affective, embodied, and itinerant performance. As TLC walks in the city, guiding tourists through the terrain of San Francisco's Financial District and beyond, they open the possibility for discourses of breast cancer to feel more present in the lives of those with whom they come into contact. Those, I believe, are risky steps worth following—closely.

5

Identification and Imagined Communities

The problem with all global issues . . . is that . . . if it seems remote and cold and unattractive and far away and to not have anything to do with my daily life, then why should I care? Life in my face, in my immediate vicinity is *so challenging* and *so demanding* and *so time consuming,* you know, do I really care about something three thousand or fifteen thousand miles away?

—Kim Haddow, producer of the toxic tour video *Matamoros*

For residents of the United States, Los Estados Unidos Méxicanos (Mexico) promises a relatively affordable international vacation destination for practically any tourist desire. Some tourists travel for the warmer weather and temperate waters at the country's many beaches and resorts, including places such as Acapulco, Cancún, and Puerto Vallarta. Nature lovers watch thousands of gray whales migrate along the waters of the Baja California Peninsula, swim with dolphins in Xel-Hà, or hike in the Copper Canyon of Chihuahua. Heritage tourists visit to learn about "ancient cultures" at the pyramids of Teotihuacán, the Mayan archaeological sites in Uxmal and Chichén Itzá on the Yucatán Peninsula, and the artistic legacy of Oaxaca. And, for those tourists more interested in a cosmopolitan experience, the capital, Mexico City, is one of the largest urban centers in the world.

Depending on one's location as a tourist or resident in either country, the borderlands may seem more or less salient. In 1994 the North American Free Trade Agreement (NAFTA) was established to make some of these connections more apparent in the name of strengthening economic relations between the United States, Mexico, and Canada. NAFTA, however, was—and continues to be—an experiment. As the nonprofit organization Public Citizen notes, "never before had a merger of three nations with such radically different levels of development been attempted. Plus, until NAFTA 'trade' agreements only dealt with cutting tariffs and lifting quotas to set the terms of trade in goods between countries. But NAFTA contained 900 pages of one-size-fits-all rules to which each nation was required to conform all of its domestic laws."[1] Since before its enactment, grassroots communities in all three nations have protested that NAFTA would hurt environmental, labor, and consumer standards. Now that the agreement has been in place for more than a decade, evidence is beginning to mount that further legitimizes earlier concerns.

NAFTA began at the forefront of an international trend of a wave of transnational economic treaties, signaling a decline in the nation-state as the primary organizing principle of government. Prior to this shift, Benedict Anderson suggested that we should consider nations as "imagined communities . . . because, regardless of the actual inequality and exploitation that may prevail in each, the nation is always conceived as deep, horizontal comradeship."[2] Anderson's articulation of "imagination" with "community" helps us to appreciate more fully how an abstract concept such as a "nation" can foster a palpable and meaningful feeling of presence. This powerful insight into the significance of how we rhetorically constitute our identities has catalyzed broader discussions about the affiliations with which we identify and how they influence the risks we are willing to take as a result. Engaging Anderson's argument in the era of NAFTA, this chapter will explore some of the broader consequences of a transnational imaginary, one that challenges social movement activists to reinvent their approach to and abilities to foster feelings of identification.

In a sense, the challenge for any modality of toxic touring is to create an embodied rhetoric of identification that, in turn, motivates tourists to reimagine who and what matters to their community. To clarify, identification with someone, someplace, or something requires that we recognize and, subsequently, feel a connection or an affinity. Kenneth Burke notes that identification is a motive grounded in the ideal of unity, inspired precisely because we are divided and alienated from each other, from the Earth, and from our own thoughts and practices. In other words, although the process of identification involves a striving for unity, it never promises to deliver complete transparency or clarity. "Identification is compensatory to division."[3]

In her analysis of international discourses of sustainable development, Tarla Rai Peterson emphasizes the importance of identification to environmental communication: "Burke suggests that social dilemmas such as environmental conflict arise from the failure to form adequate bonds of identification among those most interested in environmental advocacy as well as between that group and the larger public. Sustainable development has become so popular because it allows people to select a point of identification between themselves and others from whom they must otherwise remain alienated."[4] As such, a "reimagined community" may serve as a point of identification between communities, such as those of tourists and tour hosts. In response to the ways NAFTA disciplines relations between nations, toxic tours offer a means of fostering alternative connections through a sense of identification between grassroots communities, organizations, and advocates.

To explore this process of fostering transnational identification further, I examine a toxic tour that travels between two places divided politically by the U.S./Mexico border and geographically by the Rio Grande: the southernmost U.S. town in Texas (Brownsville) and the northernmost town in the Mexican state of Tamaulipas (Matamoros). Although my participant observation on one of these tours will eventually bear on my analysis, this chapter departs from the previous two by focusing on a toxic tour that is offered within the format of a short documentary video. *Matamoros: The Human Face of Globalization* was produced by the Sierra Club, primarily from footage taken during a series of toxic tours of Matamoros in 2001 that attempted to raise awareness of the local effects of NAFTA. I also draw on interviews with those who produced the video to ask these toxic tour "guides" about their own goals and concerns with this mode of advocacy.

Toxic tours are constituted by and circulated through various media, including videos and the internet. By following the lead of toxic tour hosts, I feel compelled to provide an in-depth interpretation of a toxic tour that does not require going to the site of contamination or production. As noted previously, although going to such places is significant, the structure of feeling present should not be confused with physical co-presence. Through comparing these different modalities of interaction, I aim to consider the possibilities and limitations of toxic tours as they are or are not constituted by media. In doing so, I imagine advocacy tourism as a performance of witnessing and as means to foster identification. The motivation for the specific tactical maneuvers engaged in this chapter is to challenge the oppressive consequences of globalization.

Global/Local Dynamics

Globalization is an ambiguous term. In a sense, globalization has been pervasive as long as people, governments, and products have traveled. The Roman Empire was a variation of globalization. The New World was "discovered" and colonized by Europeans attempting to globalize Indian spices more efficiently. The triangular slave trade between Africa, the Caribbean, and American colonies was globalization. Even more pervasive today, everyday practices such as eating Thai food in the United States constitute globalization. In these times, however, the term *globalization* is generally used to indicate economic, cultural, and political patterns that are not necessarily "new" but which have never been witnessed before on such a large scale.[5]

The effects of the current pattern of globalization appear paradoxical. On the one hand, globalizing trends lend themselves to the construction of what Gloria Anzaldúa calls "borderlands," which are "physically present . . . where the space between two individuals shrinks with intimacy."[6] This reaction alludes to a condensed feeling of space and time that, in turn, invites people to feel more connected with each other across the globe. On the other hand, as William Greider points out, globalization "evokes benumbed resignation . . . overwhelms . . . [and] makes people feel small and helpless," as if space and time are now too vast to imagine and our connections with each other are simply too much to digest.[7] Our current period of globalization thus enables feelings of both connection and alienation, in which the social construction of borderlands between publics and nations becomes more apparent and our sense of agency is increasingly tested. These contradictory feelings are based in part on the relationship between the global and the local.

"Global and local," as Stuart Hall notes, "are the two faces of the same movement from one epoch of globalization."[8] The terms *global/local* and *local/global* reflect an acute appreciation of this interconnection. In this spirit, Rob Wilson and Wimal Dissanayake suggest that we track the character of the global/local by paying attention to a "new world-space of cultural production and national representation which is simultaneously becoming more globalized (unified around dynamics of capitalogic moving across borders) and more localized (fragmented into contestatory enclaves of difference, coalition, and resistance) in everyday texture and composition."[9] Considering the impact of global/local dimensions, therefore, offers a means of following not only how globalization matters to specific publics and places but also how specific publics and places matter to the broader economic patterns and cultural politics of globalization.

For environmentalists, the interrelated tensions of the global/local are particularly pressing. "Environmental problems," as Andrew Light and Eric Higgs remind us, "were one of the first areas of social theory and policy to clearly be bound within a global problematic, challenging any hope of solving them through local solutions."[10] Environmental concerns often require global solutions, such as how the reduction of greenhouse gases depends on international cooperation. Further, seemingly "local" issues, such as an oil spill, air pollution from an incinerator, or the extinction of a species, have ecological ramifications that reverberate globally; as I explored in the last chapter, they also tend to be precipitated by transnational corporations and policies. Recognizing the interconnectedness of ecology regarding both causes and impacts, in part, is what has made popular—for better and for worse—the adage, "Think globally, act locally."[11] Because questions of the global/local are particularly important for the environment, addressing the contradictory feelings of connection and helplessness so often evoked by globalization seems necessary for communities mobilized by environmental injustices.

One of the primary challenges to addressing global/local environmental concerns democratically has been the ways this trend has transformed our relationship with embodiment. As indicated both by Anzaldúa and Greider, our physical access and barriers to bodies of each other, land, and thought have shifted with globalization. In turn, transnational politics of domination and resistance have also been transformed to some degree, and a demand to create democratic political alliances among publics to counter oppressive practices has increased. Broadening Anderson's concept of "imagined community" beyond the nation-state, Wilson and Dissanayake emphasize the need to identify emerging acts of "transnational solidarity" from a global/local perspective: "What we would variously track as the 'transnational imaginary' comprises the as-yet-unfigured horizon of contemporary cultural production by which national spaces/identities of political allegiance and economic regulation are being undone and imagined communities of modernity are being reshaped at the macropolitical (global) and micropolitical (cultural) levels of everyday existence."[12]

One way for political alliances to negotiate the communicative and democratic challenges posed by globalization is by appropriating dominant modes of operating, including media technologies. The cultural politics of transnational media, however, remain undetermined. "[W]hile the media can destroy community and fashion solitude by turning spectators into atomized consumers or self-entertaining monads," Ella Shohat and Robert Stam explain, it can also " 'deterritorialize' the process of imagining communities," enabling "community and alternative affiliations."[13] The varying impact of media can be attributed to some degree to the wide range of media producers, from multinational corporations to governments to revolutionary movements.[14] Like all encounters, in other words, media can inform, distort, deflect, reflect, and invent interpretations of global and local life.

Further complicating matters, as Mitsuhiro Yoshimoto points out, "[t]o some extent, 'globalization of image culture' or 'global image culture' is a misleading phrase or an oxymoron since on a fundamental level globalization and image are inseparable from each other."[15] Global tourism is a prime example. As indicated previously, although it is not the sole sense involved, the visual does pervade our tourist experiences; this is why so much of tourist studies focuses on sight. Visual media guide us in our decisions of where to go (and not to go), how to get there, what to value once we are there, and which places, people, or ideas we should remember once we have left. From placards to brochures to posters to films to websites to photographs to guide books, media help constitute our global/local tourist journeys.

I would emphasize, however, that just as tours are not reducible to sight, the importance of the image to globalization does not reduce the experience solely to the visual. Even global media are impossible to engage with only the sense of sight. Consider, for example, the sounds we hear and the ways our bodies lean toward or jump away from a screen.[16]

Further, despite the power that "resides with those who build, disseminate, and commercialize" global/local media systems, Shohat and Stam remind us that "[a]ll the technological sophistication in the world . . . does not guarantee empathy or trigger political commitment."[17] Likewise, Susan Sontag argues:

> There are hundreds of millions of television watchers who are far from inured to what they see on television. They do not have the luxury of patronizing reality. . . . [Yet, c]itizens of modernity, consumers of violence as spectacle, adepts of proximity without risk, are schooled to be cynical about the possibility of sincerity. Some people will do anything to keep themselves from being moved. How much easier, from one's chair, far from danger, to claim the position of superiority. In fact, deriding the efforts of those who have borne witness in war zones as "war tourism" is such a recurrent judgment that it has spilled over into the discussion of war photography as a profession.[18]

Although the possibilities for democratic change exist as a result of our current global technologies, the direction and the impact of media in public culture are far from determined.

Among various media technologies, documentaries deliberately aim to inform and, often, to persuade audiences of a particular worldview. Documentaries, Bill Nichols notes, have "the intent . . . to mobilize viewers to act in the world" and, as such, have a "much closer alliance with rhetoric than aesthetics."[19] Recognizing the subjective influence that is embedded to some extent in the production and distribution of all communication, this definition lays no claims to objectivity. The use of documentaries by social movements to "mobilize viewers" with "a committed eye" positions them as desirable and potentially efficacious modes of communication that are relatively more affordable to circulate with broader audiences.

Witnessing

Whether or not one is considering a global context, an invitation to identify with people, places, and arguments asks the tourist to *witness* what is going on in a way that invites him or her to feel implicated in the fate of those people, places, and arguments. Yet, as critical categories, "tourists" and "witnesses" tend not to signify the same thing. Whereas tourism literature tends to ignore noncommercial advocacy tourism—thus undercutting the potential of a tourist as a powerful political subjectivity—witnessing literature has generally been endowed with the assumption that the act of witnessing is political and therefore somehow distinct from practices of pleasure, such as tourism. Advocacy tourism such as toxic tourism, however, suggests that the tourist may serve as a witness. The aim of toxic tours, as Giovanna Di Chiro argues, "is to take action to change what the eyes witness."[20] Considering witnessing as a mode of operating, therefore, is pertinent to appreciating more fully the rhetorical possibilities of toxic tours.

For the most part, witnessing has traditionally been defined as an act of hearing and seeing oral and written evidence through firsthand experience.[21] "Bearing witness," as Jan Cohen-Cruz points out, "uses heightened means to direct attention onto actions of social magnitude, often at sites where they actually occur, and from a perspective that would otherwise be missing."[22] As such, social movements have found witnessing to be a persuasive mode of communication, either in the form of people "on the ground" bearing witness to their own situation and experiences or by inviting those who live farther away from particular sites and conditions to witness "a perspective that would otherwise be missing." At minimum, therefore, the potential rhetorical efficacy of providing opportunities to witness is to suggest alternative modes of viewing and acting in the world—much like those of the tourist.

One of the most effective and recent examples of mobilizing witnesses and witness discourse for social change is "Witness for Peace." Begun in 1983, the organization formed to protest U.S. aid to the Contra war in

Nicaragua. The goal was "to establish a permanent North American presence in the war zone"; delegates "would be expected to live with Nicaraguans, share the risks of Contra violence, 'face death if need be,' and become first-hand sources of information on Nicaraguan alternatives to the U.S. government." As Christian Smith notes, witnessing became "a tactic, it seemed, that transformed people, that disturbed and electrified U.S. citizens into fervent political action against their own government."[23] Thus, beyond hearing, seeing, and feeling risks through firsthand experience, the witness is an important figure in politics because he or she can potentially take action afterward, reporting, testifying, and relating to others that which has been witnessed.

In the environmental movement, Greenpeace is perhaps best known for its use of witnessing as a tactic of resistance. Started in 1971, the organization articulates "green" concerns to a pacifist ethic of "peace." The landmark event that catapulted them into the international spotlight drew on the Quaker tradition of "bearing witness" by chartering a boat to protest a nuclear test site on the island Amchitka in the northwest Pacific. This approach to social change involved "expressing opposition simply by turning up and being seen at the site of the activity to which they object."[24] Much more than engaging in a "simple" act, however, as DeLuca argues, Greenpeace activists enact "critique through spectacle," in which an "image event" is created to capture the media's attention enough to motivate them to circulate photographs and stories about Greenpeace's action to broader audiences who, in turn, might help foster social change.[25]

In her book on Argentina's "Dirty War," Diana Taylor challenges us to consider the act of bearing witness as social and engaged rather than passive and disinterested: "Witnessing entails the acceptance of the 'heavy weight of sorrow,' and it entails responsibility. And it's not without its own risks. *Se paga por ver* (one pays for looking) . . . witnessing, however singular and limited, is vital. It might help broaden the scope of the possible, expand the audience, and allow for a wider range of responses. . . . My role in this drama is not to keep quiet, but to be a better *spect-actor*." Taylor emphasizes that witnessing, as a mode of political subjectivity, entails both responsibility and risk, watching and acting. Rather than maintaining a distanced gaze through which we ignore atrocities, witnessing suggests the need to explore "what we are trained to overlook." In this act of seeing, the witness risks identification with the fate of other people, places, and events. To illustrate this point, Taylor provides examples from her fieldwork in Argentina during the "Dirty War." She argues that spectacles of domination were orchestrated to disempower people through acts of violence that aim to prohibit sensual—and efficacious—reactions. In a context of public torture, abduction, and surveillance, Taylor observes, "people dared not be caught seeing," such that "the triumph of the atrocity was that it forced people to look away—a gesture that undid their sense of personal and communal cohesion even as it seemed to bracket them from their volatile surroundings."[26] In order to challenge such atmospheres of intimidation predicated on the power to isolate people from each other, bearing witness to atrocities offers a vital mode of resistance.[27]

Witnessing also exceeds the visual. Yes, as Taylor points out in two languages, "*se paga por ver*/one pays for looking." Yet, as her examples illustrate, *se paga por oír*/one pays for hearing and *se paga por hablar*/one pays for speaking.[28] Further, I want to reassert the importance of a fully embodied communication perspective, one that enables us to consider the additional risks of "facing death if need be," of placing our bodies, our health, our sanity, and our hearts at sites that we might otherwise avoid. In other words, although seeing and hearing are consequential practices, I do not want to ignore yet another truth: *se paga por ir*/one pays for going. Examining the use of toxic tour videos goads us to reflect on the stakes of these costs.

"The Human Face of Globalization"

The eleven-minute video *Matamoros* was recorded primarily during a series of toxic tours hosted on February 16, 2001. The participants included the Sierra Club's Board of Directors, staff, and other volunteer leaders from across the United States; local residents from Brownsville; and local residents from Matamoros. "Despite its woes," Peterson points out, "the region retains a rare beauty. Western desert, northern, coastal, and tropical plants, are concentrated within the semi-arid and subtropical climate of this unique ecosystem."[29] With that context in mind, let us turn to the toxic tour.

"This Experiment"

The tour begins with a visual sign of the Sierra Club logo announcing that it is a Sierra Club presentation. While we listen to the sounds of wind, a black screen with white lettering appears. The words read: "In 1994 the United States, Canada, and Mexico launched NAFTA, the North American Free Trade Agreement." A few moments later, the next screen cuts to the words: "NAFTA allows U.S. companies to build factories in border towns like Matamoros, Mexico, without having to comply with Mexican or U.S. environmental laws." Next, faint voices can be heard, and the screen cuts again, to finish the elliptical thought: "the results of this experiment are beginning to take their toll." This brief introduction provides the tourists with a pre-trip warning: we are about to bear witness to "the results of this experiment" called NAFTA, and these results are found in "border towns like Matamoros." Finding corporations somehow "above the law," without any democratic accountability, looms ominously in this suggestive beginning to our journey.

Then, what we see begins to match the sounds we have been hearing: a dirt road appears with children playing and a woman walking. They all appear to be Mexican. The air is filled with gray smog, and the road is lined with small homes, a car, a bulldozer, and debris blowing in what appear to be heavy winds. The tour cuts to another series of black screens with white letters: "MATAMOROS: THE HUMAN FACE OF GLOBALIZATION"; "NARRATED BY EDWARD JAMES OLMOS."

Our guide, the narrator who has not yet spoken, is about to join us. We are told nothing about him besides his name. From this alone, however, many might recognize him. Olmos is a high-profile, critically acclaimed actor, catapulted into mainstream media circles in the 1980s by his role on the television series *Miami Vice*. In the United States, there are few Latino or Latina actors with greater notoriety.

We never see Olmos on the tour. His role, though limited to a voice-over, is vital. The choice of Olmos over other stars signals the importance of identity to the cultural politics of the video: his voice embodies the Borderlands. Even if one did not know that Olmos is a U.S.-born Latino, he sounds like a man who speaks English fluently with a Latino accent. In the context of a toxic tour on NAFTA based on local experiences at the Mexico/U.S. border, Olmos's visual absence does not preclude the feeling of his presence throughout the tour. His voice serves as the primary guide, inviting us to follow his lead into the ways the boundaries—and the stakes—of these two countries blur.

With a quick tracking shot of the side of a road and then an aerial shot of the border, Olmos begins the toxic tour with one simple line: "Cross over the border from Brownsville, Texas, into Matamoros, Mexico, and the world changes." Picking up on the tone of allusion, Olmos differentiates the place we are about to visit from the place where we have been.

Maquilare: "To Assemble"

Olmos continues by offering an overview of the detrimental changes in public health, environmental conditions, taxes, and labor since NAFTA began. His words and the quick flashes of images of pollution from Matamoros are reinforced by the words of a European American, Dan Seligman, whom we are told is head of the Sierra Club Responsible Trade Program.

Returning to an aerial shot of the border, we see, in the center of the image, two roads bridging the Rio Grande, both heavily trafficked and passing through border patrol stations (see figure 6).[30] This view invites us to imagine the border as a more fluid space than we might feel it to be on the ground, stopped by border patrols, searching for our passports. The details of everyday life shrink. The meandering river runs with both nations bordering the same water. The traffic indicates that people and goods likewise flow between the two countries. The sky appears the same across the landscape. This view, as one might assume, is not usually part of one's toxic tour experience by bus or on foot. One immediate advantage of video, therefore, quickly becomes apparent: it is able to provide a tour in ways most would not experience otherwise.

Of course, we have been warned of the dangers of the aerial perspective again and again—at least since the ancient myth of Icarus's fall. "The voyeur-god created by this fiction," as de Certeau points out, "exists as a temporary status for us mortals."[31] Thus, although "seeing the whole" may provide a more holistic perspective of how fluid border life is, it can also obscure pedestrian acts below. As if aware of this constraint, however, the tour quickly favors the view from the ground for most of the rest of the journey.

Figure 6. Aerial image of border between Matamoros, Tamaulipas, Mexico, and Brownsville, Texas, U.S. Image from *Matamoros: The Human Face of Globalization.* Copyright © Sierra Club, distributed by The Video Project, 2001. Used by permission.

During the aerial view, Olmos explains, in his role as guide and translator of these Borderlands, where "Matamoros" is:

> Matamoros lies in the state of Tamaulipas—just across the border from Brownsville, Texas. People have come to Matamoros from throughout Mexico, seeking jobs in one of the hundreds of new American factories. These factories are known as *maquiladoras.*

> [The view cuts to a series of tracking shots, by which we see views driving through neighborhoods, by schoolchildren, fields of debris, and then stores.]

> The name comes from the word *maquilare,* "to assemble." Since NAFTA passed, the population of Matamoros has doubled. When the job seekers arrive, some of them are fortunate to find work. But they

also find a city without clean water, sanitation, or adequate housing. The small amount of tax revenue that is generated by their employers, the *maquiladoras,* goes to the federal government, not to the cities like Matamoros. The result is that Matamoros has little funding to care for its citizens.

Seligman again reinforces Olmos's dismal view of the *maquiladoras,* and then Olmos expands on the theme of negligence with a specific example:

The Stepan Chemical Facility is owned by a company based in Chicago, Illinois. Due to its high toxicity, a facility like this should not be located anywhere near a residential area.

[Our view then pans from a residential area, right toward the factory, literally just across a set of railroad tracks. We then see two workers spilling the contents of a barrel on the ground with a caption on the screen that frames what we are seeing, a "Surveillance Video."]

A leak could be an environmental disaster.[32]

Moving back and forth between the local (e.g., Matamoros and Stepan Chemical Facility) and the global (e.g., NAFTA), Olmos and Seligman reiterate the constant flows between what is familiar (an area where people live, work, and play) and the palpable dangers caused by broader political structures of domination. Corporations have increased their plants and production, but the local government and community seem not to have benefited.

Olmos continues to describe the environmental health and safety risks to workers in the factories, concluding: "*Maquiladoras* have little regard for the impact they have on the local surrounding and people."

"The Most Vomit-Inducing Smell"

Next, Olmos's and our view focuses on the environmental pollution and the lax enforcement of environmental laws in Mexico. We are told that corporations can and have sued "the government" to pay for them to comply with environmental standards, when they do follow legal guidelines. Then we hear an unidentified voice and a new visual perspective repeating Olmos's message: we are positioned as passengers in a moving vehicle, looking out a window at sewer water, trash, dead animals, dusty roads, and small domiciles.

Once our view is heavily obscured by the grey smoke in the sky, Olmos's voice returns to explain the images we are trying to see: "Severe air pollution contributes to high asthma rates along the border. Thousands of families live in dirt-poor shacks with no running water or electricity. They construct their homes from wood pallets discarded from the *maquiladoras*." The poverty is apparent; Olmos's words neither romanticize these conditions nor somehow forget that they are global/local scenes.

We continue to pass several sites, until we reach the next stop: a pile of trash at least fifty feet high and acres wide. The visual scale of the waste is suggested in comparison to the animals, vehicles, and people around it. Birds circle above. Trucks drive toward and away from the mountainous mass, presumably transporting more trash. We continue to see smoking piles of trash without any means of containing the waste and, presumably as a result, the surrounding littered fields. NAFTA, we are told, is a short-sighted and cost-ineffective treaty for Mexico. Olmos explains how this local site is a result of global policies: "This is the Matamoros Municipal Dump. It was funded by a loan from NAFTA's development bank and was supposed to be a state-of-the-art facility with a lifespan of over ten years. Three years after it was built, it's completely full." Having linked the dump to NAFTA, a Mexican American guide from the Sierra Club, Alejandro Queral, appears and tells us, "It costs about $4 million—it's a $4 million loan to the city of Matamoros. And now you can see that Matamoros is spending a lot of money just paying off the interest because they can't pay off the whole loan." Then, images of the waste—including rubber tires on fire, emitting toxic smoke—are displayed as Olmos explains why humans can be seen scavenging the heaps of trash for anything that can be reused.

Next to the dump, our path begins to focus on a pile of cow skulls (see figure 7). Seligman returns to explain: "Cow skulls are collected by garbage pickers for resale to companies that use the bone. Their homes are right next to this huge pile of rotting, stinking cow skulls. It's the most

Figure 7. Skull pile, Matamoros, Tamaulipas, Mexico. Image from *Matamoros:The Human Face of Globalization*. Copyright © Sierra Club, distributed by The Video Project, 2001. Used by permission.

vomit-inducing smell you've ever encountered." Although toxic tourists on this tour cannot smell the skulls for themselves, Seligman attempts to make his embodied experience of the disgusting—in this case, a smell and a callousness for those who live nearby—feel more viscerally present to the audience by orally describing the odor, while the images pull back from the pile itself until we can see the surrounding children playing next to it.

A Mexican American translator, Marcos Muñoz, sits in a van as he emphasizes how NAFTA's lack of democratic accountability has led to these conditions: "There are no laws being adhered to. There is no observance of health issues, you know, related to people living here. Regulations and restrictions with regard to building a dump site are just ignored and it's just there." Seligman again repeats the message: this oppressive treatment of people, their land, and their way of life is enabled by the continual, active practice of isolating and "ignoring" what the tour is showing us.

"A Disaster for the People"

After the dump, our tour cuts to a hospital. A plaque on the wall states: "HOSPITAL AMIGO; DEL NINO Y DE LA MADRE."[33] Showing images of Mexicans who are workers and patients inside the building, Olmos tells us: "In hospitals like this one, doctors are finding an alarming incidence of neural tube disorders, severe birth defects of the brain and spine that are linked to chemical pollution." Translating for an unidentified Mexican woman, Muñoz elaborates: "From zero to fourteen years, there is a 10 percent of the population that has a health problem. And of that 10 percent, 4 percent are what might be described as severe or profound, cerebral palsy, deafness."

Two images quickly are shown of mothers holding their children suffering from toxic pollution.[34] They are striking, particularly the first one. The mother looks directly into the eyes of anyone willing and able to look as our view pans down from her eyes to the child in her arms. The child, held close to the mother's chest, is severely underdeveloped and deformed. The child's face appears almost like an oversimplified rubber doll. In this instance, it is difficult to look, at least for me. This violence to their bodies violates the seemingly sacred womb of these women and the children's right to be born into the world healthy enough to at least attempt to live a full and happy life. The knowledge that their pain is caused by the inhumanity of those who want to make more profits and, like me, who have the privilege to continue to ignore their daily struggles is almost too much to digest. It is a profane cost of our toxic love affair that feels uncomfortable to witness.

This passing scene reminds me of one of Sontag's cautionary notes about the emotions that images of bodies in pain may invoke: "Our sympathy proclaims our innocence as well as our impotence. To that extent, it can be (for all our good intentions) an impertinent—if not an inappropriate—response. To set aside sympathy we extend to others beset by war and murderous politics for a reflection on how our privileges are located on the same map as their suffering, and may—in ways we might prefer not to imagine—be linked to their suffering, as the wealth of some may imply the destitution of others, is a task for which the painful, stirring images supply only an initial spark."[35] Indeed, as it maps the global/local, this toxic tour of Matamoros highlights how people from both sides of the border and from the Borderland in between are linked. In doing so, the tourist is invited to feel this "initial spark."

Further emphasizing the link between the bodies in pain at the hospital and NAFTA's lax environmental practices, we are quickly shown a factory that can barely be seen through the surrounding smoke. Again, a lack of democratic accountability is placed at fault. Olmos notes: "Three billion dollars was initially promised by NAFTA for environmental projects to prevent what's occurred in Matamoros. Less than 10 percent of this has been spent." Seligman reiterates: "What we've seen in Matamoros, Mexico, is a paradise for these American industries, but really a disaster for the people who live in the communities around these factories."

At this point in the tour, there is a brief pause in the narration as we see several moving images of what appear to be downtown Matamoros and then the outlying areas. At the end of this silent journey, we find ourselves facing the image of the ocean and we can hear wind. Olmos returns: "As the once flourishing fishing industry, just outside Matamoros, grinds to a halt because of the pollution, the United States continues to expand to the rest of the Americas the trade agreement that helped cause this situation."

It is here, where these bodies of water and land meet, that Seligman evokes what becomes the subtitle of the video: "What we've seen in Matamoros, Mexico, is the human face of globalization." A small female Mexican child is shown eating something off a spoon and holding a soda can that appears quite large in comparison to her size. She seems oblivious to anyone watching her, the epitome of stereotypical innocence. By focusing the camera on her image after Seligman uses the phrase that serves as the subtitle of the tour, her appearance takes on a deeper significance. Although she is but one among many who are affected by NAFTA, this articulation offers a sacred symbol through which we might concretize the costs of the often more abstract idea of globalization. Who would want to hurt this child? What are we willing to do to protect her?

"For More Information"

From the questions provoked by the sight of the little girl, our attention is turned to a small group of Mexican boys walking with a soccer ball in a field of debris, again juxtaposing youthful innocence with the costs of

NAFTA. From this view, Seligman signals the end of the tour, stating: "The Bush administration now plans to expand NAFTA throughout the Western Hemisphere, all the way down to Chile, creating a Free Trade Area of the Americas. The challenge here is that we expect more communities of this sort will be created that lack the basic conditions for a decent quality of life." Not only are we asked to care about what NAFTA has done, but we are also asked to feel a sense of concern for what creating a Free Trade Area of the Americas might do. NAFTA becomes important once again not just to assess its own progress but also as a means by which to measure whether similar transnational experiments should be allowed to begin.

The toxic tour then ends with three more black screens with white letters and the sounds of kids playing and an engine running: "Since NAFTA took effect, the number of *maquiladoras* in Mexico has grown from about 2,000 to more than 3,000"; "90% of them are US owned"; "FOR MORE INFORMATION CONTACT: WWW.SIERRACLUB.ORG; 202-547-1141." Like other toxic tours, this one ends with a call to action. Through statistics represented literally "in black and white," the video-tour articulates the vast proliferation of *maquiladoras* owned by the U.S./us and invites tourists to find out more.

In Comparison: Field Notes from Matamoros

The hotel in Brownsville where we sleep during the weekend of the Matamoros toxic tour in which I participate is six minutes walking distance, thirty-five cents, and a picture I.D. proving my U.S. citizenship away from the Mexican border. Yet, immediately arriving in the town, it is apparent from the restaurants, dress, and languages spoken how blurred the boundaries are in the everyday lives of those inhabiting this Borderland space.

Before arriving in Brownsville, I receive an e-mail that is sent to all the proposed participants with the subject header: "EVERYTHING YOU NEED TO KNOW ABOUT BROWNSVILLE MEETING." Regarding the toxic tour, the organizers promise a unique and important event: "The tour is the backbone of the entire weekend. Upon registration, participants will be divided into at least seven groups, each with its own destination. We promise each group a unique experience and will allow for time after the tour for participants to share what they experienced."

The toxic tour I attend is the one by the ocean that concludes the video tour. My guide is Father Ruben Becerra, a Mexican priest from Matamoros. The brief description I am e-mailed prior to flying into town states: "Many communities along the border have received thousands of new families that lack housing. To fill the need, families form squatter camps on public land. This visit will involve interviews with families and workers in their homes. Followed by presentations by local group leaders." Father Becerra and our European American translator tell us that we are scheduled to tour a local dumping area, a fishing squatter camp, a toxic waste site, the Matamoros Municipal Dump, and Father Becerra's church. Seventeen of us pile into a van that functioned much like the chartered bus from the toxic tour in southern Louisiana, except with a more rugged and intimate atmosphere.

Having heard that the Sierra Club and accompanying media might be touring, someone somewhat cleaned up the local dumping area before we arrived. This absence of our first stop spoke to the power of toxic tours to raise awareness and accountability. As the Executive Director of the Sierra Club, Carl Pope, noted afterward: "Like [Mexican President Vincente] Fox's visit, the arrival of the Sierra Club Board of Directors in Matamoros had a momentary impact—some of the sites on our itinerary were actually cleaned up for our appearance. If President Bush and the CEOs of the major corporations with a presence on the border were to make a regular habit of visiting the *maquiladora* zone, that small step would probably improve the situation more than NAFTA has."[36]

At the fishing squatting camp there are lots of children, particularly boys playing soccer (*fútbol*); however, I don't notice the little girl from the video who symbolizes "the human face of globalization." Now, I will not forget her.

We pass the dump and the skulls. The smells and scale are difficult to put into words. They are disgusting. We also conclude our tour, as promised, at the priest's church for an alliance-building meeting that is uplifting and inspiring. The story I want to focus on, however, is about our attempt to tour the toxic waste site.

To call it a "toxic waste site" is a euphemism. We are told that it was adopted as a toxic dump by NAFTA businesses and, although it had been out of use for over a decade, no one had bothered to clean it up. Father

Becerra is attempting to convince our driver, another Mexican man, to keep driving down the dirt road we are on. As they continue (in Spanish), it is clear to me that our driver doesn't believe it is possible due to the condition of the road. A few people, including the driver and the priest, exit the vehicle to test the ground. Several side conversations start. And then, out of the corner of my eye, I see a 4x4 that had been following our vehicle zoom past us—and sink. A groan and sounds of surprise arise from all of us in the van.

Our driver comes back to the van and explains (in English) that he had *told* the priest the mud was too wet. Now the priest, who had presumably gotten into the 4x4 to make his point, is stuck. Everyone's anxiety rises. We are near no phone or town. It could take hours to pull the vehicle out of the mud. Comments of surprise and exasperation abound (*"Why* did he do that?"; "We're *never* getting out of here"; "Are you *kidding?*"). But, slowly, most of us begin to exit the van.

When I step down onto the ground, my foot begins to sink. I hadn't realized how soft it was. I turn the corner to have a better look at the stuck vehicle and to figure out how I might help. Everyone pushing is covered in mud. It is a desperate scene. Some people speak only Spanish, some only English; few of us knew both, and to varying degrees. This range of cultural backgrounds exacerbates the usual solution-oriented commands that tend to erupt from such scenarios. The confusion and the ground continue to muddy our plans for about an half and an hour.

Finally, one of the Matamoros residents on the tour finds a long, synthetic strap to attach to the van, and the smaller vehicle is pulled out successfully. After the immediate dilemma is resolved, Father Becerra sits up against the front bumper of the car, seemingly exhausted, and asks the translator to help him explain. She walks over, with her feet covered in mud so that they look as large as clown shoes. The rest of us gather around them in a half circle. The priest begins with a tone of tenderness that he had not expressed before that moment with us: "The reason I wanted you to see the dump *so much* . . . [*He pauses for translation*] is because the dump is such a tragedy for our community."[37]

You will not find this story or, as a result, the toxic dump itself, included in the eleven minutes of the video *Matamoros*. I'm not sure I would want it to be. Unless you were there, it would be challenging to appreciate the way the transportation situation reflected the local conditions, the strength of Father Becerra's will, and the value of this collective experience. In such a short video, taken out of context, the scene could erroneously appear to make our guide look disorganized or unfamiliar with the local roads—indeed, I worry that my own retelling of it here could led to the same conclusion. The toxic tour I participated in that day was not efficient. But it was worthwhile, at least for myself, because it reminded me that these are the hardships of everyday life and that tremendous willpower is required of those who are struggling against toxic polluters. Life can be muddy, both literally and metaphorically. That is part of what makes me feel connected to humanity—knowing that life doesn't always happen as we plan it.

I share this story in the hopes of continuing to emphasize the spontaneity that sometimes occurs on toxic tours and to illustrate the ways that physical co-presence does not guarantee a "better" tour. It was a *different* tour. The video tour was a compilation of "highlights" from the tours that took place that day. As such, like the one I just described, it offers a partial representation. Neither toxic tour is more "complete." To ask for such a tour is to miss the point. Both tours taught me more than I would have known otherwise. Both have the potential to spark action.

In Conversation: Making the Video

Kim Haddow, a European American and Sierra Club's then Senior Media Strategist, initiated the project of recording the toxic tours. She explained in an interview her reasons for wanting to do so, which are worth quoting at length:

> One of the things that I have done since working with the Club . . . is really try to dare a heavily pencil-press-influenced organization. They're a very literate organization and a big believer in the printed and written word. And what they didn't have—despite the fact that this is the organization that invented the coffee table book—they didn't have many visuals. . . . [Yet,] when you have the environ-

ment and you have *everything*—you have all of the beauty in the world plus you have all of the degradation in the world—to be able to visually show people what should be valued and protected and the threats, to visually depict the threats or the lack of concern or the lack of decision making or just the total destruction of things have wrought—I mean, *people get it. . . .* That old adage about a picture being worth a thousand—make it about a million. So, I am totally committed to telling as many tales about the environment as we can visually. It is a way to broaden our audience. It is a way that you don't need jargon: you can just *show* people, you know. If you want to show the consequences of the *maquiladoras,* show people living next door to it, show what happens when you work in it, show the stream on the outside of it. Enough said.[38]

Haddow encourages the Sierra Club to create more visual texts not only because they can (since the environment suggests powerful ways to depict both the picturesque and the grotesque), but also because "people get it." She implies that visual texts speak to audiences in a way that moves them. Furthermore, as she points out, the format of a video or other mediated text potentially broadens the audience of tourist-witnesses by moving people who are not interested in jargon. As Haddow explains when describing different environmental advocacy tours, "The philosophy behind them all is the same: *show them.*"[39]

When I ask Haddow to clarify why creating videos is particularly important for global issues, her answer sounds reminiscent of TLC's tactic of "making links": "People who have to drink polluted water are human beings. And I think the thing that visuals can do in terms of global issues is to bring them home and to bring them closer, but to also find common ground. It is that we're *all* part of that community. . . . What our job is to do is to connect the dots. And what I think that video can do in a way that I think that nothing else can do is humanize it, make us understand we're all in this thing together, and *really, really,* demonstrate that the consequences are not as far away or generations removed as we like to think they are." In her reference to "connecting the dots," Haddow is addressing the sense of helplessness that people sometimes feel in reaction to global problems. Her response also suggests that part of the answer is tied to the question of *identification* with reimagined communities, reminding audiences that "we're all part of that community" in order "to bring them closer."

Haddow produced *Matamoros* in conjunction with Adam Werbach of Act Now! Productions. Werbach notes that the first decision they made was to ask who the intended audience would be and what the goal of creating the video was.

> We basically tried to look at it as an output. In other words, what does the community need and what can really be useful? Rather than simply creating a diary of the Board of Directors' trip, [we decided it wouldn't be] . . . a camp video or a vacation video. . . . A camp video would sort of show the Board of Directors and what their experiences were and how they went through the experience, through their eyes. This video, obviously, provides an omniscient narrator through the voice of Edward James Olmos. It looks at the issue and gives a very clear and compelling statement about why *maquiladoras* and border pollution needs to be dealt with. So, it goes from the camp video into an advocacy piece. . . . Once we decided to make it an advocacy video, we wanted to cover the issue, give it background, and do all the things that weren't covered—or may have been covered in the tour, but we never saw.[40]

These choices should not be taken for granted. First, Werbach recalls that the community's goals became the motivation for those involved in the production. The producers of this video chose to listen to grassroots environmental justice activists and to develop the video as a tactical process of alliance building.

Second, Werbach suggests that an advocacy video might more efficiently depict the issue by providing an omniscient narrator with an explicit advocacy message in contrast to a diary format. To help enhance the feeling that the person watching the video is on a tour, the film eliminates the other tour participants from view, adds the voice of an omniscient guide, and includes additional background information. As such, the video provides its own toxic tour. In this sense, the video does not attempt to replicate an exact copy of the original tours; rather, it offers its own toxic tour to experience altogether, one that is no less significant.

In Response: After the Tour

The impact that the initial seven toxic tours had for the Sierra Club's Responsible Trade Campaign was significant. In fact, three months after the toxic tour, "the Sierra Club, in cooperation with the Sierra Club Foundation, created Beyond the Borders—a three-year, $1 million grant program aimed at countering the ill effects of free trade."[41] These results again give credence to the idea that being physically present in a place can enable people to feel the presence of a particular community in a way that may be politically efficacious for the hosts.[42]

One of the people who saw the video early on is Domingo González, a Mexican American and self-described border activist who was vital to organizing the toxic tours.

Pezzullo: Do you feel like if a person saw the film that he or she would know what it was like to visit Matamoros?

González: Oh, yes.

Pezzullo: Yes, OK. And do you feel like it captures—

González: —*if* they came on a toxic tour. The problem is that most people don't come to *see* those kinds of things, unless it's an organized tour.

Pezzullo: Right. So, it was helpful for people who cannot go on a toxic tour?

González: Exactly. Audiences that are outside of the region who want to get close to the issues.

Pezzullo: Right. And, then, do you feel like it captures "the human face of globalization," like it says it does? Do you feel like it humanizes globalization well?

González: I think so.

Pezzullo: Do you think it could be used for a Mexican audience, if it was translated into Spanish? Or, do you think it would have to change a little bit?

González: Well, depending on the audience—I was very surprised that a lot of people in Matamoros itself had never been out to those areas of town. . . . It was a surprise to them to see squatter camps and people living on the city dump and things of that sort. . . . The story is very, very large; but, in a short film, I think it did what it can do, in one of those short topic films. If it was a little bit longer, it might look into a more complex subject like the possible links between pollution and birth defects, things of that sort.[43]

González points out, as I did in addressing the United States, that Mexican areas that are toxically assaulted are hidden even from those residents who live in nearby areas. For these residents, the initial tours became the first occasion for some people to witness these conditions and their effects on people who live in them. González further claims that the tours, both on and off video, are venues to help people "*see* those kinds of things." Further, he notes how the video's brevity may limit its possibilities. Conversely, I would suggest that the brevity of the video tour makes it more amenable to the organizing meetings for which it is intended and, thus, to discussion subsequent to a screening. Such postscreening discussions, in turn, can augment an invitation for further identification and, then, perhaps, for feeling the presence of the lives and struggles of those who have been witnessed via the video tour.

González's perceptions were reinforced by Werbach's account of a film festival at which more residents of Matamoros saw the video.

Werbach: And I think that if there's a fault to our film, it's far too one-sided and bleak. You know, . . . that's what the *worst maquiladoras* in the dumps look like. But, that's not what *maquiladora* life is. And it is an advocacy piece and it's meant to pull the heart strings . . . but, it's not what Matamoros is. I've actually showed it to people from Matamoros and they hate it. . . . Because that's not what Matamoros looks like. So, that's another discomfort with it. Actually, . . . they don't hate it, they understand it; but, they hate that people are going to be seeing this as the place where they're from. . . .

Pezzullo: Did they articulate another vision that they would like you to include?

Werbach: . . . They said simply—it's probably easier or better for you to talk to folks from there—is that it just wasn't all of Matamoros and you should show the good stuff too. And, I think they're right. It's a piece that holds up as an advocacy video; but, it certainly doesn't hold up as journalism.[44]

Werbach's concerns about toxic tours echo those of other voices I have heard and read throughout this project. Since every toxic tour I have participated in has ended with a call to action, I agree with Di Chiro that subsequent action is one of the primary goals of toxic tours.[45] Again, such an imperative may provide motivation to construct shorter videos such as this one in order to allow people the opportunity to focus more time on what to do rather than on the tour itself.

Without delving into how objective or "balanced" journalists are today, Werbach's stance as a nonjournalist belies the fact that the stakes of this documentary are high and that the people involved in toxic tours, at every level, are not participating in these struggles in an attempt to provide "just the facts." When people organize toxic tours to a particular site, they attempt to persuade people to take sides as a result of placing our physical bodies, health, sanity, and hearts in spaces that we might otherwise avoid. Toxic tours onscreen similarly ask people to take sides; although they do not entail all of the same risks, video toxic tours do entail the risk of exposing one's eyes, ears, and self to the choice to become involved with a place and a people that might otherwise be avoided. Although these different media of communication inscribe bodies of people and environments differently, both provide the tour participant an opportunity for identification with the communities, places, and arguments shared on the tour. As a result of this opportunity for identification, the possibility of provoking the enthymematic and performative "what if" is reopened: What if I lived in a community polluted by toxins? What if my child was born with a brain outside his or her skull? What if the people I loved had to live near vomit-inducing smells? Would I do something in response or even visit?

Although I have heard others question the productivity of toxic tours, from my own experiences listening to those who host them, I do not believe that this practice would be so prevalent if this tactic did not produce or at least pose the possibility of beneficial results for the hosts. When I tried to tell González about Werbach's story of sharing the video with other people from Matamoros, I fumbled for words so as to not lead his response, because I wanted to know if this feeling of self-consciousness resonated with him.

Pezzullo: . . . they were a bit—
González: —that they only showed the worst parts of Matamoros?
Pezzullo: Yes.
González: Of course! . . . We're not the Chamber of Commerce. [I laughed.] . . . The Chamber of Commerce has a lot of money to do those kinds of things.[46]

Although González does not speak for all people living in areas that are featured on toxic tours, I believe his voice is worth noting as yet another, important perspective. Both Werbach's and González's responses confirm that people from Matamoros might not identify with the video *Matamoros*. Yet, again, the goal for the documentary was not to show "Matamoros" but to create a documentary film that would be useful for advocacy purposes. In part, González suggests that what is useful about the video tour is the opportunity to portray what would not be witnessed otherwise, what the Matamoros Chamber of Commerce would probably edit out of its video.

In this sense, the video invites viewers to appreciate what de Certeau calls a sense of "space" (*espace*), in addition to learning more about the area as a "place" (*lieu*). "In short," de Certeau suggests, "space is a practiced place." He elaborates on this distinction within the context of stories: "In our examination of the daily practices that articulate . . . experience, the opposition between 'place' and 'space' will rather refer to two sorts of determinations in stories: the first, a determination through objects that are ultimately reducible to the being-there of something . . . , the law of a 'place' . . . ; the second, a determination through operations which, when they are attributed to stone, tree or human being, specify 'spaces' by the actions of historical subjects. . . . Stories thus carry out a labor that constantly transforms places into spaces or spaces into places."[47] I would suggest that it is through the video's performance of stories that it carries out the labor of moving between places and spaces, between being-there and operations. Further, in the context of a broader conversation about toxic tours, it is worth considering how this touristic movement retains the possibility of invoking identification, whether or not it is shared in the same space and time.

Conclusions

In our current era of globalization, it has become critical to imagine international and transnational communities through which to resist decentralized patterns of domination over vast geographical areas. As the physical presence of Borderlands proliferates even beyond national borders, we will increasingly face the choice of whether to feel further connected or to feel overwhelmed by the differences (racial, ethnic, national, economic, etc.) that we physically encounter. In this context, toxic tour videos have become an increasingly common organizing tactic in order to "connect the dots" or "link" people rather than to divide us. Shohat and Stam note what they perceive to be the usefulness of multicultural films: "Since cultural identity, as Stuart Hall has pointed out, is a matter of 'becoming' as well as 'being,' belonging to the future as well as the past, multicultural media could provide a nurturing space where the secret hopes of social life are played out . . . a space of community fantasies and imagined alliances."[48] The toxic tours discussed in this chapter suggest that part of recognizing these articulations and thus reaffirming our self-identity as agents of democratic social change is to imagine our communities as both global and local, or "global/local." *Matamoros* and the tours on which it was based were produced in consideration of the ways in which global treaties such as NAFTA shape local cultures by undercutting democratic accountability. The overwhelming costs, not the benefits, from these global arrangements, according to toxic tour guides, do not reach the local governments or many of the everyday people affected by these decisions. Toxic tours provided on and off film suggest how local communities might embrace global solidarity with other local communities in order to find strength, personal growth, and perspective to resist domination from transnational polluting corporations.

I have argued that the tourist may serve as a useful mode of political subjectivity in environmental justice struggles, because touring shifts the perspective of those who tour—or so is the hope of the host community. On the types of toxic tours I addressed in chapter 3 via Louisiana's Cancer Alley, "outsiders" are invited in to tour a toxically assaulted community. The tactic on the part of the hosts is to articulate their lived experiences in their concrete world to the visitor's sense of agency by placing the tourist in close proximity with the toxically assaulted area and by sharing people's stories, homes, and perspectives. The assumption is that, during the tour, previous notions of the sacred and the profane might be denaturalized as the host community's struggles become more present to the tourists. On the types of toxic tours I addressed in chapter 4 via San Francisco, California, the toxic tour format is reversed, such that "the attraction" is the toxically assaulting industries rather than the toxically assaulted communities. The assumption is that by focusing on the industries that enable toxic pollution and their co-opting practices, the injustices of their actions might feel more present to those who participate in and come across the tour.

Given the relative cost, ephemerality, and physical fixity of these two modes of touring, it is politically prudent to consider if toxic tours on video—or, by implication, other media technologies—can open up similar possibilities. In one sense, I have already suggested that they cannot. The risks of a tourist traveling to a place and witnessing a video tour about that same place are different. Most significantly, the safety promised by maintaining one's physical distance cannot be ignored. Physical distance from the harmful health effects of short-term toxin exposure matters to the tour experience. It also is less likely that the video tourist will build personal relationships with people in the video (who live in other parts of the world) or have spontaneous encounters during a screening with people from the communities toured (though this depends on the context of the recording). At the risk of sounding redundant, therefore, the video tourist *does not* experience the toxic tour *as if* he or she were on the tour filmed or recorded.

Yet, the feeling of presence is not guaranteed even with literal co-presence. As I have shown, toxic tour participants who travel to a site might miss a specific smell, person, or place that could help them more fully appreciate the preciousness of a place or a people. Further, the video's material rhetoric as a durable, mobile, and relatively affordable mode of communication is useful politically. Documentaries of toxic tours, like other toxic tours I have described, provide a means by which to witness places, people, and behaviors that might not be otherwise witnessed. In addition to being able to reach broader audiences, videos may help those who participate in toxic tours that require literal co-presence to remember what they have witnessed (and have not).

My point is that pollution makes a difference to our bodies in a way that images of pollution cannot—and vice versa. As Conquergood states matter-of-factly: "Opening and interpreting lives is very *different* from opening and closing books."[49] Personally, I have yet to find an image of the Grand Canyon or the Sistine Chapel that is able to make me feel like I do when I am standing inside these breathtaking environments. I also value few objects more than my photographs of family and friends. Likewise, I am writing this book with the hopes that my own written words and the visual images reproduced on these pages might portray a sense of presence about bodies in pain that might not be otherwise for those of you engaging me on this journey. Losing all faith in the verbal or visual ability to translate experiences would mean, at minimum, that we should never read a book derived from an ethnography, and I cannot imagine that such drastic measures would be productive. These various ways of operating need not be any more or less valuable; they just are undeniably different.

Through video, in other words, tourists may be offered a concentrated and deliberate—though still partial—representation of a particular community's everyday life. The absence of proximity, in other words, does not exhaust the possibilities of presence or identification as affective mobilizing tactics. I have highlighted numerous moments throughout my analysis to portray how video tours offer opportunities for *identification with* the people who live with severe environmental injustices, without requiring the physical presence of the tourist at the site of environmental injustices. Sometimes the rhetoric of the video tour appears to reinforce what other toxic tour participants are asked to witness. For instance, *Matamoros* articulates the rhetoric of "the human face of globalization" to one particular child, suggesting the importance of making abstract notions appear as if they are palpable. This tactic is frequently used in non-video toxic tours (e.g., the Louisiana vista of Holy Rosary Cemetery with Union Carbide in the background or RavenLight's exposed mastectomy scar in the streets of San Francisco). Sometimes, however, the way that video tours invite participants to feel present varies from that of other toxic tours. Consider, for example, the aerial shot. This perspective enables the video tourist to witness that which many tourists do not on other toxic tours. Seeing images of the Mexico/U.S. border from above provides a tangible image with which video tourists might be able more readily to feel as if the messiness of everyday life below is more manageable, more tractable and, thus, even if just for a moment, more present.

This chapter illustrates how toxic tours aim for a sense of identification between tourists and tour hosts in order to reimagine their sense of community. This affective response may be enabled by a closing call for action or by the way guides, residents, and other activists repeat, amplify, or illustrate the need to believe that the communities toured matter. I have argued how, sometimes, the stories shared—even when not shared in person—can transform our understanding of ourselves and of others. As a result, although the material rhetoric of a video differs from that of a tour, the invited political subjectivity of the video tourist remains called to feel present, invested as if the life of communities witnessed—both real and "imagined" but, nevertheless, vulnerable—are no longer remote.

The aim of all toxic tours is to catalyze social change in ways that might improve the bodies of people, land, and thought most severely affected by toxic pollution. According to *Matamoros,* the "experiment" of NAFTA has led to disastrous environmental effects: the pollution of the air, water, land, and bodies (with increased asthma, birth defects, cancer, etc.). Through the embodied rhetoric of the video tour, tourists are invited to witness vulnerability, to see, to hear, to smell (insofar as smells are described), and to feel the corporeal pain of the planet and of those who have lost or are losing loved ones. In the end, even if there is no meeting planned after the viewing, the video tour itself invites tourists to do more.

The possibilities of feeling presence in relation to physical presence are particularly relevant to the political context of mobilizing environmental justice activism during a time of increased globalization. I began this chapter noting that our current era of globalization enables simultaneous feelings of connection and helplessness. Some days, therefore, it may seem quite easy to act as if local life is all that matters and that international treaties are of no concern to us. Yet the toxic tours addressed in this chapter suggest that the costs of believing we are helpless or unaffected are extremely high. To the degree to which we wish to reduce, deter, and avoid those effects, we must find ways to rejuvenate our capacity as a people to feel as if every person, every place, and every way of life matters. Such a challenge provokes us to risk performing an attitude of political optimism—despite the fact that no one individual can share a sense of identification with everyone everywhere all the time or in a way that erases the divisions between us and each other, the Earth, or even our own thoughts and practices. Sometimes this idealistic attitude requires us to find ways to feel as if we are present, even when we are not physically so. For, in the end, possibilities of political subjectivity and agency rest on an investment in some sense of "being there," not necessarily physically, but in imagined alliances with communities around the globe. Without this structure of feeling of presence, I would suggest that we are all much too vulnerable to patterns of isolation, alienation, and toxic assault.

For me, traveling to Brownsville and Matamoros provided a sense of everyday life that tends to be left on newsroom editing floors or not recorded at all. For example, I recall waiting for my luggage at the airport and seeing a billboard for a company promoting NAFTA. Never in all my travels across the United States had I noticed such an advertisement before. The air pollution that irritated the contacts in my eyes and the smells that made me lose my appetite on the tour are more memorable to me than the statistics that were shared during the ride. Toxic tours such as this one also help me place my everyday life into perspective. Although life feels hectic sometimes, these tours remind me how much I take for granted, how fragile those gifts are, and how vigilant I should be in my efforts to stand up for the right to clean air, water, and land.

When I saw the video, however, I truly felt like I was being offered a different tour, one that was more holistic about the problems in the area. Somehow, it was easier for me to stomach the statistics and repeated messages. Yet, the image of the little girl who represents a synecdoche for "the human face of globalization" now remains vividly captured in my memory. I do not know if I would feel so visceral in my reaction to the video if I had not traveled to Matamoros first; however, I do know that there are other places I have not visited in which advocacy videos have moved me. I also imagine that this sense of identification is part of what motivates most of my undergraduate students to tell me that they plan to travel to Hawaii and Alaska before they die. These tourist destinations have already come to signify significant spaces in their personal and national imaginaries through secondary sources.

What probably surprised me the most in my overall research for this chapter were the interviews. Most of the media producers, practitioners, and activists with whom I spoke were not only acutely aware of the political situation on the ground but also astutely reflexive about their own role in reproducing and reimagining those struggles. Talking with them helped me perceive further dimensions to both tours that had not crystallized for me previously. Despite the fast-paced nature of their final product, their actions appeared quite deliberate. In a sense, their voices and stories helped add even more texture and flesh to the tours.

In concert, all three dimensions—the video tour, the toxic tour in person, and the interview—offered me a fuller sense of Matamoros and NAFTA than I had before I began exploring. No, I do not feel as if I now am part of the inner circle of the campaign that unfolded subsequently or the group of environmental and environmental justice leaders whom I interviewed. I do feel, however, that when anyone—including you and I—shares these tours and stories with someone else as a host or a temporary "tourist," we become better able to identify with communities outside our own day-to-day understanding and with the broader social movement for environmental justice. What we do after the tour then determines which side of the movement—for or against—we choose to belong to.

Conclusion

All the Time in the World

Black, white, young, old are dying before their time. There are other ways to develop economies than to ask people to give up the lives of their children.

—Patricia Melancon of Convent, Louisiana

Indeed, who wants to die "before their time"?[1] Who wants one's loved ones to do so? I do not. Do you?

Those who host toxic tours are posing a relatively simple challenge: If you want to live, if you want the next generation of children to live, join us in the struggle to end the ongoing toxification of our world. This call is not merely one of belief or agreement (again, who is *for* toxic pollution?); rather, it beckons us to act. As such, the challenge for toxic tours is to inspire a motivated sense of agency, to translate the seemingly uncontroversial feeling that toxic pollution needs to stop into concrete practices that help prevent further pollution and provide redress for the harm we have already allowed to occur. It is valuable, therefore, to explore toxic tours if for no other reason than that they provide a grassroots model of how a tactic of resistance might enact environmental decision making in a more democratic manner.

In addition to this pragmatic instrumental goal, toxic tours tell us a great deal more. By way of conclusion, I want to emphasize the importance of unpacking the relationship between space, time, and social change. Then, I clarify how this book has illustrated the spatial dynamics involved in toxic tours, from specific locations where tours are hosted to the broader patterns of residential segregation that enable the linking of waste with certain populations. After focusing on spatial politics, I elaborate on how toxic tours negotiate the arts of timing. As a democratic tactic that enables "public time," toxic tours warrant our attention because they provide nothing short of the conditions of possibility to transform the toxic cultural politics that currently frame the ways we travel, the perceptions we hold of tourists, and the unjust environmental conditions continuing to plague both our planet and ourselves.

Tactics of Space-Time

Throughout this book I have deliberately described toxic tours as a "tactic," based on de Certeau's distinction between "tactic" and "strategy":

> I call a "strategy" the calculus of force-relationships which becomes possible when a subject of will and power . . . can be isolated from an "environment." . . . Political, economic, and scientific rationality has been constructed on this strategic model. I call a "tactic," on the other hand, a calculus which cannot count on a "proper" (a spatial or institutional localization). . . . A tactic insinuates itself into the other's place fragmentarily, without taking it over in its entirety, without being able to keep it at a distance . . . a tactic depends on time—it is always on the watch for opportunities that must be seized "on the wing." Many everyday practices . . . are tactical in character.[2]

Although de Certeau's explanation of "tactic" and "strategy" is cited often, Meaghan Morris notes that "these terms need clarification, since it is not just a matter of opposing major to minor, strong to weak, and romantically validating the latter." What a "tactic" more productively enables, she elaborates, is a way to identify localized acts that "depend on arts of timing, a seizing of propitious moment, rather than on arts of colonizing space."[3] In other words, for those occupying a position of more power, the colonization of space (namely, the privilege to make choices that shape space according to one's will) is more attainable than for others in positions of relatively less power. Conversely, for those who aim to resist dominant power relations, the arts of timing become more vital to one's hopes and actions. Neither is a somehow "perfect" solution; rather, both are messy and complicated negotiations.

It seems important to emphasize, however, that de Certeau's writings do not necessarily suggest that time and space operate exclusively from each other; instead, the labeling of certain practices as "tactics" or as "strategies" is more productively appreciated as the acknowledgment that various acts privilege one dynamic over the other.[4] In this spirit, it is useful to recall Doreen Massey's argument that articulating space and time together as "space-time" is important, because it "inherently implies the existence of the lived world of a simultaneous multiplicity of spaces: crosscutting, intersecting, aligning one another, or existing in relations of paradox or antagonism." From this perspective, both space and time shape history and are imbued with power relations.[5] Although one may play a more dramatic role in a particular moment, neither exists in isolation.

In a sense, this book has mapped a spatial story. To begin, I explored particular places that have become sites of struggle, from regions and cities (e.g., southern Louisiana, San Francisco, and Matamoros) to specific stops on tours (e.g., "that cemetery," "this corporation," and "those smells at the dump"). Following the cues of those who host toxic tours, I showed in chapters 3 through 5 how particular political themes (e.g., building coalitions, protesting the cancer industry, and challenging international trade agreements such as NAFTA) have varied depending on the location of the tour. Although this book has illustrated how certain shared values, practices, and goals can be found across the range of practices called "toxic tours," I also have indicated how local or place-based exigencies animate each tour in unique ways.

I also have emphasized how toxic tours involve spatial dimensions of everyday life that exceed the specificity of any one struggle. Toxic tours resist toxic spatial patterns of segregation and alienation by redefining the spaces in which we live through processes of site sacralization, corporate co-optation, and national identification. In doing so, these tours challenge colonizing Western and Enlightenment-inspired spatial dynamics by promising to create a structure of feeling present, to reduce the distance—physically and affectively—between tour hosts and tourists, oppressed and elites, bodies and minds, embodiment and sight, and the locations of study and scholarly research. Traveling, in these instances, creates palpable opportunities for communities to negotiate power. Rather than reifying some essential notion of place, toxic tours educate participants about the affective feelings for and the biological necessity of specific environments, while highlighting the cultural politics that shape and are shaped by these spatial dimensions in mobile and dynamic ways.

As such, bodies of land are intertwined with bodies of people and bodies of thought. Acknowledging these three inextricably linked facets of everyday life *as corporeal* helps highlight how each is rhetorical, dynamic, material, and interdependent on each of the others. Resisting traditionally Western and Enlightenment tendencies to disembody our sensual ways of acting and knowing in the world, therefore, remains significant to mobilizing political dissent.

Further, as I have argued, challenging conceptions of tourist practices to account for an embodied way of acting in the world that exceeds the visual addresses at least three problematics. First, a more fully embodied appreciation of tourism reminds us that even when we look, we are looking from an embodied subjectivity. All of our senses and body parts implicate each other. For example, when tourists stopped in Louisiana to take pictures of the graveyard, they needed to walk off the bus, position themselves for their desired view, and physically push a button to take a picture, in addition to speaking, smelling, and breathing along the way. Second, tours require more than merely gazing. In this book I have shared how toxic tours also involve a range of embodied practices, such as sitting, walking, listening, smelling, and proxemics. Third, decentering the visual as our primary way of engaging tourist practices may help those of us who study tourism to become more reflexive about our own culpability in privileging and, thus, perpetuating oppressive and colonial sensibilities. Doing so requires that we try to find ways to appreciate and to translate the richness of the practices we are witnessing and participating in. It suggests the need to rehearse vocabularies that might at first seem theoretically counterintuitive, as I have done with the concept of "presence."

Throughout this book, I have argued that the particular embodied rhetorics enacted through the practice of toxic tours articulate a feeling of presence. Although admittedly partial and ephemeral, affectively feeling as if someone, someplace, or something is present in our lives can significantly challenge feelings of alienation from the land and each other. The hosts of toxic tours are inspirational speakers and activists for their continued strength to challenge environmentally unjust practices; however, unlike other environmental tours, toxic tours tend not to invoke the sublime or the picturesque. Rather, they embody a pedagogical posture by inviting us to witness and to interrogate the disgusting and the grotesque through critical questions, such as: Why would a company pay to relocate a community and restore a historic slave plantation home but not admit its role in creating injustice? Why do we allow corporations that have caused cancer to frame breast cancer discourse? And why have governments sanctioned the flow of goods and services across national borders, but not people and laws to ensure environmental and public health protection?

Toxic tours also concretize or make present the sometimes overwhelmingly ambiguous and abstract terms *toxic* and *pollution* through spatial practices such as sharing stories, pointing out who has died, mapping the location of polluting industries to those who are ill, and exposing tourists to the smells and other bodily sensations of a place that are hard for most to imagine are part of the everyday lives of the tour hosts. Navigating hegemonic tendencies to portray "the toxic" as either extraordinarily beyond our reach or banally omnipresent and, thus, futile to attempt to address, toxic tours are designed to invoke a feeling of presence that will translate into significant action. Identifying how social perceptions and physical effects of pollution are perpetrated, create harm, and can be stopped is vital to their success.

Although clearly indebted to such spatial dynamics, toxic tours also imply a complex relationship with the arts of timing and of temporality. I now want to highlight two general temporal patterns: one focuses on the cultural, political, and economic context leading to the need for toxic tours; the other focuses on revealing how toxic tours negotiate the arts of timing. In doing so, I hope to illuminate how time-space (or space-time) influences the cultural politics of pollution, travel, and environmental justice.

Time Bombs

"Modern societies," according to Jérôme Bindé, "suffer from a distorted relationship to time." Namely, a "logic of 'just in time'" enables the dominance of a "tyranny of emergency," or what he calls "emergency time," in which everything from "communication to finance" is expected at "the speed of light" or "[r]eal time, the absolute zero of temporal distance." Bindé also claims that those in decision-making positions have fallen into a pattern of enacting quick and dramatic decisions with little deliberation or prudence involved. The stakes of this approach to public life, he argues, are such that "citizens of today are claiming the rights of citizens of tomorrow" by focusing on short-term solutions without long-term analysis of consequences.[6] Bindé's analysis of the future costs of this temporal logic is sobering, especially for those who are willing to admit that all of the profound discoveries in science and technology still do not include a way for humans to exist outside of Earth or without relatively healthy habitats.

Bindé's argument seemingly echoes the environmental belief in the precautionary principle, in which it is suggested that when there are doubts or uncertainties about the effects of specific practices on the environment we require to live, we would do best to err on the side of caution until we can be more confident that our short-term desires do not preclude the existence of our future lives or generations.[7] However, Sandra Steingraber emphasizes that any cautionary challenges to systemic patterns of toxification should not be confused with individual acts of environmental self-disciplining in everyday life. She calls the idea that all we need to counter the toxification of the world is to give up consuming high-"risk" items or to buy a healthy home environment with environmentally sound products "the myth of living safely in a toxic world." Instead of aspiring "to become the ecological equivalent of the boy in the bubble," Steingraber insists, we must struggle for systemic change in the industries and governments that continue to pollute bodies of land (including the water cycle and our food chain) in addition to our own bodies.[8] This type of transformation would take into account long-term implications of our collective acts as a body politic, requiring that we live more deliberately and act more democratically—even if it means slowing things down.

In these complicated and contradictory times, however, Bindé's hope to work toward a more unhurried life is not enough. In fact, the time line of toxification is usually quite slow. As noted previously, the public health effects of toxins might not manifest themselves in the short-term. Further, chemical and biological spans of time often influence institutional responses. Whereas public health threats tend to create a sense of exigence to act "now" in response to crises or catastrophic events like tsunamis, hurricanes, and militaristic attacks, the latent effects of toxic pollution are apt to pose a risk sometime "in the future" and, in turn, are often rationalized not to require immediate reaction—thus deferring action indefinitely. Reflecting the effects of toxins themselves, therefore, the institutional response to them often constitutes a sense of latent exigency in which there is an acknowledgment, either tacitly or explicitly, of an urgent need to do something—just never now.[9]

What is particularly remarkable in communities showcased on toxic tours is that they have been toxically assaulted to the degree that some of the detrimental effects on bodies of people and land have already become apparent to those living there. Damage to the Earth has become palpable not only through shocking sites but also through vulnerable bodies. These communities have already faced the dilemma of communicating their corporeal pain, including a range of public health effects (e.g., cancer, respiratory problems, and birth defects) and the degraded quality of life lived every day (e.g., with vomit-inducing smells, visible eyesores, and the sounds of industry barreling through their neighborhoods).

What is absent from these tours, in a sense, is as important as what is present. Since some toxins damage one's physical capacity for memory, the stakes of holding onto times past may become all the more precious. Toxic tours also provide precautionary reminders of what is yet to manifest itself within those communities and elsewhere as a result of our toxic culture. Absences, such as a graveyard marking the death of loved ones, a scar where a breast once existed, or indistinguishable body parts of a child born with birth defects, constantly defer more absences that inevitably will grow if we continue on our current path.

In addition to latent costs, time moves quite slowly in relation to toxically assaulted communities in another way. Toxic tours often teach or remind us how environmental injustice is an extension of repeated historical patterns of oppression that continue to plague our world, including the "-isms" based on dominant perceptions of social pollution, such as racism, classism, sexism, and ethnocentrism. Further, these oppressive logics of social pollution have manifested themselves repeatedly within our own lifetimes. Noting how a petrochemical plant moved on top of a community, for example, Darryl Malek-Wiley pointed out on the toxic tour of southern Louisiana that "this happens time and time again."[10] On the toxic tour in San Francisco, standing in front of a public relations agency, Judith Brady likewise observed, "One of their favorite gimmicks is to create what we call an astroturf organization. They create phony grassroots groups, and it is through those phony groups that they give their live voice to the public. They've done it many times." After one major television network aired a story in which Domingo González hosted a toxic tour, the "president of the Matamoros *maquiladoras* association repeatedly denied the possibility that working conditions and industrial effluent may be linked to high rates of birth defects among *maquila* workers' children."[11] The repetition of these patterns of literal and metaphorical pollution on the part of dominant institutions and figures signals the resilience of these issues and the pervasive cultural norms that enable this toxic configuration to continue.

Time in everyday life or political decisions may be fast-paced for those occupying dominant positions of power, as Bindé describes; however, when "convenience" for the government and corporations requires institutions to move slowly (because, to be honest, what is faster than doing nothing?), we are reminded to complicate the "tyranny of 'just in time'" by asking: "just in time" for whom? In order to dismantle "the myth of living safely in a toxic world," therefore, we need to reevaluate what alternative ways of operating are necessary to account for long-term effects *and* to enable fast solutions for those who are being toxically assaulted. This book was written with the belief that toxic tours provide one model of how to aim for both.

Public Time

Like the oppressive relations that provoke them, toxic tours implicate a sense of time as well as space. As Barbara Brenner noted at the beginning of the TLC tour in San Francisco, "I'm here because it's time, it's way past time for people concerned about cancer to start making connections." This sense of time signals how toxic tours work as what de Certeau calls "tactics." Seizing upon and constituting the best "time to act" from the perspective of grassroots communities of resistance is the goal of toxic tours. A feeling of presence is, moreover, as much about time as it is about space. For another person, place, or idea to matter to us, we require not only the feeling of shared togetherness, or a connection between "there" and "here," but also a shared sense of time insofar as it entails the sense that *when* something happens "there," it matters "here." For toxic tours, invoking a sense of presence ideally helps mobilizes action because doing so makes people, places, and things feel closer *and* more urgent to address.

Believing we are living in a time that is opportune—or long past overdue—to challenge alienating and oppressive patterns of toxification, however, does not mean that anti-toxic environmental justice activism is easy. As Malek-Wiley stated on a toxic tour during the first term of U.S. President George W. Bush, reflecting the exasperation many environmental activists feel in the current political climate, "right now, we're losing the war on the environment. . . . It's time to get up and get moving. And it's tough." For those who have not been involved but might become involved in the movement for environmental justice, media producer Kim Haddow also identifies one of the primary constraints to global activism as the relationship between time and space: "Life in my face, in my immediate vicinity is *so challenging* and *so demanding* and *so time consuming,* you know, do I really care about something three thousand or fifteen thousand miles away?"[12]

Given the many directions our lives pull us simultaneously and the reality that most anti-toxic activism is not glamorous or quickly rewarding, it seems worthwhile to revisit the question: of all the possible ways to resist, why tour? If anything, "the touristic" colloquially refers to someone who is traveling for pleasure; pejoratively, it implies an attitude relegated *solely* to tourists, one *not* shared by local residents or people with more intimate relationships to a place ("Riding on the trolley is the touristic thing to do"; "She has a touristic relationship to the city"; "He has such a touristic attitude about everything"). In this sense, the "touristic" implies superficiality—particularly in terms of time: a whirlwind experience of an "outsider" passing through one or more destinations, quickly checking off what otherwise might be savored as a unique envelope of time in one's life like a haphazard afternoon of errands ("Braided hair on the beach in the Caribbean, Check"; "Ate Italian food in Florence, Italy, Check"; "Photographed the Grand Canyon at sunset, Check"). Rather than dwelling in the nuanced utterances of each moment, this attitude seems to hold that an erasure of one's soul is needed to make room for the cultural capital one might hope to feel or to receive from others when one returns home. When framed by this perception of touring as superficially toxic, as established in chapter 1, popular cultural depictions and scholarly writings about tourism tend to constitute a broader tourist imaginary with portrayals of the tourist in the role of the buffoon unwilling to adapt or the opportunistic adventurer adept at cultural infiltration and exploitation.

For communities that have been toxically assaulted, however, the time it takes to participate in a tour is more than they usually have to share in environmental decision-making processes.[13] Tours, at least toxic tours, matter in part *because they are time-consuming.* Rather than placing the onus on residents to travel to government buildings or other meeting centers and to bring evidence to make their case, toxic tours place the responsibility back on those who are privileged enough to live in other areas. They require other activists, lawyers, scientists, media, corporate employees, and governments to take the time—usually at least three to four hours, in addition to any time required to travel to a location—to listen to the people who are suffering, to witness how their environments have been degraded, and to bring their own bodies into contact with the effects of toxic pollution. Although most toxic tour films or websites provide a relatively quicker event for its participants, toxic tours tend not to be fast-paced productions. Toxic tours require dialogue between guides, drivers, and the people who open their homes and lives to the tourists. They are based on the scheduling of itineraries and the willingness to be open to spontaneous interactions that the tours enable. Furthermore, even though toxic tours on film or the Internet require less time than a tour in person (because they are shorter and tend to involve less effort for participation), those tours do require more time than not engaging toxically assaulted communities at all. As some of the moments shared in this book have illuminated, toxic tours also involve a range of emotional energies that run counter to a fast-paced way of acting in the world, including the patience to wait for logistical matters, the ability to enjoy a sense of humor, and the willingness to listen to painful, personal testimonies.

As part of the broader social movement for environmental justice, these forums enable opportunities for grassroots activists to express their perspectives and, it is hoped, to influence those involved in making decisions about their lives, including government officials, media, corporate executives, scholars, and other communities that might be inclined to join and to further their cause. Toxic tours not only create a space to bring together diverse people or "stakeholders" (to borrow a term used frequently by the EPA) but also help foster a relationship to time that is necessary for the enactment of more just and democratic relations. This shift also enables us to examine more closely the stakes of the often long and mundane practices involved in environmental decision making.

More specifically, toxic tours ideally foster "public time." Drawing on the writings of Cornelius Castoriadis, Henry Giroux argues, "public time demands and encourages forms of political agency based on a passion for self-governing, actions informed by critical judgment, and a passion for linking responsibility and social transformation. Public time renders governmental power explicit."[14] Applied to the idea of toxic tours, the requirement of "public time" for self-government speaks to how hosts of toxic tours have created maps of their communities, traced toxic patterns of pollution, and voiced their perspective on how governments and corporations should change the way they define "business as usual." These complex acts involve critical judgment in which everything is questioned and weighed against the value of human and ecological life. Finally, all of this effort requires passion—from the tour guides, the people who open up their lives on the tours, and, when successful, the tourists themselves—for the right to self-determination and the desire to hold those in decision-making positions accountable for the costs of our toxic culture. As a result, governmental power is rendered explicit, including the right to know, the right to participate, the right to provide independent expertise, the right to prevention, the ability to provide clean up, and who has the burden of proof. Valuing "public time" along with our sensual and spatial ways of acting and knowing in the world seems vital to the enactment of political dissent.

Invoking and delineating these characteristics of "public time" reminds us of the interconnection between space-time and radical democratic ideals. Although a democratic framework is far from new, "[d]emocracy," as Chantal Mouffe reminds us, "is our most subversive idea because it interrupts all existing discourses and practices of subordination."[15] The power and importance of such critical interruptions highlight the linkage between self-reflexive grassroots reclamations of democratic culture and an ethic of accountability or responsibility. "Being able to act," as Bindé notes, "also means being able to answer for our actions, to be responsible. Out of this coincidence between a forward-looking approach and an ethical choice emerges the need for a temporal change in the notion of responsibility."[16] Achieving a more democratic and just world by making toxic-polluting industries and governments more accountable requires us to make judgments that challenge ongoing spatial patterns of oppression *and* to transform our sense of temporality in relationship to the future.

However, gaining a temporal sense of urgency that would foster a more compelling ethic of accountability does not happen overnight. It will not spontaneously appear in any top-down mandate. It is a cultural shift in attitudes and practices that requires us to locate grassroots practices of political dissent that may help foster a more just and compassionate way of life.

Further, bringing various publics together does *not* promise to erase differences, as if that were a desirable goal. Instead, in a fundamental sense, part of the significance of toxic tours is the opportunity to create *contact zones* between various publics that tend to operate in worlds segregated from one other. Mary Louise Pratt defines a "contact zone" as "an attempt to invoke the spatial and temporal copresence of subjects previously separated by geographic and historical disjunctures, and whose trajectories now intersect. . . . A 'contact' perspective emphasizes how subjects are constituted in and by their relations to each other. . . . [It stresses] copresence, interaction, interlocking understandings and practices, often within radically asymmetrical relations of power."[17] Both spatially and temporally framed, the bringing together of differences on toxic tours enables the juxtaposition of uneven relations and resources that exist between publics. It also reminds us that, in the drama of our daily lives, feeling a sense of presence can create palpable effects.

Time to Tour

Toxic tours have not erased the existence of environmental injustices, because, like all tactics of resistance, they have rhetorical limits. In this book I have highlighted at least two broad areas of concern. First, toxic tours do not clean up communities. As Di Chiro observes in her earlier work on toxic tours, toxic tours do not help the movement for environmental justice if nothing comes of them. She rightly notes that the performance of "bearing witness" means little to the material conditions of the lives of people who are toxically assaulted if no one is "taking action" as a result. A transformation is required from agreeing that toxic pollution is bad to doing something about it. Results are not guaranteed. Likewise, as indicated by Werbach and my colleague who spoke of toxic tours in a worst-case scenario as working in a manner akin to the logic of zoos, if no actions follow, the toxic tour itself could foster a damaging experience for residents, who, as a result, may feel further discouraged and exploited. If the final result for the tourists is a sense of, "Well, c'est la vie—if it has to happen to someone, thank God it's not me,"[18] then a toxic tour might serve only to exacerbate the feeling of alienation a tourist feels in relation to the communities toured.

Second, as Sontag argues about photography as a mode of communication, the act of sharing another's life should not be conflated with the belief that one knows what it is like to be that person. Yes, presumably, a person who participates in a toxic tour will appreciate more fully the struggles and hopes of the hosts than would a person who is not from that location and who has not toured at all. Yet a toxic tour cannot—and need not—promise complete transparency. As Scarry reminds us, pain itself is incommunicable—that is part of its power. The best a host can do is describe what his or her pain feels like, and the best a tourist can do is try to imagine what that pain must be like with compassion. This vulnerable and precious process of translation, however, should not be mistaken for immediacy. Such a naive assumption, for example, may enable a government employee, a journalist, or a coalition partner from a more established environmental organization to forget that working together is not about being "the same"; rather, working together in political alliances is grounded in the possibility that in and across specific envelopes of space-time, different groups of people might be able to work together toward inventing a better world. The goal of democratic movements is not to erase the diversity of the *demos;* it is rather, as Laclau and Mouffe argue, to "expand the chains of equivalents between the different struggles against oppression" and, as a result, to foster the just negotiation of public culture for a diversity of people.[19]

Of course, these rhetorical limitations of toxic tours are mitigated by the fact that they do not exist in isolation. Toxic tours are just one tactic enacted by the environmental justice movement. Other venues and practices continue to matter, such as electing government officials (who set agendas), forming and maintaining Citizen Advisory Boards (which make decisions about toxically assaulted places), publicizing right-to-know information about toxic chemicals, staging media events, engaging in grassroots organizing, and lobbying for more just legislation—to name just a few. Toxic tours work in synergy with these and other ways of operating to educate and to mobilize alliances.

Still, toxic tours can be distinguished from other practices of environmental decision making in three ways. First, toxic tours blur distinctions made between high and low culture, influencing the epistemologies and evidence that come to bear on environmental decision making. For example, the toxic tour in chapter 3 highlighted through the mode of touring itself how, in an area of the country better known for Mardi Gras, alligators, and Cajun cooking, grassroots communities are critically analyzing the rhetorical frames offered by corporations such as Shell and are finding ways to challenge them by testing their own air quality and gathering their own information about their health conditions. Rather than ignoring the historical slave plantation being preserved (Ashland estate), the toxic tour included it as a brief stop to illustrate how more traditional tourist practices of sight sacralization are connected to the cultural politics of polluting the surrounding communities. I noted in chapter 4 how toxic tour hosts drew on touring as an inventive cultural resource to blur boundaries between dominant notions of who tours and who is toured by turning attention back on the industries that tend to remain invisible in the hidden abode of production. Chapter Five focused on how a toxic tour provided through film may question high/low cultural distinctions about touring itself and the politics of immediacy. Further, all the tours discussed aimed to create a sense of identification between tourists and tour hosts in order to reimagine their sense of community, challenging racial and national distinctions about who "belongs" and who does not.

Toxic tours also remind us of the importance of *embodiment* to public life. It is not that institutionalized practices such as government hearings or other social movement tactics such as media events are somehow not embodied; rather, toxic tours emphasize *the value of corporeal knowledges* by inviting people to visit places (in person, on film, or via the internet). By *showing* participants what they believe to be the problems of toxic pollution through *doing* a tour, toxic tours embody a *performance*-centered approach to environmental decision making. "The performance paradigm," as Dwight Conquergood argues, "privileges particular, participatory, dynamic, intimate, precarious, embodied experience grounded in historical process, contingency, and ideology. Another way of saying it is that performance-centered research takes as both its subject matter and method the experiencing body situated in time, place, and history."[20] As a result, "[p]roximity, instead of purity, becomes the epistemological point of departure and return."[21]

Recognizing this performance paradigm in toxic tours, I chose to engage in participant observation. Although it may be more limited than a focused study of any one place, this multi-sited approach provided me access to the practice of toxic tours in a way that is impossible to gain from secondary texts and to the opportunity to provide an overall assessment of this practice across various sites. It also became illustrative, as I discussed in chapter 5, in my own assessment of the differences between toxic tours offered in person and on film.

Although toxic tours provide only partial representations of a particular location, they still speak to a faith people have in the act of sharing through doing something together. This epistemological attitude is akin to the now-famous scene from *Erin Brockovich* in which the corporate lawyers are invited to drink a glass of water from the toxically assaulted community, or when a resident on a toxic tour I attended in Cincinnati goaded another tour participant by saying, "If you don't think the river is polluted, you're welcome to walk in it." It also resonates, to recall some examples shared in this book, with the frustration and the exasperation of the priest in Matamoros when we could not physically reach the toxic dump he wanted us to visit. And the importance that RavenLight places on exposing her mastectomy scar in public. And the way Margaret Evans in Norco, Louisiana, pointed out that Shell was not providing a "green belt" to protect her community from their pollution—because we could see the tree dying in her mother's yard.

In summary, toxic tours provide an inventive and provocative way to cultivate public time, and therefore we would do well to follow them closely in order to more fully appreciate the shifts in culture that they are engendering. Toxic tours challenge resilient traces of high/low political and cultural distinctions that might otherwise discount the value of practices such as tourism as pivotal to the ways we make decisions about the environment. Since the politics of domination surely are not solely grounded in "high" or "official" motivations, the politics of dissent must render explicit these blurred boundaries. Motivated by democratic impulses to increase the number of voices involved in environmental decision making, toxic tours also create political alliances between the tourists and the hosts in anticipation of building a more effective environmental justice movement. As a result, toxic tours also suggest the possibility that tourism may serve more admirable desires, such as inspiration for counterhegemonic resistance, passion for self-governance in civic decision making about public life, and a desire to educate others about the fate of one's home or way of living. Rather than being a "negative," "dark," or "tragic" practice of travel, this sensual way of knowing and acting in the world offers hope of an end to our self-defeating patterns of toxic pollution.

Epilogue

And the Struggles Continue . . .

Homeland Insecurities

After a toxic tour, the Environmental Community Liaison to the Louisiana Attorney General's Office, William Fontenot, was forced to retire after twenty-seven years of service. Two weeks earlier, he had served as a local guide of a small group of graduate students from Antioch College on a toxic tour of a Baton Rouge neighborhood in Cancer Alley that was in the process of being bought out by the ExxonMobil refinery. According to the professors leading the trip, the students were touring the region to learn about environmental racism and environmental justice in the Mississippi Delta. Their experiences, field notes, and photographs were for use in subsequent, course-required PowerPoint presentations. After they met with the local mayor, the next tour stop was directly across from the facility at a house where the owner had refused relocation. When the students began taking photographs from the sidewalk, "a pair of off-duty officers from the Baton Rouge sheriff's and police departments, wearing their official public service uniforms, but in the employ of ExxonMobil," pulled up and detained the group; "fulltime ExxonMobil security officials soon joined the detention team."[1] The group was detained for more than an hour, even though it is *not* illegal—with or without permission—to take pictures of chemical plants from outside a company's property on a public sidewalk. On Monday, April 4, 2005, Fontenot was told he would have to retire or be fired, which would cost him his pension and right to health insurance.[2] He chose the former option.

Two days later, Darryl Malek-Wiley sent out a mass e-mail with the news and the following note: "The petro-chemical industry put poisons [in] Louisiana's air water and land every day. The tours that Willie, I and other[s] have given over the years are a way to expose the massive scale of the petro-chemical industry in Louisiana to interested person[s] from other parts on the United States and the world. If the petro-chemical industry was really interested in homeland security they would be working to move to greener chemistry and inherently safe technologies."[3] Malek-Wiley's words reminded me of Bradley Angel's message after 9/11, that in addition to the people who were killed that day, "we also need to be . . . seeing story after story in the paper about—the other victims of terrorism."

Indeed, given events like this one and others like it across the country, it seems timely to reconsider what would make this country a safer place to live. Is it really stopping students from taking photographs? Is it ending toxic tours? Somehow, as both of these activists note, although the United States has come to recognize the terrorists who kill us quickly, we are unwilling to take a stand against the terrorists who are killing us slowly.[4] Instead, we have begun to criminalize those who question these slower— but equally deadly and far more common—terrorist acts.

The spirit of the law enforcement officials' concern is understandable: if a terrorist wanted to cause harm to a great number of people in the United States with minimal supplies on his or her end, targeting one of these petrochemical industries would be an effective approach. This is why environmental advocacy groups from international (e.g., Greenpeace) and local arenas (e.g., North Carolina Waste Awareness and Reduction Network, "NC WARN"), as well as the General Accounting Office and other government agencies, have brought attention to the potential use of chemical facilities as terrorist targets. Bill Moyers also reported in a story called "Homeland Insecurity" that the Chemical Security Act was passed to monitor these facilities more closely.[5] Senator Jon Corzine (D-N.J.) stated the justification for the act: "According to the Environmental Protection Agency (EPA), there are 123 facilities where a release of chemicals could threaten more than one million people. There are more than 750 additional facilities where such a release could threaten more than 100,000 people."[6] The effects of an attack on these facilities would be devastating.

Yet, by intimidating toxic tourists and their guides instead of addressing the source of the potential terrorist targets (i.e., eliminating toxic producing industries), the government is challenging the right of residents in toxically assaulted communities to share their views with those who live farther away. This makes no one safer. Isolation, as I have argued, enables those of us privileged enough not to live in toxically assaulted communities to more easily alienate ourselves from the costs of toxic chemical production as we know it. One of the primary ways we can challenge such alienation is through toxic tours. Rather than restricting the freedom of students, government employees, and residents to share their perspectives on toxic tours, why not restrict the industries and government facilities from creating such hazardous sites in the first place? With the latter approach, we could protect our nation not only from potential attacks that we cannot predict but also from the actual and ongoing toxic attacks that are occurring every day on our planet and our bodies.

Unnatural Acts

A second, more widespread tragedy affected Cancer Alley in September 2005: Hurricane Katrina. Yet as most media outlets, social movement activists, and even the president of the United States have now recognized, the devastating impact of this category 5 hurricane was grossly exacerbated by human choices. The impact of Hurricane Katrina was not natural.

Katrina's aftermath highlighted issues that environmental justice activists have long been pointing out on toxic tours and elsewhere. People of color, people in poor communities, and people who are ill or with disabilities within the United States did not have adequate access to resources, transportation, or information prior to the storm. One would have realized this if one had participated in a toxic tour. This book is grounded in the belief that toxic tours have come about as a result of a geographical and emotional distance existing between mainstream or dominant culture and the communities that are bearing the brunt of our polluting practices. The breach of the levees in New Orleans after Katrina literally forced the nation to observe how our current "sink or swim" attitude can lead to extreme tragedy.

The storm also brought many people to the region for relief efforts, government planning, and media coverage. Reporters rushed to the area to provide eyewitness accounts of the tragedy. The president was initially criticized for only flying over the area in a plane, and eventually he appeared moved by public pressure to revisit the area on the ground to take a "tour" of the flood zone. Somehow, in response to this tragedy, going there, stop by stop, issue by issue, mattered in our public culture. This response appears to reinforce the pedagogical and political value of toxic tours.

Finally, it seems worth noting that as this book goes to press, the extent of the toxic chemical damage is unknown. On September 15, 2005, the EPA issued a public advisory warning that included the following: five major oil spills had occurred in the New Orleans area; they had already collected 20,286 household hazardous waste and orphan containers; a leaking 55-gallon drum containing chloroacetic acid was identified by air surveillance; initial floodwater analysis revealed hexavalent chromium, arsenic, and lead levels that exceeded EPA drinking water standards; and five Superfund sites were being assessed, including one that remained underwater.[7] As the toxic tour described in chapter 3 showed, these hazards existed in the area well before Hurricane Katrina. As long as U.S. culture finds certain populations expendable, the toxification of our air, land, and water will continue—and vice versa: as long as we treat the Earth as expendable, certain populations will continue to be exploited. Events such as this one should remind us that it is naive to believe that the negative social and environmental impacts of such practices can remain contained.

Appendix: Contact Information for Advocacy Groups

For more information on toxic tours or on how to support toxically assaulted communities, contact:

Jesus People Against Pollution (JPAP)
Charlotte Keys (Founder and Executive Director)
P.O. Box 765
Columbia, MI 39429
Phone: (601) 736-0686
Fax: (601) 736-7811

Sierra Club Environmental Justice Grassroots Organizing Program
Darryl Malek-Wiley (Organizer)
14732 Sweetwood Ct.
Baton Rouge, LA 70816-2873
Phone: (225) 925-8650
E-mail: darryl.malek-wiley@sierraclub.org
Website: http://www.sierraclub.org/environmental_justice/

Toxic Links Coalition (TLC)
Bradley Angel (Executive Director)
GreenAction Office
One Hallidie Plaza, Suite 760
San Francisco, CA
Phone: (415) 248-5010, cxt. 108
Fax: (415) 248-5011
Website: http://www.toxiclinks.net/

Notes

Introduction

1. Mayfield's quote is from the film *Laid to Waste: A Chester Neighborhood Fights for Its Future*. For more on Chester's environmental justice struggles, see Cole and Foster, *From the Ground Up*.

2. MacCannell, *The Tourist*, 10.

3. Jordan, "Report from the Bahamas"; Kincaid, *A Small Place*.

4. See chapter 2.

5. Quotations such as the following are indicative of this cynicism: "Ecotourism is touted as more socially responsible than mass tourism, but the backpacker and the conservationist remain wealthy intruders in the native's homeland." Peña and Mondragon-Valdéz, "The 'Brown' and the 'Green' Revisited," 313. Suspicious responses to the use of tourism for progressive ends are understandable. Rather than "creating a magnet for foreign currency," tourism has "created a new kind of dependency" in which "the international politics of debt and the international pursuit of pleasure have become tightly knotted together." Enloe, *Bananas, Beaches, and Bases*, 31, 32.

6. Moore's film depicts, in the light of GM's downsizing of automobile workers in Flint, the development of a tourist theme park aimed to spark the local economy. "Auto-World" offered an indoor replica of the town before it became so economically depressed and a mechanical display in which an autoworker sings to a factory machine. Sayle's film portrays a variety of narratives about tourist endeavors, including swimming as a mermaid at the local aquarium, golfing, and hosting community fairs with a "heritage" theme.

7. "Tourism itself is the world's number one employer, accounting for 10 percent of jobs globally. If it were a country, it would have the second largest economy, surpassed only by that of the United States." Honey, *Ecotourism*, 9.

8. "Welcome to U.S. Industry's Spectaculars," *Life*, August 17, 1962, 19.

9. John E. Frazer, " 'Plant Tours'—A Vacation Extra," *Reader's Digest*, July 1966, 19.

10. J. F. Ross and J. Lorenzo, "A Vacationer's Guide to American Know-How," *Kiplin-*

ger's Personal Finance Magazine, May 1992, 116. Additionally, factory managers are encouraged to organize plant tours because they "allow senior executives to build a better understanding of a site's performance potential, to assess a competitor, to rally the frontline workforce, and to communicate the company's performance, strategy, and current challenges." David M. Upton and Stephen E. Macadam, "Why (and How) to Take a Plant Tour," *Harvard Business Review,* May/June 1997, 98. See also Michael Schrage, "That's the Ticket," *Fortune,* September 3, 2001, 236.

11. Larabee, *Decade of Disaster,* 51. Another recent trend has been for research organizations to offer tours of toxic facilities in order to foster education and discussion about land use. See, for example, the Center for Land Use Interpretation (http://www.clui.org/) opportunities to tour toxic facilities from the Hanford Nuclear Reservation to the DuPont Hagley Museum.

12. "Human sacrifice zones" share two characteristics: "1) they already have more than their share of environmental problems and polluting industries, and 2) they are still attracting new polluters." Bullard, *Confronting Environmental Racism,* 12.

13. Layne, "In Search of Community," 26.

14. Higgins, "Race," 252.

15. "Articulation" is an important theoretical concept I use throughout this book. By "articulation" I mean to reference what Hall defines as "the form of the connection that can make a unity of two different elements, under certain conditions . . . a linkage which is not necessary, determined, absolute, and essential for all time." Qtd. in Grossberg, "On Postmodernism and Articulation," 141. Ernesto Laclau and Chantal Mouffe also note that when articulations occur, the elements themselves are modified as a result. Laclau and Mouffe, *Hegemony and Socialist Strategy* (2nd ed.), 105.

16. I borrow this phrase from Mary Douglas: "If cleanness is a matter of place, we must approach it through order. Uncleanness or dirt is that which must not be included if a pattern is to be maintained. To recognize this is the first step towards insight into pollution . . . it involves no special distinction between primitives and moderns: we are all subjects to the same rules. But in the primitive culture the rule of patterning works with greater force and more total comprehensiveness. With the moderns it applies to disjointed, *separate areas of existence*" (emphasis added). Douglas, *Purity and Danger,* 40.

17. Rita Harris is a Sierra Club environmental justice organizer in Memphis, Tennessee. The quote is from a survey I created and implemented. Pezzullo, "Mapping," 9.

18. D. Willis, "Medical Incinerator Is Causing Environmental Harm, Group Says; 'Toxic Tour' Travels to Area Industrial Sites," *Baltimore Sun,* February 2, 1998, 3B.

19. Terry Harris is a lawyer and environmental justice activist. Pezzullo, "Mapping," 10.

20. For more on "tactics" as rhetorical performances of resistance, see the Conclusion. This move borrows from Michel de Certeau's writings. Drawing from Toulmin, Perelman and Olbrechts-Tyteca, and others, de Certeau argues that rhetoric "describes the 'turns'

or tropes of which language can be both the site and the object, and, on the other hand, these manipulations are related to the ways of changing (seducing, persuading, making use of) the will of another (the audience)." De Certeau, *Practice,* xx; see also 206 n. 22.

21. Reich, *Toxic Politics,* 142–47.

22. Ibid., 1. See also Carson, *Silent Spring.*

23. When I talk with people who work in the EPA on environmental justice issues, they have usually participated in at least one toxic tour. As part of the Environmental Justice Small Grants Program, the EPA provides funds to facilitate toxic tours, such as grant no. EQ-993450-01, the Anacostia Watershed Society's request for funds for "[a]n environmental justice tour of D. C. for 32 members of the Coalition on Environment and Jewish Life" (19) (http://www.epa.gov/compliance/environmentaljustice/grants/pdf/success.pdf); grant no. EQ-996891, with the stated purpose "to develop an active Woodland Acres Chapter of Mothers for Clean Air That would increase community awareness of air and solid waste hazards, identify environmental justice issues, and gather additional information on pollution sources in or near the community" (32) (http://www.epa.gov/compliance/environmentaljustice/grants/pdf/success.pdf); and in Huntington Park, California, grant no. EQ-999684-01-0 was "to provide students with critical skills and hands on experience in environmental problem solving" (71) (http://www.epa.gov/Compliance/resources/publications/ej/ej_smgrants_emerging_tools_2nd_edition.pdf). In fiscal year 1998 a grant was awarded to a grassroots group in San Antonio, Texas, in part, to organize a toxic tour (http://www.epa.gov/compliance/resources/publications/ej/grants/ej_smgr_recipients_98.pdf). At the fifteenth meeting of the National Environmental Justice Advisory Committee (NEJAC), environmental justice activist Connie Tucker provided a toxic tour of Anniston, Alabama (http://www.epa.gov/compliance/resources/publications/ej/nejacmtg/transcript_atl_052400.pdf). The Airbeat Project of Roxbury, Massachusetts, also suggests toxic tours as a useful tool in their EPA handbook, "Planning and Implementing a Real-time Air Pollution Monitoring and Outreach Program for Your Community" (http://www.epa.gov/ORD/NRMRL/Pubs/625R02012/625R02012.pdf). All websites available at www.epa.gov.

24. *EPA Transcript of the NEJAC Meeting in Atlanta, Georgia, Vol. II* (May 24, 2000), 11–71, http://www.epa.gov/Compliance/resources/publications/ej/nejacmtg/transcript_atl_052400.pdf.

25. For a concise but useful introduction to the historical association of tourism with "low" culture and how this linkage often is predicated on the contrasting fetishization of "high" culture as nation building, see Franklin, *Tourism,* 67–73.

26. R. Williams, *Resources of Hope,* 4, 13. Tellingly, although Williams claims that "[c]ulture is one of the two or three most important words in the English language," he asserts: "Nature is perhaps the most complex word in the language." R. Williams, *Keywords,* 87, 219.

27. Kelley, *Race Rebels,* 4.

28. Di Chiro, "Bearing Witness," 296.

29. Charlotte Keys, interview with author, November 20, 2001.

30. As a critical category, presence exceeds the ontological. From a rhetorical perspective, the heuristic value of "presence" is perhaps nowhere stated more clearly than in the collective and individual work of Perelman and Olbrechts-Tyteca. In summary, Perelman argues: "What an audience accepts forms a body of opinion, convictions, and commitments that is both vast and indeterminate. From this body the orator must select certain elements on which [she or] he focuses attention by endowing them, as it were, with a 'presence.' This does not mean that the elements left out are entirely ignored, but they are pushed into the background. . . . Things present, things near to us in space and time, act directly on our sensibility. The orator's endeavors often consist, however, in bringing to mind things that are not immediately present. . . . To make 'things future and remote appear as present,' that is, to create presence, calls for special efforts of presentation." Perelman, *New Rhetoric,* 17. As Perelman and Olbrechts-Tyteca emphasize, therefore, presence should not be confused with presentation, because physical co-presence does not guarantee a sense of presence, and vice versa. Perelman and Olbrechts-Tyteca, *New Rhetoric,* 117–18; see also Perelman, *Realm of Rhetoric,* 35.

For more on "presence" from a rhetorical perspective, I recommend Karon, "Presence in the New Rhetoric"; Leroux, "Perceiving Rhetorical Style"; and Murphey, "Presence, Analogy, and *Earth in Balance.*"

Jacques Derrida and Iris Marion Young have eloquently critiqued Western philosophy's tendency to fetishize "presence." Derrida, *Speech and Phenomena* and *Writing and Difference;* Young, "The Ideal of Community."

As a result, I want to emphasize that I am invoking a sense of presence that is both partial and ephemeral. As Stuart Hall notes: "If Derrida is correct in arguing that there is always a perpetual slippage of the signifier, a continuous 'deference,' it is also correct to argue that without some arbitrary 'fixing' or what I am calling 'articulation,' there would be no signification or meaning at all." Hall, "Signification, Representation, Ideology," 93. Articulation theory, therefore, enables us to appreciate when meaning is present—however partial, undetermined, and temporary it might be.

31. "Structure of feeling" is one of Raymond Williams's most notable contributions to cultural studies, and one that he develops throughout much of his work. He defines it as when "we are concerned with meanings and values as they are actively lived and felt. . . . We are talking about characteristic elements of impulse, restraint, and tone; specifically affective elements of consciousness and relationships: not feeling against thought, but thought as feeling: practical consciousness of a present kind, in a living and interrelating community." R. Williams, *Marxism and Literature,* 132.

By "affective" I am referring to Grossberg's elaboration on Williams's "structure of feeling" to consider "the nature of the concern (caring, passion) in the investment, . . .

the way in which the specific event is made to matter." "Affective organizations," as Grossberg emphasizes, "are a complex and contradictory terrain, but one that the Left ignores at its peril." Grossberg, *We Gotta Get Out,* 82, 83, 87.

32. "To be sensual, I think, is to respect and rejoice in the force of life, of life itself, to be *present* in all that one does, from the effort of loving to the breaking of bread." Baldwin, *The Fire Next Time,* 62, emphasis in source.

33. C. Kaplan, *Questions of Travel,* 170.

34. Leopold, *A Sand County Almanac,* 239.

35. For further discussion see chapter 1.

36. In chapter 2, I expand on how this system of thinking perpetuates cultural attitudes about "social pollution" in relation to not only women but also people of color, lower-income communities, and the ill.

37. My emphasis on embodiment throughout this book lends itself to the larger project that McKerrow calls "embodied rhetoricity," which, he notes, resonates with Marvin's "embodied literacy" and Conquergood's "embodied practice"—and, I would add, with Madison's "embodied writing." Whatever the name, the importance of a rhetorical sensitivity to embodiment is to recognize the vital role of bodies in all communicative practices. McKerrow, "Corporeality and Cultural Rhetoric"; Marvin, "The Body of the Text"; Conquergood, "Rethinking Ethnography"; Madison, "Performing Theory/Embodied Writing."

38. Scarry, *Body in Pain,* 15.

39. Hofrichter, "Introduction: Critical Perspectives," 1.

40. During a talk in spring 2004 at Indiana University, Bloomington, Cynthia Enloe argued that her "feminist curiosity" goads her to focus on the term *militarization* in her own work rather than words such as *empire* and *the military* because *militarization* emphasizes the ongoing process by which a place becomes militarized *as a process,* one that is not necessarily inevitable or closed to debate. Following her lead, I have begun to articulate my work as a study of the *toxification* of our world. See also Enloe, *Maneuvers,* 281.

41. Gregory Clark argues that tourist experiences were part of how people living in the United States began to identify as "Americans." Clark, *Rhetorical Landscapes.* With modernity, tourist encounters have only increased. As MacCannell observes, institutions such as the courtroom, the stock exchange, mental hospitals, and army bases are now designed for tourists to visit. "The becoming public of almost everything—a process that makes all [women and] men equal before the attraction—is a necessary part of the integrity of the modern social world." *The Tourist,* 50. See also chapter 1.

42. For evidence of Warren County cited as the birthplace of the movement and elaboration on the story itself, see Pezzullo, "Performing Critical Interruptions."

43. Environmental justice leader Benjamin Chavis qtd. in Grossman, "People of Color Environmental Summit," 278.

44. Bullard and Wright, "The Quest for Environmental Equity," 42. The history of the

environmental movement is less homogeneous and more complicated, of course. For a more recent and elaborated discussion of the relationship between these two movements see Sandler and Pezzullo, *Environmental Justice and Environmentalism.*

45. For further study of the leadership role of women in community-based movements for environmental justice as opposed to the mainstream environmental movement, see Di Chiro, "Defining Environmental Justice"; Dunlap and Mertig, *American Environmentalism;* T. Kaplan, *Crazy for Democracy.*

46. Gottlieb, *Forcing the Spring.*

47. *Proceedings,* 103.

48. Cole and Foster, *From the Ground Up,* 20.

49. Bryant, *Environmental Justice,* 6.

50. Hofrichter, introduction to *Toxic Struggles,* 5.

51. Bullard, *Unequal Protection,* 11. An all-too-often-overlooked history of democratic thought is that "Benjamin Franklin and Thomas Jefferson borrowed from Indian social organizations when seeking inspiration for a new political system. The Iroquois League (or Six-Nation Conference)—a near neighbor of the thirteen colonies—had almost two centuries of political unity prior to the American Revolution. Their constitution long predated the American version." O'Connor, "Promise of Environmental Democracy," 48.

52. Gibbs, *Dying from Dioxin,* xxi, emphasis added. Gibbs, formerly a resident of Love Canal, New York, gained national attention in the late 1970s through her struggle to relocate her community as a result of dioxin pollution. Since then she has become a vital leader of the community-based anti-toxic movement. Initially, Gibbs established the Citizens' Clearinghouse for Hazardous Waste; the name was subsequently changed to the Center for Health and Environmental Justice. Since it appears that the anti-toxics movement itself has increasingly privileged the rhetoric of "environmental justice," I have done so in this book with the intention of indicating the most inclusive discourse. For more on anti-toxic movements see Gottlieb, *Forcing the Spring;* and Moses, "Farmworkers and Pesticides."

53. Laclau and Mouffe, *Hegemony and Socialist Strategy* (1st ed.), 153, 176. In *Image Politics,* Kevin DeLuca suggests that the diversity of the struggles that constitute the environmental justice movement lend themselves to Laclau and Mouffe's theory of radical democracy, in which a range of struggles may join in political alliances against a common foe or ideology. According to Laclau, the radical democracy line of argument in their text is primarily Mouffe's contribution. Laclau, *New Reflections,* 180. Mouffe has continued to develop this concept. The importance of a radical and plural democracy, according to her, is that it "proposes a reformulation of the socialist project that avoids the twin pitfalls of marxist socialism and social democracy, *while providing the left with a new imaginary,* an imaginary that speaks to the tradition of the great emancipatory struggles but that also

takes into account recent theoretical contributions by psychoanalysis and philosophy" (emphasis added). "A new imaginary," as Mouffe defines it, "*is what we are struggling for. A vision of a future better than our past.*" Mouffe, "Hegemony and New Political Subjects," 32–33. This ideal is precisely what Mouffe calls the "paradox of democracy": "since the very moment of its realization would see its disintegration . . . such a democracy will therefore always be a democracy 'to come,'" a possibility to build toward. Mouffe, *The Return of the Political,* 8. See also Mouffe, *The Democratic Paradox.*

54. Cole and Foster, *From the Ground Up;* Ferris, "A Call for Justice"; Lavelle and Coyle, "Critical Mass Builds."

55. Setterberg and Shavelson, *Toxic Nation,* xiii.

56. For more information see *United Church News* (online edition), June 2002, " 'Toxic Tour' Marks 15th Anniversary," http://www.ucc.org/ucnews/jun02/toxic.htm.

57. "Interview: Barry Hill and Vernice Miller-Travis discuss problems of environmental racism and EPA policy [Tavis Smiley, 9–10 A.M. ed.]," *National Public Radio,* April 22, 2004.

58. The civil rights backlash was immediate and continues into the present day. For accessible accounts of civil rights backlash see J. Williams, *Eyes on the Prize;* and Chideya, *Don't Believe the Hype.* For accessible accounts of the environmental backlash and the environmental degradation enabled by George W. Bush's first term as president see Helvarg, *The War against the Greens;* and Kennedy, *Crimes against Nature.*

59. The program I participated in was through the School for International Training (SIT) in the fall of 1994. The assignment was a month-long research project culminating in a final paper and presentation titled "Ecotourism: A Case Study of Amboseli National Park."

60. My own observations are verified in a published study of tourist perceptions using surveys. It noted "over 40 per cent of the respondents visited a Maasai village during their stay in or near the reserve. . . . Overall, visitors (84 per cent) felt this type of recreation/cultural opportunity should be made available to all reserve tourists." Henry, "Carrying Capacity," 51.

61. Of all the ethnic groups in Kenya and Tanzania, Maasai are those most commonly represented on postcards, usually with red henna in their hair and beaded necklaces around their bare chests. On the coast at the time, it was common for European female tourists to hire men who dressed in this attire as prostitutes. For what it's worth, one Maasai man (who always wore T-shirts and jeans) told me that these images and prostitutes often were not ethnically Maasai; they just posed as such. For more on the complicated cultural politics of Maasai and tourism, see Bruner, *Culture on Tour;* Robert A. Pool, "Heartbreak on the Serengeti," *National Geographic,* February 2006, http://www7.nationalgeographic.com/ngm/0602/feature1/index.html.

62. R. Williams, "Base and Superstructure" and *Marxism and Literature.*

63. For more on the usefulness of participant observation research in studying publics, see Pezzullo, "Resisting 'National Breast Cancer Awareness Month.' "

64. "Ethnography is by no means the sole method of pursuing this goal; but . . . if one recognizes that the crucial insights for the pursuit of alternatives will be found . . . in a new reading of popular practices and of the reappropriation by popular actors of the space of hegemonic sociocultural production, then one must concede that the task of conceptualizing alternatives must include a significant contact with those whose 'alternatives' research is supposed to illuminate." Escobar, *Encountering Development,* 223.

65. Judith Brady, phone interview with author, October 12, 2001.

66. The goal of a "multi-sited ethnography" is "to examine the circulation of cultural meanings, objects, and identities in diffuse time-space. This mode defines for itself an object of study that cannot be accounted for ethnographically by remaining focused on a single site of intensive investigation. It develops instead a strategy or design of research that acknowledges macrotheoretical concepts and narratives of the world system but does not rely on them for the contextual architecture framing a set of subjects." Marcus, *Ethnography through Thick and Thin,* 79—80. On the similarities of ethnographers and tourists, much has been written; see, for example, Edensor, "Staging Tourism" and *Tourists at the Taj;* and MacCannell, *Empty Meeting Grounds.*

67. Whiteness is a social construction that often consolidates power for those who are assumed "white" and obscures more complex ethnic histories (e.g., my ancestors were at least Italian, German, Native American, French, Swiss, Welsh, and Irish). A large body of literature on the invention of "whiteness" and "white privilege" exists, including T. W. Allen, *Invention of the White Race;* Frankenberg, *Social Construction of Whiteness;* Ignatiev, *How the Irish Became White;* Roediger, *The Wages of Whiteness;* and Segrest, *Memoir of a Race Traitor.*

68. This quote is excerpted from a series of sixty-second public service announcements (PSAs) entitled *Ordinary People Doing Extraordinary Things.* They were produced by Greenpeace U.S.A. and aired by the VH-1 cable music channel throughout Earth Day 1990.

69. Conquergood, "Performing as a Moral Act," 5, 9—11.

70. Madison, "Ch. 8," 149. On the ubiquity of performance in the contemporary academy and what it may offer critical ethnography, see Madison and Hamera, *Sage Handbook;* and Madison, *Critical Ethnography.*

71. Clifford, "Traveling Cultures," 105.

72. Voice—who, how, and why one is speaking—has been critical to environmental justice struggles. In representing the environmental justice movement, therefore, it is important to cite the voices of those involved in the movement, particularly the voices of people of color and of working-class status. I have attempted to honor this ethical rhetorical position throughout this text by not claiming to speak for people in toxically

assaulted communities. As Linda Alcoff reminds us, however, "speaking for others"—even when we do cite their own words—is a complicated act. She leaves us with the following question to assess the political implications of representation: "Will it enable the empowerment of oppressed peoples?" Alcoff, "The Problem of Speaking for Others," 29. Likewise, in a sense, what I am asking is, Are toxic tours enabling the empowerment of oppressed peoples? If so, how? I want to reemphasize, however, that this study is only partly about the environmental justice movement. It also is a critical analysis of a communication practice, namely, tourism, and of the cultural politics of "toxicity" more broadly.

73. S. Hall, "Notes on Deconstructing 'the Popular,'" 453.

74. "Cultural performances," as characterized by Kirk Fuoss, are temporally framed, spatially framed, programmed (i.e., they follow an order of activities), communal, "heightened occasions" involving "display," both reflexive and reflective, and scheduled, publicized events. Fuoss, *Striking Performances / Performing Strikes,* 173–74. See also R. Bauman, "Performance." Cultural performances are relevant to this study insofar as it is through them that "many people both construct and participate in 'public' life. Particularly for poor and marginalized people denied access to middle-class 'public' forums, cultural performance becomes the venue for 'public discussion' of vital issues central to their communities, as well as an arena for gaining visibility and staging identity." Conquergood, "Rethinking Ethnography," 189.

Chapter 1

1. *Vacation,* dir. Harold Ramis (Warner Brothers, 1983); *European Vacation,* dir. Amy Heckerling (Warner Brothers, 1985); *Vegas Vacation,* dir. Stephen Kessler (Jerry Weintraub Productions and Warner Brothers, 1987); *Christmas Vacation,* dir. Jeremiah S. Chechik (Hughes Entertainment and Warner Brothers, 1989); *Crocodile Dundee,* dir. Peter Faiman (Paramount Pictures, 1986); *Crocodile Dundee II,* dir. John Cornell (Paramount Pictures, 1988); *Crocodile Dundee in Los Angeles,* dir. Simon Wincer (Vision View Entertainment and Paramount Pictures), 2001.

2. Bourdieu, *Distinction.*

3. Bond is a character created by novelist Ian Flemings and brought to international fame through cinema by producers Albert R. Broccoli and Harry Saltzman in 1962; today he is nothing short of an international cultural icon. Though he doesn't necessarily "blend in" like an undercover spy, he is portrayed as the universal epitome of desire for (read: heterosexual) women of any nation and able to stop international threats in a variety of contexts that call for a wide range of skills. Bristow is the female protagonist in a currently popular U.S. television series, *Alias.* In comparison to Bond, though she too is

portrayed as deadly and sexy, Bristow also is renowned for multiple disguises and fluency in more than a dozen languages.

4. Tyler, *The Accidental Tourist* (New York: Ballantine Books, 1985 / 2002); *The Accidental Tourist*, dir. Lawrence Kasdan (Warner Brothers, 1988).

5. Tyler, *The Accidental Tourist*, 31, 334, 12.

6. "All tourism includes some travel but not all travel is tourism" (59). C. M. Hall and Page, *Geography of Tourism and Recreation*, 59. *Traveling* is a much broader term that might include immigration, business travel (from driving to work in the morning to flying across the country for a meeting), and everyday practices such as walking to the grocery store or taking a bus to the mall.

7. Judith Brady, interview with author, October 3, 2001.

8. Mulvey, "Visual Pleasure and Narrative Cinema."

9. Adams, *The Sexual Politics of Meat* and *The Pornography of Meat;* Baker, *Picturing the Beast.*

10. Urry, *The Tourist Gaze.*

11. Crawshaw and Urry, "Tourism and the Photographic Eye," 177–78, 179.

12. I am not alone in doing so; most notable to me are those who provide such criticisms informed by a performance studies perspective. Edensor, *Tourists at the Taj;* Desmond, *Staging Tourism;* Crang, "Performing the Tourist Product"; and Kirshenblatt-Gimblett, *Destination Culture.* In addition to performance scholars, see Johnston, "(Other) Bodies and Tourism Studies"; and Crouch and Desforges, "The Sensuous in the Tourist Encounter." On this subject, see also MacCannell's argument that while Urry has named one important logic of "the gaze," there are other "gazes" to explore, such as Lacan's "second gaze." MacCannell, "Tourist Agency." Exceeding tourist literature, it has been "demonstrated that, beginning with the ancient Greeks, our Western culture has been dominated by an ocularcentric paradigm, a vision-generated, vision-centered interpretation of knowledge, truth, and reality." Levin, *Modernity and the Hegemony of Vision,* 2.

13. Ocularcentric accounts of tourism obviously also ignore the experiences of blind tourists. Susan Wendell astutely cautions us against accusations of ocularcentrism based on discourses of ableism, because she believes they do a disservice to, for example, deaf people, who do depend more on sight than on hearing. A discussion of more than the visual, however, would seem to benefit people who do rely heavily on sight, insofar as most also use embodied senses that exceed their vision, including touch, taste, etc. Wendell, *Rejected Body.*

14. Conquergood, "Rethinking Ethnography," 30.

15. Behar, *Vulnerable Observer.*

16. Adam Werbach, interview with author, February 19, 2002. For more see chapter 5.

17. Similarly, another toxic tour organizer states: "It's our responsibility as tour organizers not just to feed the interest in 'what's the ugly side of a corporation' but to show

the solution side. The 'toxic tour' label is a problem because of the risk of sensationalism. One of the problems of doing a political tour like this is that you can sell difference and you can sell inequity and that's gross, you know, 'come see the poor people, come see the toxic sludge.' But that just reinforces the idea that 'I am privileged and I don't have to live like that'; it doesn't have a useful political message." Di Chiro, "Bearing Witness," 286–87.

18. Mullan and Marvin, *Zoo Culture*, 88.

19. Desmond, *Staging Tourism*, xix.

20. Beardsworth and Bryman, "The Wild Animal in Late Modernity."

21. Echtner and Prasad, "Context of Third World Tourism Marketing," 679.

22. Desmond, *Staging Tourism*, 5, 11.

23. Z. Bauman, "From Pilgrim to Tourist," 29–30.

24. "Tourism," Caren Kaplan insists, "must not be separated from its colonial legacy, just as any mode of displacement should not be dehistoricized or romanticized" (*Questions of Travel*, 63); thus, she traces the distinctions between a range of traveling practices, including the exile, the tourist, the nomad, and the theorist. Yet, Franklin and Crang challenge the assumption that leaving and returning to a static home is the modus operandi of a tourist, noting, for example, that some refugees feel like tourists on part of their journey. Franklin and Crang, "Trouble with Tourism."

25. Bruner, *Culture on Tour*, 17.

26. Lippard, *Lure of the Local*.

27. Given global flows of migrancy, Chambers argues that "home" might be "a mobile habitat" where "neither the points of departure nor those of arrival are immutable or certain." Similarly, Wise states that home "is not the place 'we come from'; it is a place we are." Likewise, Anzaldúa describes her own sense of home as akin to a turtle, traveling with her wherever she goes on her back. Chambers, *Migrancy, Culture, Identity*, 5; Wise, "Home," 108; Anzaldúa, *Borderlands / La Frontera*, 43.

28. Enloe elaborates on how, in many cultures, "being feminine has been defined as sticking close to home. Masculinity, by contrast, has been the passport for travel." *Bananas, Beaches, and Bases*, 21. See also Lippard, *Lure of the Local*.

29. MacCannell, *The Tourist*, 11.

30. Enloe, *Bananas, Beaches, and Bases*, 19.

31. Kincaid, *A Small Place*, 14, 19–20, 15.

32. Again, tourist literature here is assuming the context of commercial tourism, not advocacy tourism. For now it is perhaps worth noting that I do not mean to reference Kincaid's assessment as a means of saying that this is indeed the relationship between *every* tourist and *every* native (nor do I necessarily believe that is her intention); rather, I believe this caricature is drawn to illustrate a larger political and ethical picture of the privileges of the tourist.

33. By using the phrase "everyday life" I mean to invoke two of the most common academic referents for the term: Michel de Certeau's understanding of "'ways of operating' or doing things" (*Practice*, xi) and Henri Lefebvre's theory of "what is humble and solid, what is taken for granted and that of which all the parts follow each other in such a regular, unvarying succession that those concerned have no call to question their sequence." As one form of leisure, Lefebvre argues, tourism is "a temporary break with everyday life," motivated by "the prospect of departure, the demand for evasion, [and] the will to escape." Lefebvre, *Everyday Life*, 24, 54, 85. Ben Highmore notes that the ongoing popularity of this concept arises from its power "to make the invisible visible," especially "the lives of those who have been sidelined by dominant accounts of social life." Highmore, *Everyday Life Reader*, 1–2.

34. MacCannell asserts that while he believes some tourists find their everyday lives uninteresting, he hopes the majority of tourists are not leaving home because they live banal or awful lives. *The Tourist*, 25. This observation does not necessarily negate Kincaid's standpoint regarding visiting someone else's everyday life; further, I believe both authors would agree that the privileges of all tourists (e.g., First-World tourists visiting Third-world tourists) are not equal in terms of frequency, accessibility, and luxury.

35. Rothman, *The Devil's Bargain;* Kirshenblatt-Gimblett and Bruner, "Tourism"; A. P. Russo, "Vicious Circle."

36. These concerns are well documented. For a popular article that describes these historical transformations and current attempts to curb these negative effects, see William Least Heat-Moon, "Beyond the Valley of Wonders," *National Geographic,* January 2005, 98–117.

37. Desmond, *Staging Tourism,* 15, 29.

38. Bruner, *Culture on Tour,* 194. In sharing an experience from his ethnographic research of tourists on a ride to the Ngorogoro Crater in Tanzania, Bruner also notes that tourist industry attempts to isolate and silence do not always succeed (98).

39. Jordan, "Report from the Bahamas," 312.

40. Solnit, *Wanderlust,* 15. Solnit also points out the public memorialization of famous philosophers' walks in central Europe: "the celebrated Philosophenweg in Heidelberg where Hegel is said to have walked, the Philosophen-damm in Konigsberg that Kant passed on his daily stroll (now replaced by a railway station), and the Philosopher's Way Kierkegaard mentions in Copenhagen" (16).

41. Tourism as a leisurely practice was recorded as early as the wealthy citizens of ancient Greece and the Roman Empire who traveled to thermal baths and other places of enjoyment; allegedly, the first tour book found was published in 1130 by a French monk and concerned traveling to Spain for religious purposes. Honey, *Ecotourism,* 7.

42. Foley and Lennon, *Dark Tourism,* 7.

43. Graburn, "Tourism," 29.

44. Although he reached a smaller number of clients, Thomas Cook created tourist opportunities and advertising for women as early as 1901. Enloe, *Bananas, Beaches, and Bases,* 28–31.

45. Franklin, *Tourism,* 36.

46. Clark, *Rhetorical Landscapes,* 26, 25.

47. Likewise, Roderick Nash's history of the concept of "wilderness" provides evidence of how the creation of such places was predicated, at least in part, on arguments of national pride. Nash, *Wilderness and the American Mind.* See also Pretes, "Tourism and Nationalism."

48. Neumann, *On the Rim,* 8.

49. Enloe, *Bananas, Beaches, and Bases,* 28.

50. Without guides, tours often still involve an interpretive framing of the journey, such as through travel guides, markers at the site, other tourists, the structure of the site itself, etc.

51. MacCannell, *The Tourist,* 203.

52. De Certeau, *Practice,* 123.

53. Bowman, "Performing Southern History."

54. MacCannell, *The Tourist,* 14.

55. Ibid., 192; see also Bowman, "Performing Southern History."

56. Edensor, *Tourists at the Taj,* 70, emphasis added.

57. On dominant, resistant, or negotiated dispositifs, see S. Hall, "Encoding/Decoding."

58. Although Edensor (*Tourists at the Taj*) cautions that tactics are not necessarily a heroic or unconstrained activity, de Certeau's understanding of tactics remains useful for imagining the relevance of spatial and temporal dimensions to resistance.

59. Di Chiro, "Bearing Witness," 297; Di Chiro, "Beyond Ecoliberal 'Common Futures,'" 229.

60. William F. Schultz, "Conscientious Projectors: Tourists with an Eye on Human Rights Can Make a Difference," *Nation,* October 6, 1997, 31.

61. Grossberg, *We Gotta Get Out;* Reagan, "Coalition Politics."

62. Shohat and Stam, "From the Imperial Family," 166.

63. Di Chiro, "Bearing Witness," 275.

64. Lippard, *On the Beaten Track,* 2, 118.

65. Foley and Lennon, *Dark Tourism,* 3, 12.

66. Their work and label of "dark tourism" has already begun to be mobilized in subsequent studies. Strange and Kempa, "Shades of Dark Tourism."

67. MacCannell, *The Tourist,* 40, emphasis added.

68. Linenthal, *Preserving Memory.*

69. Blair, "Challenges and Openings."

70. Qtd. in Honey, *Ecotourism,* 26 n. 5.

71. MacCannell, *The Tourist,* 40–41.

72. The tour as political statement is provocatively embodied in the film *Margaret's Museum,* which centers on Margaret, who loses her grandfather, brother, and husband to the occupational hazards of working in coal mines. Her tourist museum, which frames the beginning and end of the narrative, denaturalizes what Marx calls the "hidden abode" of production by displaying body parts of her deceased loved ones pickled in jars with a sign outside that reads: "The Price of Coal." Though dramatized to a grotesque, abject extreme, it is the cultural and political potential of this type of appropriation of tourism as a mode of communication that seems under-recognized. I am grateful to Della Pollock for introducing me to this film.

73. Pezzullo, "Mapping," 7.

74. Qtd. in Olwig, "Reinventing Common Nature," 393.

75. Davis, *Spectacular Nature,* 231.

76. Worth noting is the importance of technology's role in enabling environmental tourism, particularly transportation. In addition to the creation of camping equipment that was easier to carry and to use for hikers walking in less-developed areas (involving titanium and other durable, light innovations), the invention of the automobile helped foster more accessible and convenient travel for a larger number of people. Further, airplanes caused nothing short of a revolution for the tourist industry more broadly, including environmental tourism. In other words, as traveling to more remote places has become easier, people have gravitated to them. Honey, *Ecotourism;* Nash, *Wilderness and the American Mind.*

77. Honey, *Ecotourism,* 25. See also Kouis, "Tourism and the Environment"; Bauer, "Tourism and the Environment"; Markwell, " 'An Intimate Rendezvous with Nature?' "; McGehee, "Alternative Tourism and Social Movements"; Khan, "ECOSERV"; Holden, "In Need of New Environmental Ethics"; Kim and Kim, "Implications of Potential Green Tourism Development"; and Waitt, Lane, and Head, "Boundaries of Nature Tourism."

78. Di Chiro, "Bearing Witness"; see also Di Chiro, "Beyond Ecoliberal 'Common Futures,' " 229.

79. Di Chiro, "Beyond Ecoliberal 'Common Futures,' " 223.

80. Qtd. in R. McManus, "Happy Trails: Celebrating a Century of Adventure," *Sierra,* May/June 2001, 40. See also Olwig, "Reinventing Common Nature"; and Nuttal, "Packaging the Wild."

81. For examples of environmental education centers see Franklin, *Tourism,* 2003. Carol Adkins and Bora Simmons argue that the difference between the overlapping missions of outdoor, experiential, and environmental education may be "its focus on developing the core concepts and skills that environmentally literate citizens need for responsible action." Adkins and Simmons, "Outdoor, Experiential, and Environmental Education: Converging or Diverging Approaches?" (ERIC Clearinghouse on Rural Education and Small Schools, EDO-RC-02-1, 2002, August).

82. *New York Times,* August 17, 1969, 61; *New York Times,* November 8, 1969, 18; *New York Times,* December 3, 1969, 56.

83. T. Spears, "Tours to Focus on Pollution in the City," *Toronto Star,* May 3, 1989, B7.

84. There are too many toxic tours on the internet to cite here; they can be found easily by using the key words "toxic tour" on any search engine. At the time of this writing, sponsors of a few of the more prevalent sites are Texas Public Employees for Environmental Responsibility, Citizens for a Better Environment, Greenpeace, and Cornell University.

85. Depoe and Delicath, introduction, 2–3.

86. Laclau and Mouffe, *Hegemony and Socialist Strategy* (1st ed.), 153, 176.

Chapter 2

1. Britney Spears, *Toxic,* by Cathy Dennis (Jive, November 18, 2003).

2. For government TRI reports, see http://www.epa.gov/triexplorer/. For information on the limitations and possibilities of this data as it currently is defined, collected, and distributed, see http://www.scorecard.org/general/tri/tri_gen.html. The production of toxic chemicals is supported by a variety of industries from extracting metals to manufacturing, or "refining," chemicals. According to 2002 TRI data, the top producers were all mining industries: Red Dog Operations—Mine Facility (Arkansas); Newmont Mining Corporation (Nevada); BHP Copper N.A. San Manuel Operations (Arizona); Kennecott Utah Copper Mine Concentrators and Power Plant (Utah); and Barrick Goldstrike Mine (Nevada). In addition, the usual corporate suspects made it to the top 100, such as: BASF (Texas); BP Chemicals, Inc. (Ohio); DuPont (Texas, Mississippi); Monsanto (Louisiana); and Chemical Waste Management (Oregon, Alabama, California). Environmental Defense Fund (EDF), "Facilities Releasing TRI Chemicals to the Environment," 2004, http://www.scorecard.org.

3. Freeze, *Environmental Pendulum,* 8.

4. Bishop, *Pollution Prevention,* 7.

5. Freeze, *Environmental Pendulum,* 8.

6. By "chemical industry" I refer to manufacturers that produce chemicals as either products or by-products. The American Chemical Society is quicker to distance itself from this broader label, accurately pointing out that other industries, such as mining and electric power, are larger producers of toxic chemicals than what they refer to more narrowly as "the chemical industry"—though they admit to massive amounts of nitrate compounds, ammonia, dioxin, and lead. "Government Concentrates," *Chemical and Engineering News,* July 7, 2003, 13.

7. "In 1996, sales of the U.S. chemical industry amounted to $372 billion, while those of all western Europe taken together amounted to $495 billion and of the Japanese chemical industry, $216 billion. On a value-added basis, the chemical industry accounts

for about 11.3 percent of U.S. manufacturing and produces about 1.9 percent of U.S. gross domestic product. The preeminence of the U.S. chemical industry is not reflected in size alone. The chemical industry is one of the largest in term of R&D [research and development], spending an estimated $18.3 billion in 1996. . . . The commercial success of the chemical industry in the United States is a story of a constellation of factors." Arora, Landon, and Rosenberg, *Chemicals and Long-Term Economic Growth,* 71.

8. "BASF Appoints Director of Media Relations for North American Operation," *Washington Post,* December 19, 2001, http://financial.washingtonpost.com/.

9. "DuPont Taiwan Celebrates Company's 200th Anniversary with Photo Exhibit," *DuPontWebsite,* January 8, 2002, http://www.dupont.com/news/daily/2002/dn01_08_02b_pf.html.

10. Setterberg and Shavelson, *Toxic Nation,* 4.

11. Bryant, *Environmental Justice,* 46, 47.

12. Freeze, *Environmental Pendulum,* 8.

13. Reich, *Toxic Politics,* 142–47.

14. Government Accounting Office, May 2, 2000, Letter Report, GAO/HEHS—00-80.

15. Although the details vary, the lack of knowledge about the health effects of what are classified as "toxic chemicals" persists. Cheryl Hogue, "Genes, Computers, & Chemicals," *Chemical and Engineering News,* October 13, 2003, 50–53.

16. Government Accounting Office, June 2005, "CHEMICAL REGULATION: Options Exist to Improve EPA's Ability to Assess Health Risks and Manage Its Chemical Review Program," *Report to Congressional Requesters,* GAO-05-458, http://www.gao.gov/index.html.

17. With physical illnesses related to contagion and contamination (such as sicknesses associated with toxins, sexuality, etc.), there has often arisen a historical pattern of labeling and stigmatization of people marked as "polluted." Reich, *Toxic Politics;* Douglas, *Purity and Danger.* Moreover, as a result of their study of the people living in the Mohawk territory of Akwesasne, Alice Tarbell and Mary Arquette argue that the dangers of pollution "include effects on economic, social, psychological, cultural, spiritual, and community health." Tarbell and Arquette, "Akwesasne," 102.

18. Grossman, "People of Color Environmental Summit"; Di Chiro, "Defining Environmental Justice"; Brown and Mikkelsen, *No Safe Place;* Novotny, "Popular Epidemiology"; and O'Brien, "When Harm Is Not Necessary."

19. Andrews, *Managing the Environment,* 242, emphasis added. This connection persists. For example, see the first "commonly asked question" addressed in a basic handbook on toxins: "Is there a cancer epidemic?" Harte, Holdren, Schneider, and Shirley, *Toxics A to Z,* ix. In 2000 alone, U.S. industries emitted 100 million pounds of carcinogens. Niaz Dorry and Nityanand Jayaraman, "Chemical Industry versus Public Interest: Redefining the Public Debate on Chemical Security," No More Bhopals Alliance (June 2004),

9, http://www.greenpeaceusa.org/multimedia/download/1/543878/0/ACCCoalRep. For more on cancer see chapter 4.

20. The authors emphasize that the media attention to this troubling finding about one of the nation's favorite obsessions should not obscure our attention from the broader amount of evidence in the book about humans and wildlife, including "the larger concern about diverse hazards stemming from altered hormone levels during early development." Colborn, Dumanoski, and Myers, *Our Stolen Future,* 175, 253.

21. Marilyn Berlin Snell, "Theo Colborn: A Controversial Scientist Speaks on Plastics, IQ, and the Womb," *Mother Jones,* March/April 1998, 30–31.

22. Phillip Landrigan and Lynn Goldman, "Another View of Children's Health," *Chemical and Engineering News,* July 21, 2003, 3.

23. For more about the effects of toxic pollution on children, see Brown and Mikkelsen, *No Safe Place;* Colborn, Dumanoski, and Myers, *Our Stolen Future;* and Wargo, *Our Children's Toxic Legacy.*

24. Setterberg and Shavelson note that toxins played a role in a wide range of popular media, including television shows (*thirtysomething*), films (*Fletch Lives,* the *Toxic Avenger* movies, and *Tootsie*), novels (*White Noise, Strong Motion, Always Coming Home,* and *Floating Dragon*), theater (*The Speed of Darkness*), and newspapers (as commonplace metaphors for everything from bad parenting to police informants). *Toxic Nation,* 111–13. This list, of course, is partial and has only grown since the early 1990s.

25. In general, this book follows the lead of the EPA and community activists in categorizing nuclear waste, though toxic, separately from the general category of "toxic chemicals." At times, however, these histories collide politically and culturally.

26. Sanderson, *X-Men Updated Ed.,* 9.

27. De Falco, *The Hulk,* 21.

28. Cole and Foster (*From the Ground Up*) note that the environmental justice movement itself has expressed concerns about turning to legal redress when it is done at the expense of grassroots mobilization. For more on the cultural politics of these two films, see Pezzullo, "Articulating Anti-Toxic Activism to 'Sexy' Superstars."

29. Perhaps this is an exaggeration. One of the risks of writing on contemporary political issues is that the cultural landscape is constantly changing. U.S. President George W. Bush and Vice President Dick Cheney have received much criticism for their environmental policies, and it is unclear at the time of this writing that they have minded their anti-environmental, pro–toxic chemical industry image.

30. Field, "Risk and Justice," 81.

31. In his writings about everyday life, Lefebvre argues that women's magazines are the exemplars of blurring boundaries between the banal and the fantastical: "The best examples of social make-believe are to be found in . . . women's magazines, where experience and make-believe merge in a manner conducive to the reader's utter bewilderment. Indeed, a single issue may include practical instructions on the way to cut out and

sew up a dress . . . alongside a form of rhetoric that invests clothes and other objects with an aura of unreality: all possible and impossible dresses, every kind of dish . . . " Lefebvre, *Everyday Life,* 85–86.

32. Soon after, in 1972, the First United Nations Conference on Human Environment was held in Stockholm, creating the United Nations Environment Program. During this time, new U.S.-based environmental organizations were formed, including the Natural Resources Defense Council (1970), Friends of the Earth (1970), the Public Interest Research Group (1970), and Greenpeace (1971). In addition, more environmental legislation was passed, such as the Occupational Safety and Health Act (1970), the Endangered Species Act (1973), the Resource Conservation and Recovery Act (1976), and the Toxic Substances Control Act (1976).

33. Margaret Mead, "Women and Our Plundered Planet," *Redbook,* April 1970, 64, 60, 57.

34. See, for example, Marjie Driscoll, "Kids Meet the Wilderness," *McCall's,* October 1972; Rajalakshmi Jagadeesan, "T.L.C. for Earth," *Ms.,* September/October 1991; Elizabeth Larsen, "Granola Boys, Eco-Dudes, and Me," *Ms.,* July/August 1991; Ralph Nader, "America's Unsung Heroines," *Ladies' Home Journal,* July 1976; Beverly Paigen, "1991 'As They Grow' Awards," *Parents,* March 1991; "Take Our Environmental Quiz: Children (And Parents Too!)—Put Your Eco-Savvy to the Test!" *Good Housekeeping,* September 1993.

35. See, for example, Andrea Rock, "Toxicville," *Ladies' Home Journal,* September 1999; "Our Toxic Waste Time Bomb," *Reader's Digest,* March 1986; Michael Tennessen, "Into the Toxic Cloud," *Reader's Digest,* July 2000; "Thousands Die in West African Toxic Disaster," *Jet,* September 8, 1986.

36. "This Is What You Thought: 88% Fear a Chemical Disaster," *Glamour,* July 1985, 23.

37. Dunlap and Mertig, *American Environmentalism;* Joe Miller, "Earth Day at 30: Greener, Cleaner and Growing," *Raleigh (N.C.) News and Observer,* April 21, 2000; Jonathan Rauch, "There's Smog in the Air, But It Isn't All Pollution," *Washington Post,* April 30, 2000, B01.

38. Glen Martin, "Earth Day Report Card—We Still Care, Sort of," *San Francisco Chronicle,* April 22, 2000, A1.

39. Earth Day is increasingly noted as a commercialized, spectacle endeavor. Goldman and Papson, *Sign Wars.* "The failure of Earth Day . . . [is] that ecology, like any 'politics,' has become a question of attitude and investment, as if investing in the 'correct' ideological beliefs, even demonstrating it, was an adequate construction of the political. Within the new conservative articulation of the frontier, political positions only exist as entirely affective investments, separated from any ability to act." Grossberg, *We Gotta Get Out,* 279. I note it here as a sign of the popularity of "environmentalism" as a discourse.

40. L. J. Shrum, John A. McCarty, and Tina M. Lowrey, special issue of *Journal of Ad-*

vertising 24, no. 2 (1995). Again, I note this phenomenon as an indication of the popularity of "environmentalism," not necessarily as a sign of good intentions. For the most part, I agree with Goldman and Papson regarding the motivation for "green" advertising: "Advertisers want to signify environmental concerns because they see dollar signs in environmentalism" (*SignWars,* 194).

41. As Goldman and Papson remind us, "The Discovery Channel, the Learning Channel, Turner Broadcasting Services, as well as the Public Broadcasting System, sustain a continuous flow of nature programs" (*SignWars,* 201).

42. Originated by Jake "the Snake" Roberts, the "DDT" wrestling move has now permeated WWE (formerly WWF) culture such that three wrestlers have been known for using a variation in this "finishing move": Gangrel for the "Big DDT," Cactus Jack for the "Double-Arm DDT," and Christian for the "Modified-Reverse DDT."

43. Darnovsky, "Green Living in a Toxic World," 219.

44. In the context of "safety discourses," the interpellation of women into this gendered attitude about risk management is well described in R. Hall, " 'It Can Happen to You.' "

45. "Beauty Detox," *Mademoiselle,* February 1992; Randy Blaun, "Saving Face," *Good Housekeeping,* June 1996; R. Caras, "Protecting Pets from Poisons," *Ladies' Home Journal,* October 1979; Karyn L. Feiden, "The Hidden Health Dangers That Lurk in Your Home," *McCall's,* April 1999; Roberta Israeloff, "The Poison-Control Crisis," *Parents,* September 1995; Gerald M. Knox, "Accidental Poisoning! What Should You Do?" *Better Homes and Gardens,* February 1976; Laura Flynn McCarthy, "The Light Factor," *Vogue,* January 1987; Katherine Pritchard, "What to Do If a Child Swallows Poison," *McCalls,* April 1977; Norman Rollins, "Lifesaving News about the Poisons in Your Home," *Good Housekeeping,* April 1977; S. M. S., "Indoor Air," *Vogue,* January 1987; Wendy Schmid, "Acid Reign," *Vogue,* March 1997; Gene Church Schulz, "How to Poison-Proof Your Home," *Parents Magazine,* May 1977, 42–43, 60.

46. Lois Marie Gibbs, "Do You Jog beside a Freeway? Staying Healthy in a Toxic World," *Ms.,* May 1984.

47. Davis, *Spectacular Nature,* 146–47.

48. Grossberg, *We Gotta Get Out,* 306.

49. Hofrichter, "Cultural Activism," 87.

50. The political ambiguity of what to do about toxins is reflected in this synopsis of toxic pollution policy: "If the 1970s was, in the environmental policy arena, the decade of pollution control, and the 1980s was the decade when pollution policies began to shift toward such approaches as waste minimization and marketing incentives, then the 1990s has clearly come to be defined as the decade of pollution prevention. But legislation and policy directives notwithstanding, policymakers are still asking just what pollution prevention means." Gottlieb, *Forcing the Spring,* 7. The 1990s, of course, did not resolve this

question; if anything, events since the turn of the century have reminded us that not everyone agrees that pollution prevention is our primary approach.

51. Douglas, *Purity and Danger,* 3.

52. C. Kaplan, *Questions of Travel,* 170.

53. This phrase is borrowed from Butler, *Bodies That Matter.*

54. Grosz, *Volatile Bodies,* 14.

55. For example, the connection of women with the grotesque has historically been linked to reproductive processes such as menstruation and birth. Douglas, *Purity and Danger;* M. Russo, *The Female Grotesque;* Shildrick, *Embodying the Monster.*

56. Over at least the last thirty years, scholars have increasingly attempted to unlearn these legacies of the body, particularly Plato's conception of the soul and the body and Descartes's writings on the mind and the body. Plato's writings divide humans into souls and bodies. Ultimately, Plato believed that human senses could not be trusted to discern the difference between bad and good. Plato, *Gorgias,* 102–3; see also Plato, *Phaedrus,* 28. Further, Plato claims the soul is imprisoned in the body. Thus, only in death will humans be free from the sinful lusts and earthly desires our bodies draw us toward. Plato, *Cratylus,* 54. Descartes's philosophy maintains a similar split, yet his writings focus on the mind more than the soul. Famous for the adage "I think, therefore, I am," Descartes most strikingly concludes that because his mind is separate from his body, he can exist without the latter. Descartes, *Discourse on Method.*

57. Crowley, "Afterwards," 358.

58. Similarly, many ecofeminists have emphasized that it is unhelpful to conceive of ecofeminism as a body of thought positing that women are essentially "closer" to nature. Connie Bullis, for example, argues that ecofeminism "functions as a material, historical grounding to encourage a better understanding of how current discourse evolved and how it oppresses"; thus "[t]he radical potential of ecofeminism lies in its ability to critique several narratives within . . . environmental discourses." Bullis, "Retalking Environmental Discourses," 125, 130.

59. Soap ads from the nineteenth century similarly perpetuated the association between blackness and uncleanliness. See S. Hall, *Representation,* 241.

60. "A pattern of labeling and stigmatization has been recorded for various 'strange' diseases: for mental illness, tuberculosis and cancer, venereal diseases, and handicapped persons in general. Recent fears about AIDS have similarly created patterns of stigmatization and discrimination, raising deep cultural fears about 'contagion, contamination, and sexuality' (Brandt)." Reich, *Toxic Politics,* 170.

61. Higgins, "Race," 252, 262. Similarly, women in U.S. history who have spoken out too much or too loudly have been referred to by patriarchy's supporters as "not knowing their place."

62. Douglas, *Purity and Danger,* 40.

63. Dyer, *White,* 39, 45.

64. Mills, "Black Trash," 84.

65. Stallybrass and White, *Politics and Poetics,* 125.

66. Bakhtin, *Rabelais and His World.*

67. Miller, *Anatomy of Disgust,* 18. I am grateful to D. Soyini Madison for giving this book to me.

68. Reich, *Toxic Politics,* 260. The same could be said of people with disabilities; see Wendell, *Rejected Body,* esp. chapter 3.

69. Sontag, *Illness as Metaphor,* 72.

70. Scarry, *Body in Pain,* 1, 22, 14, 9.

71. Ibid., 14, 6.

72. Ibid., 22.

73. Some argue that communication's inability to be transparent is indicative of the value of communication itself as a mode of translation. Striphas, "Communication as Translation."

74. Sontag, *Regarding the Pain of Others,* 112, 116–17.

75. Ibid., 125–26.

76. Scarry, *Body in Pain,* 4, emphasis added.

77. MacCannell, *The Tourist,* 192–93. John Frow cautions us against overly romanticizing gift economies, particularly when we do cross-cultural research involving a range of obligations and entitlements. I hope the arguments of this chapter and the preceding one have provided sufficient context for the specificities of toxic tours. Frow, *Time and Commodity Culture.*

Chapter 3

1. See the epilogue for updates on New Orleans.

2. Many have argued that the 1896 "separate but equal" ruling reinscribed racist sanctions. For a compelling analysis of this case see Robinson, "Forms of Appearance of Value."

3. Roach, *Cities of the Dead,* 182.

4. Wright, Bryant, and Bullard, "Coping with Poisons," 111, 114.

5. For further evidence of the initial reports regarding environmental racism, see Bullard, *Confronting Environmental Racism* and *Unequal Protection;* Bullard and Wright, "The Quest for Environmental Equity"; Grossman, "People of Color Environmental Summit"; Lavelle and Coyle, "Critical Mass Builds"; United Church of Christ Commission for Racial Justice, *Toxic Wastes and Race;* U.S. General Accounting Office, *Siting of Hazardous Waste Landfills.*

6. I consider toxic tours "cultural performances" because they generally function as what Turner describes as "active agencies of change, representing the eye by which cul-

ture sees itself and the drawing board on which creative actors sketch out what they believe to be more apt or interesting 'designs for living.'" Likewise, toxic tours rhetorically invent more livable designs for life. Turner, *Anthropology of Performance,* 24. This move reflects agreement with an increasing number of scholars who argue that tourism, defined more broadly, should be appreciated as a performance.

7. Schechner, *Performance Theory,* 120.

8. MacCannell, *The Tourist,* 44–45. *Sight* sacralization can be more fully appreciated in the less ocularcentric sense of *site* sacralization, a process involving an entire embodied way of life in a particular space and not just what the eyes can see. Out of respect for MacCannell's profound writings on tourism and to avoid confusion, however, I retain the original wording of this phrase.

9. In "Tour Guide Performances as Sight Sacralization," Elizabeth C. Fine and Jean Haskell Speer further emphasize the importance of tour guides' verbal performances to this transformative process. Although tour guides may have written themselves scripts, I agree that such self-conscious or "staged" performances are constitutive rather than "fake," potentially generative rather than simply reflective. Reflecting on Richard Schechner's company, The Performance Group, Turner writes: "Schechner aims at *poiesis,* rather than *mimesis:* making, not faking." Turner, *Anthropology of Performance,* 93. For more on the importance of this perspective to performance studies see Conquergood, "Ethnography, Rhetoric, and Performance," 84.

10. Goldman Prize, 1999, "Margie Eugene-Richard," http://www.goldmanprize.org/recipients/recipientProfile.cfm?recipientID=131.

11. For more on Eugene-Richards's story and the stories of the region, see B. L. Allen, *Uneasy Alchemy;* S. Lerner, *Diamond;* and Roberts and Toffolon-Weiss, *Chronicles.*

12. The Group of Ten includes the Sierra Club, the Sierra Club Legal Defense Fund, Friends of the Earth, the Wilderness Society, the National Audubon Society, the National Resources Defense Council, the Environmental Defense Fund, the National Wildlife Federation, the Izaak Walton League, and the National Parks and Conservation Association. For a period of time during the Reagan administration, these major national environmental organizations met weekly to coordinate their efforts against the ongoing environmental backlash.

13. Gulf Coast Tenant Leadership Development Project, letter to Jay D. Hair, January 16, 1990, 1 (copy in author's possession). For an interesting roundtable discussion including environmental justice and environmental activists subsequent to these letters, see "A Place at the Table," *Sierra,* May/June 1993.

14. Philip Shabecoff, "Environmental Groups Told They Are Racist in Hiring," *New York Times,* February 1, 1990, 20A.

15. See, for examples, Bullard, *Confronting Environmental Racism* and *Unequal Protection;* Gottlieb, *Forcing the Spring;* Schwab, *Deeper Shades of Green;* Dowie, *Losing Ground;* Hurley,

Environmental Inequalities; Di Chiro, "Nature as Community"; Chicago Surrealist Group, "Three Days."

16. *Proceedings,* 84. This "one Sierra Club member" is most likely Bryant's friend and fellow activist Darryl Malek-Wiley. Malek-Wiley is a European American Sierra Club member who was one of the original signers of the first letter to the Group of Ten; he is the primary toxic tour guide this chapter focuses on.

17. Ibid., 99, 101.

18. Ibid., 99, 100.

19. Ibid., 105, 106.

20. For more on the environmental justice movement's criticisms and the environmental movement's response to them since, see Sandler and Pezzullo, *Environmental Justice and Environmentalism.*

21. T. Noah, "Sierra Club Takes an Edifying Tour of Black America: Its Hired Guide John McCown Shows Environmentalists a Polluted Rural-Landfill," *Wall Street Journal,* June 24, 1993, A1, A5.

22. This article is cited as evidence of the environmental movement's shortcomings in its ability to engage social justice. Dowie, *Losing Ground,* 168–70.

23. Keys interview. For a powerful video on her community, including a toxic tour provided for a journalist, see the film *Environmental Justice.*

24. Qtd. in Dowie, *Losing Ground,* 170. John McCown attended the tour described in this chapter. In the fall of 2004 he resigned from the Sierra Club for personal reasons.

25. These principles are published in Sandler and Pezzullo, *Environmental Justice and Environmentalism.*

26. Those attending primarily represented the initial six Sierra Club Environmental Justice Grassroots Organizing Program sites: Memphis; Washington, D.C.; Los Angeles; Detroit; Arizona/New Mexico; and central Appalachia.

27. Jenny Coyle, "Growing Justice," *Planet: The Sierra Club Activist Resource,* July/August 2001, 4.

28. Perhaps the most popular referent in recent history is Spike Lee's film about the Million Man March, *Get on the Bus,* in which the bus line was named "The Spotted Owl." The film repeatedly cuts to the side of the bus, panning its logo as an apparent means of articulating the "endangered" state of black men with the high-profile Pacific Northwest environmental controversy. Interestingly, Benjamin Mohammed (formerly Reverend Benjamin Chavis Jr.) has served both as a pivotal leader of the environmental justice movement and as a leader in the Nation of Islam; he was Louis Farrakhan's second in command at the Million Man March.

29. Kelley, *Race Rebels,* 57, emphasis added.

30. "The discourse between the tour guide and tourists varies among expressive, referential, conative, poetic, metalingual, and phatic functions." Fine and Speer, "Tour Guide

Performances," 77. Erik Cohen suggests that the tour guide's role has four principal components: (1) instrumental (e.g., providing direction, access, and control); (2) social (e.g., offering tension-management, integration, morale, and animation); (3) interactionary (e.g., as a "middle man" who both integrates and insulates the tour group and a logistical coordinator); and (4) communicative (e.g., selecting "points of interest," sharing information, interpreting, and "fabricating"). Cohen, "Tourist Guide."

31. Sayre, "Pursuing Authenticity," 125.

32. Since this tour, Malek-Wiley was hired by the Sierra Club—on the recommendation of a committee constituted by both local environmental justice activists and Sierra Club volunteers and staff—as an environmental justice organizer in the region. For more information about his work or contact information, see Sierra Club, *Environmental Justice,* http://www.sierraclub.org/environmental_justice/.

33. Norco is an acronym for the New Orleans Refinery Company, which purchased a plant in 1916 in a place named Sellers at the time. In 1925, Norco was established.

34. Smith was the founder of Black Voices for Peace and the National Black Environmental Justice Network. He died of cancer on April 28, 2006. These fliers announce "Suffer the Little Children: The Celebrity Tour to 'Cancer Alley,' Louisiana," to be held on June 9, 2001. The list of attendees includes famous figures such as writer Alice Walker, actor Mike Farrell, attorney Johnnie Cochran, and Congresswoman Maxine Waters. For more information on this toxic tour, including individual stops and testimony from celebrities after the tour, see newspaper coverage, in addition to an informative online version of this tour at Greenpeace's website. Lance A. Foster, "Greenpeace and Cancer Alley [editorial]," *The Advocate,* June 22, 2001, News, 6-B, S; Chris Frink, "Residents Wary of Greenpeace Visit," *The Advocate,* June 8, 2001, News, 1-B; Emily Kern, "Pollution Spotlight: Greenpeace Brings Tour of 'Cancer Alley' to BR, Plaquemine," *The Advocate,* June 10, 2001, Metro Edition, 1-B; Mary Swerczek, "Greenpeace Visits Chemical Corridor; Celebrity Activists See Plants, Neighbors," *New Orleans Times-Picayune,* June 10, 2001, 1; Greenpeace, "Celebrities to Tour 'Cancer Alley,' Louisiana," http://greenpeaceusa.org/toxics/canceralleytour/celebritytourtext.htm.

35. This language borrows from Thomas B. Farrell's assertion that "rhetoric, despite its traditional and quite justifiable association with the preservation of cultural truisms, may also perform an act of critical interruption where taken-for-granted practices of a culture are concerned." Farrell, *Norms of Rhetorical Culture,* 258. For an elaboration of how social movements perform critical interruptions, see Pezzullo, "Performing Critical Interruptions."

36. J. L. Austin calls a "performative utterance" one which "indicates that the issuing of the utterance is the performing of an action"; it "is not to *describe* my doing of what should be said in so uttering to be doing or to state that I am doing it: it is to do it"; in this exploration, he asks when "can saying make it so?" Austin, *How to Do Things with Words,*

6, 7. In other words, the performative "enacts or produces that to which it refers." Diamond, introduction, 4.

37. Motavalli, "Toxic Targets," 34. For more information on the July 2002 Shell settlement with Norco, see *Fenceline: A Company Town Divided,* cited in B. L. Allen, *Uneasy Alchemy,* 166.

38. MacCannell, *The Tourist,* 44.

39. Sue Williams, e-mail to author, January 13, 2002.

40. For more on the use of the Bucket Brigade in Norco, see Wright, "Race, Politics, and Pollution."

41. *Random House Webster's Unabridged Dictionary,* 2nd ed. (New York: Random House, 2001), 2127.

42. S. Hall, "Signification, Representation, Ideology," 109.

43. McKerrow, "Corporeality and Cultural Rhetoric," 107.

44. Miller was a labor organizer for the Oil, Chemical, and Atomic Workers.

45. In the early 1980s, "BASF Corporation, the U.S. subsidiary of the German multinational BASF, was on a union-busting spree across the country." Schwab, *Deeper Shades of Green,* 234. The BASF lockout of workers in Geismer, a town downriver from Baton Rouge, lasted three years and, in that time, brought together workers, environmentalists, and civil rights activists. It was the longest "lock-out" in U.S. labor history. R. Wilson, "A Labor-Environmental Alliance: Louisiana's OCAW Local Union Joins Forces with NTC," *Toxic Times: The Newsletter of the National Toxics Campaign* 3 (1990): 22–23.

46. MacCannell, *The Tourist,* 44.

47. Local environmental justice activist Margie Richard (now Eugene-Richard) also "suggests that 'Cancer Alley' is not appropriately descriptive, because it does not suggest the range of illnesses in her community; she calls her community simply Death Alley." Qtd. in B. L. Allen, *Uneasy Alchemy,* 28.

48. MacCannell, *The Tourist,* 105, 44.

49. For a provocative series of articles on historical preservation and waste, see Bookspan, "Junk It, or Junket?"

50. "The plantation was built by Duncan Kenner in 1840 for his new bride, Anne Guillelimine Nanine Bringer. . . . Kenner named his home 'Ashland' after Henry Clay's Kentucky home. . . . In addition to preserving the 'great house,' archaeological digs have been conducted on the sites of the sugarhouse and two of the 30 slave cabins that once stood. . . . 'The Ashland-Belle Helene archaeological project . . . provides insight into the processing of cane in the sugarhouse and about the life of African Americans who toiled and lived on the plantation,' state archaeologist Thomas H. Eubanks writes." K. Martin, "Touring Great Houses; Two Antebellum Homes to be Opened for Tour," *Baton Rouge Advocate,* October 2, 1995, 1C, emphasis added.

51. Fine and Speer, "Tour Guide Performances," 86.

52. Many sources criticize this reiterated performance of enshrining *Gone With the Wind*. Two of my favorites are Baldwin, *The Evidence of Things Not Seen;* and Patricia J. Williams, "The Stochastic Aptitude Test," *Nation,* May 21, 2001, 11.

53. Bullard, *Confronting Environmental Racism,* 12—13, 23.

54. MacCannell, *Empty Meeting Grounds,* 179.

55. Bowman, "Performing Southern History," 155.

56. MacCannell, *The Tourist,* 9, 10.

57. *Green: A Film about Environmental Injustice.* More information on this project and its awards is available at http://www.twobirdsfilm.com.

58. MacCannell, *The Tourist,* 45.

59. Schwab, *Deeper Shades of Green,* 419.

60. Cox, "Cultural Memory," 4, 14.

61. Wright, Bryant, and Bullard, "Coping with Poisons," 126—27.

62. Patraka, *Spectacular Suffering,* 8.

63. Swerczek, "Greenpeace Visits Chemical Corridor," 1.

Chapter 4

1. Gramsci defines hegemonic "common sense" as historically constructed yet taken-for-granted societal beliefs. Gramsci, *Selections.*

2. Douglas and Wildavsky, *Risk and Culture,* 58.

3. Proctor, *Cancer Wars,* 1. According to the American Cancer Society: "This year [2001] about 553,400 Americans are expected to die of cancer, more than 1,500 people a day. Cancer is the second leading cause of death in the US, exceeded only by heart disease. In the US, 1 of every 4 deaths is from cancer." *Cancer Facts and Figures 2001,* 4. GreenAction estimates that "[c]ancer mortality has risen from 5% of American deaths a hundred years ago to 25% today. Lifetime rates for Americans have risen from one in four people in 1960 to 1 in 2 for men and more than 1 in 3 for women." GreenAction, "Stop Cancer Where It Starts! Action Alert Fact Sheet," http://www.greenaction.org/cancer/factsheet.shtml.

4. Steingraber, *Living Downstream,* 47.

5. American Cancer Society, *Cancer Facts and Figures 2001,* 11.

6. Y-ME National Breast Cancer Organization, 2001, http://www.y-me.org/cancerInfo/cancerInfo.html.

7. AstraZeneca, 2001, "AstraZeneca US. History," http://www.astrazeneca-us.com/about/history.asp.

8. "Corporate Profile: The Arranged Marriage," *The Independent* (London), February 24, 1999, 5; N. Pandya, "Jobs & Money: Jobs: Company Vitae: AstraZeneca Which This

Week Held Its AGM and Posted First Quarter Profits of Pounds 694m—Up 12%," *The Guardian* (London), April 28, 2001, 23.

9. Pandya, "Jobs & Money," 23.

10. National Breast Cancer Awareness Month, 2001, "Help Promote NBCAM," http:www.nbcam.org/promote_healthsite.cfm.

11. AstraZeneca, 2001, "New Survey Finds Few Employers Provide On-Site Breast Cancer Screening," http://www.astrazeneca-us.com/news/article.asp?file=2001102701.htm.

12. This is an area of extensive debate that I do not have the space or expertise to address here. The breast cancer movement, however, has begun to find evidence to counter the breast cancer industry's encouragement of mammograms. See, for example, Barbara Brenner and Barbara Ehrenreich. "The Pink-Ribbon Trap: Breast Cancer Activism Has to Go Beyond Simply Encouraging Women to Get Mammograms and Joining Support Groups." *Los Angeles Times,* December 23, 2001, http://www.commondreams.org.

13. National Breast Cancer Awareness Month (2005), "NBCAM Board of Sponsors," http://www.nbcam.org/about_board.cfm.

14. King, "An All-Consuming Cause," 138.

15. Focusing on the Bay Area, see Klawiter, "Racing for the Cure" and "From Private Stigma to Global Assembly."

16. A disturbing trend has been to attribute the cause of cancer to women who have not "made the 'proper' dietary and reproductive choices," i.e., who have not been "skinny women and good mothers." Yadlon, "Skinny Women and Good Mothers," 645–46.

17. Not surprisingly, few still allege that "studies have never shown a clear association between environmental toxins and elevated rates of the disease." B. H. Lerner, *Breast Cancer Wars,* 267.

18. For more about the problematic assumptions made in studies of hereditary breast cancer, see Condit, Condit, and Achter, "Human Equality," 92–94.

19. Steingraber, "Social Production of Cancer," 31.

20. Goldman and Papson, *Sign Wars,* 193.

21. Fitts, "Pathology and Erotics," 4, 9. This trend to contemplate breasts more than cancer often lends itself to the sexualization of the disease. In an article pointed out to me by John Delicath, Karen Lurie notes: "The cover of the February 18, 2002 issue of *Time* magazine features a naked, airbrushed, very thin woman with blond hair, shown from the waist up, standing sideways, covering her breasts with one arm while the other is awkwardly bent upward. She is staring off into space with a completely disengaged expression, like a mannequin, or a blow-up doll. One can't help but wonder," she concludes, "if breast cancer gets so much coverage because of the first word in the disease, not the second." Lurie, "Making Cancer Sexy," Alternet.org, February 27, 2002, http://alternet.org/print.html?StoryID=12507.

22. Eisenstein, *Manmade Breast Cancers,* 96.

23. K. Nyasha, "For Women under 40, Hunters Point Breast Cancer Rate Highest in U.S.," *Bayview Newspaper,* 2001, http://www.greenaction.org/cancer/pr100301.shtml. "A report from the city's Department of Public Health said that between 1988 and 1992, 60 black women in Bayview–Hunters Point ['San Francisco's forgotten southeast corner'] were found to have breast cancer—and 41 percent of them were under age 50. In the rest of San Francisco, only 22 percent would be expected to fall in that age group. The study also found elevated rates of cervical cancer but lower-than-expected rates of prostate cancer and non-Hodgkin's lymphoma among black men." C. Johnson, "Disputed S.F. Power Plant Expected to Get 1st OK: Neighbors Worry About Health Issues," *San Francisco Chronicle,* March 4, 1996, A13. "Bayview–Hunters Point has two Superfund sites, areas in which federal funds pay for toxic cleanups, and more than 100 other identified toxic waste spots. [A] task force found that all six schools in Bayview–Hunters Point had asthma rates that averaged between 15 and 20 percent. That's the highest rate in the city, and four times higher than the state average." J. B. Johnson, "Bayview Holding Breath on Plants; If Bid Is Best, S.F. Would Buy and Shutter 2 PG&E Stations," *San Francisco Chronicle,* June 8, 1998, A15.

24. For more on the beginnings of TLC see Klawiter, "Racing for the Cure" and "From Private Stigma."

25. Toxic Links Coalition, "Toxic Links Coalition Home Page," 2001, http://homeflash. net/~dlscism/toxiclinks/home_text.html.

26. Ibid.

27. Proctor, *CancerWars,* 255, 266.

28. Judith Brady, "Cancer Industry Tour," sfbg.org, November 10, 1999, http://www. sfbg.com/News/34/06/6other.html.

29. Similarly, "GE and Du Pont, rivals for the leads in Superfund toxic sites, sell more than $100 million worth of mammography machines every year (GE) and much of the film used in those machines (DuPont)." Proctor, *CancerWars,* 257.

30. GreenAction, "Action Alert: Stop Cancer Where It Starts!" (2001), http://www. greenaction.org/cancer/pr100301.shtml.

31. Toxic Links Coalition, videotape from Stop Cancer Industry Tour, San Francisco, 1997. I would like to thank TLC activist Judith Brady for lending her sole copy.

32. TLC's campaign's centerpoint is the annual toxic tour; however, it is a multi-pronged effort. For example, coalition activists have also protested the Susan G. Komen "Walk for the Cure" event, which according to Judith Brady, is also focused on corporate commodification and co-optation of the breast cancer movement. Although the Komen Foundation has accomplished good things, "What they don't see is that 'business as usual' is why we have cancer"; namely, "[t]here's no talk about prevention, except, in terms of lifestyle, your diet for instance. No talk about ways to grow food more safely. No talk

about how to curb industrial carcinogens. No talk about contaminated water or global warming." Qtd in Mary Ann Swissler, "The Marketing of Breast Cancer," alternet.org, September 16, 2002, http://www.alternet.org/story/14014/.

33. According to TLC activists I interviewed, the number of those attending steadily grew until 2001, when the numbers were slightly smaller. Although the cause was uncertain, many assumed the drop in attendance was occasioned by the events of September 11.

34. Di Chiro, "Bearing Witness," 281. Judith Brady notes that, for some, the lunch hour during a weekday makes the tour more difficult to attend: "The tour is held during a lunch hour in the middle of the week because it doesn't really make sense to visit corporate offices on the weekend. That makes finding the time to join the hour-and-a-half tour difficult, but if you can be a part of this Cancer Industry Tour, you owe it to yourself to be there." GreenAction, "Unmasking Cancer," http://www.greenaction.org/cancer/pr103002.shtml.

35. See S. Rubenstein, "S.F. Rally against Cancer High Rates in Bayview–Hunters Point," *San Francisco Chronicle,* September 22, 1995, A21; Syracuse Cultural Peace Workers, "Peace Calendar" (Syracuse, N.Y.: Syracuse Cultural Workers, 2002); Breast Cancer Oral History Action Project, *Who Holds the Mirror?*

36. Toxic Links Coalition pamphlet, 2001.

37. After I participated in a tour, I provided Judith Brady with a copy of the videotape. In addition, I subsequently discovered that TLC owned a tape of a previous tour; however, that tape did not record the entire event. TLC has also uploaded on the internet some images from the 2002 toxic tour. Toxic Links Coalition, "Photos from the 8th Annual Cancer Industry Tour" (2002), http://www.toxiclinks.net/thumbnails.html.

38. TLC annually obtains a permit from local police to demonstrate publicly.

39. In their study of ACT UP, Adrienne E. Christiansen and Jeremy J. Hanson argue that the exigencies and constraints of AIDS have motivated activists to draw on the comic frame. This may help explain actions of those cancer activists who also face incredible tragedy and choose to respond comically by providing "tours" and wearing costumes. Christiansen and Hanson, "Comedy as Cure for Tragedy," 167.

40. DeLuca, "Unruly Arguments," 17, 22. Employing inventive visual resources is a tactic with a long history in most social movements. Recall, in addition, how depression-era labor strikers used mock performances. Fuoss, *Striking Performances/Performing Strikes.* Also, recall how early preservationists and conservationists drew upon images and political theater. Nash, *Wilderness and the American Mind.*

41. Edensor, *Tourists at the Taj,* 143.

42. Chakrabarty, "Open Space/Public Space," 26, qtd. in Edensor, *Tourists at the Taj,* 59–60.

43. RavenLight, conversation with author, October 3, 2001.

44. The politics of displaying mastectomy scars is beyond the scope of this project. For feminist analysis of the cultural politics of displaying mastectomy scars and breasts, see Lurie, "Making Cancer Sexy"; Fitts, "Pathology and Erotics"; and Cartwright, "Community and the Public Body."

45. In explaining her choice of tactics, RavenLight states: "Wouldn't you think that if one in eight people had one arm or one leg, we'd ask what's going on? I'm too angry to die. I bare my de-breast in a fierce political stance. Breast cancer has been hidden under heavy layers of shame, guilt, and puffs of cotton stuffed inside empty bras for too many decades. I choose to use my body to put a face on this hideous disease." Breast Cancer Oral History Project, *Who Holds the Mirror?* 14–15.

46. DeLuca, "Unruly Arguments," 11.

47. BCA's role in countering NBCAM is called their "Think Before You Pink" campaign. This T-shirt is part of BCA's line of products that encourage women with breast cancer: "Identify yourself as a breast cancer activist. Dress the part—wear a Breast Cancer Action hat, shirt, and pin proudly." Breast Cancer Action, "BCA Logo Merchandise" (2005), http://www.bcaction.org/Pages/Membership/BCALogoMerch.html.

48. The first quote is excerpted from the second speaker, Medea Benjamin from Global Exchange; the second is from Marie Harrison from GreenAction, a resident of Bayview/Hunters Point.

49. Edensor, *Tourists at the Taj,* 105.

50. Cohen, "Tourist Guide," 166.

51. Edensor, *Tourists at the Taj,* 51.

52. Solnit, *Wanderlust,* 9.

53. De Certeau, *Practice,* 97, 98. As a result of these choices and displacements, the walker "condemns certain places to inertia or disappearance and composes with others spatial [arrangements]"; this "discreteness" infers a creative, noncontinuous, or individually distinct path that leads to what he calls the "phatic" aspects of walking, or "a rhetoric of walking." By "phatic" de Certeau "means the function, isolated by Malinowski and Jakobson, of terms that initiate, maintain, or interrupt contact, such as 'hello,' 'well, well,' etc. . . . which is an effort to ensure communication" (*Practice,* 99). Therefore, as a communicative act, walking serves as a metaphor and a literal possibility for engagement with others, a means to negotiate contact.

54. Reich, *Toxic Politics,* 186. Reich elaborates insightfully on this pattern in social conflicts throughout his text.

55. Miller, *Anatomy of Disgust,* 2.

56. Aristotle, *Rhetoric and Poetics,* 32.

57. See, for example, Chaloupka, *Everybody Knows;* Goldfarb, *The Cynical Society;* Jacoby, *The End of Utopia;* and Eliasoph, *Avoiding Politics.* For more on political dissent subsequent to 9/11 see Ivie, *Democracy and America's War on Terror.*

58. C. Le Grand and N. O'Brien, "Upset Court Attacks 'Unethical' Pro-Lifers," *The Australian,* April 1, 1998, 5; P. Swift, "Going to Extremes in the Debate over Abortion," *Buffalo News,* November 21, 1998, 7C; B. Knickerbocker, "Animal Activists Get Violent," *Christian Science Monitor,* August 29, 1997, 5; C. Pesce, "Holding the 'Radical Line': Animal Group Shocks Even Its Supporters," *USA Today,* September 3, 1991, 3A.

59. MacCannell, *The Tourist,* 40.

60. Brady is also the editor of and a contributor to a collection of essays on women with breast cancer, *One in Three: Women with Cancer Confront an Epidemic.*

61. Stauber and Rampton, *Toxic Sludge Is Good for You!* 82.

62. Perhaps because it was assumed that everyone knew who he was, Angel was only introduced by name. A former field anti-toxic organizer for Greenpeace, he now is the executive director of GreenAction.

63. Like Malek-Wiley, Angel ultimately emphasized the need for tour participants to get involved after the toxic tour. Although the tour is the primary cultural performance through which TLC attempts to influence public debate, observers and participants at the tour were handed fliers with information about how to become more involved with each group in the coalition. In addition, each speaker reinforced the need for participants and observers to do more after the tour. As a result, the tour functioned as a "cultural performance" whose implicit rhetorical structures, as Richard Schechner explains, lead to overt social dramas, which lead to implicit social processes, which lead to manifest stage performances, which lead back to implicit rhetorical structures, and so on. As Victor Turner argues, this circular pattern between the overt and the implicit, the social and the stage, helps us to appreciate how any one cultural performance is part of a larger context. Schechner, *Performance Theory;* Turner, *From Ritual to Theatre.*

64. Black Eyed Peas featuring Justin Timberlake, "Where Is the Love?" (Universal International, July 28, 2003).

65. Franklin defines *communitas* as "a unique social bond between strangers who happen to have in common the fact that they are in some way traveling or 'on holiday' together." *Tourism,* 48.

66. Lorde, *The Cancer Journals,* 11.

Chapter 5

1. Public Citizen Home Page (n.d.), http://www.citizen.org/trade/nafta/.

2. Anderson, *Imagined Communities,* 7.

3. Burke, *Rhetoric of Motives,* 22. Perelman and Olbrechts-Tyteca express concern about Burke's optimism regarding "identifications," claiming they are "simply connections and rejections of connections, for the associated and dissociated concepts appear, after the operation, to remain as they were in their original state, like bricks saved intact

from a building that has been pulled down." *New Rhetoric,* 413. I believe this interpretation is oversimplified; as an enthymematic feeling, identification cannot "simply" connect and disconnect, without transformation. Rather, it seems more productive to imagine identification as a process of articulation in which two elements form a temporary unity "establishing a relation among elements *such that their identity is modified as a result.*" Laclau and Mouffe, *Hegemony and Socialist Strategy* (1st ed.), 105, emphasis added.

4. Peterson, *Sharing the Earth,* 52.

5. For an analysis of what is "new" see Cvetkovich and Kellner, *Articulating the Global and the Local.*

6. Anzaldúa, *Borderlands/La Frontera,* 19.

7. Greider, *One World, Ready or Not,* 15.

8. S. Hall, "The Local and the Global," 27.

9. Wilson and Dissanayake, *Global/Local,* 1.

10. Light and Higgs, "Politics of Corporate Ecological Restorations," 102.

11. "The radical slogan of an earlier day, 'Think globally, act locally,' has been assimilated by transnational corporations with far greater success than in any radical strategy." Dirlik, "The Global in the Local," 34.

12. Wilson and Dissanayake, *Global/Local,* 6.

13. Shohat and Stam, "From the Imperial Family," 145.

14. Castells, *The Power of Identity;* Trent, "Media in a Capitalist Culture."

15. Yoshimoto, "Real Virtuality," 109.

16. L. J. Williams, "Film Bodies"; Hawkins, *Cutting Edge.* See also Odendahl, "Embodied Views to the Visual."

17. Shohat and Stam, "From the Imperial Family," 166.

18. Sontag, *Regarding the Pain of Others,* 111–12.

19. Nichols, *Blurred Boundaries,* 47.

20. Di Chiro, "Bearing Witness," 277.

21. *Oxford English Dictionary Online,* http://dictionary.oed.com.

22. Cohen-Cruz, *Radical Street Performance,* 65.

23. Smith, *Resisting Reagan,* 76, 77, 78.

24. Warford, *Greenpeace Witness.* I am grateful to Kevin DeLuca for pointing out this connection.

25. DeLuca, *Image Politics,* 22.

26. Taylor, *Disappearing Acts,* 265 (emphasis added), 121, 123, 122.

27. "This is not to deny that there is testimony that closes off the possibility of response, or that there are responses that attempt to deny the subjectivity of the witness. The question is how to respond to those false witnesses in a way that reopens the possibility of witnessing, of responsibility." Oliver, *Witnessing,* 108.

28. Taylor, *Disappearing Acts,* 265, 27.

29. Peterson, *Sharing the Earth,* 122.

30. The Rio Grande is often rated as the dirtiest U.S. river: "Along its 1,885-mile journey the river picks up toxic tailings from mining in Colorado; radioactive tailings from bomb buildings in Los Alamos, New Mexico; and raw human sewage, factory discharges, and agricultural chemicals along the border of Texas and Mexico. Finally, there are the human bodies. Hundreds of unidentified people are dragged lifeless from the lower Rio Grande every year." Ibid.

31. De Certeau, *Practice,* 93.

32. The *maquiladoras* of the region generally include the following industries: "automotive, electrical, electronic, furniture, ceramics, textile, and chemical. . . . The chemical industry has been, and is predicted to continue as, the fastest-growing segment, with a 92 percent growth rate reported in 1990." Peterson, *Sharing the Earth,* 125. For more on the toxic materials produced and distributed in and from the region, see also Greider, *One World, Ready or Not;* and Mary E. Kelley, "NAFTA and the Environment: Free Trade and the Politics of Toxic Waste," *Multinational Monitor,* October 1993. Kelley's article notes that U.S. House Majority Leader William Gephardt participated in a toxic tour of Matamoros in 1991.

33. Roughly translated: "Friendly Hospital: For Children and Mothers."

34. These still images of mothers and their children are shown, as the video notes, courtesy of *CNN.* As Sontag points out, in a sense, journalists simply are "specialized tourists." Sontag, *Regarding the Pain of Others,* 18. Noticeably, for those familiar with the local situation, the film does reference or show "anencephaly," a condition in which children are born with all or part of their brain outside their skull, usually leading to death almost immediately. The anencephaly story broke in U.S. national media in 1991, and this *CNN* footage was aired in May 1992. One local activist highlighted in this report, Theresa de la Cruz Gomez, was "especially angry with *CNN* reporters, who 'focused on sensationalism' and sought out mothers of anencephalic infants who did not want to speak with them." Peterson, *Sharing the Earth,* 129, 130.

35. Sontag, *Regarding the Pain of Others,* 102–3.

36. Carl Pope, "Ways and Means: Big River between Us," *Sierra,* September/October 2001, 13, http://www.sierraclub.org/sierra/200109/ways.asp.

37. Although I understood this statement in Spanish and then heard it in English, my memory is in English; so, I have written it as such. Unfortunately for this retelling, I did not have an audio recorder with me at the time that would allow me to share his words in both languages.

38. Kim Haddow, interview with author, February 27, 2002.

39. Ibid. This quote is excerpted from a discussion about advocacy tours that focuses on not only problems but also solutions. All the toxic tours I have participated in offer solutions. It also would be compelling to examine other environmental advocacy tours,

such as what the Sierra Club calls a "Tour de Sprawl"; playing off the idea of the "Tour de France," these bicycle tours raise awareness about more or less sustainable ways for communities to grow.

40. Adam Werbach, interview with author, February 19, 2002. Werbach is European American and a well-known leader of the environmental movement. He is a former president of the Sierra Club (the youngest ever, at age twenty-four, from 1996 to 1998), co-founder of the Apollo Alliance, and executive director of Common Assets. More information on Werbach and Act Now! Productions is available at http://www.actnowproductions.com.

41. Marilyn Berlin Snell, "Profile: Nancy Rodríguez, Border Doctor," *Sierra,* September/October 2001, 27.

42. At the time of these interviews the film had yet to circulate broadly.

43. Domingo González, interview with author, March 8, 2002. Of note to this study, on March 26, 1992, ABC's *PrimeTime Live* ran a story hosted by Diane Sawyer in which González led a toxic tour. Afterward, the "president of the Matamoros *maquiladoras* association repeatedly denied the possibility that working conditions and industrial effluent may be linked to high rates of birth defects among *maquila* workers' children. He has asked the Matamoros city council to have González, the 'toxic tour' guide, investigated by Mexico's Interior Ministry, which human rights groups have linked to the deaths of journalists, labor leaders, and political activists." Peterson, *Sharing the Earth,* 131.

44. Werbach interview.

45. Di Chiro, "Bearing Witness."

46. González interview.

47. De Certeau, *Practice,* 117, 118.

48. Shohat and Stam, "From the Imperial Family," 167.

49. Conquergood, "Performing as a Moral Act," 2, emphasis added.

Conclusion

1. National Council of Churches, "African American Church Leaders Pledge Their Support to the Struggle against Environmental Racism," March 1998, http://www.ncccusa.org/news/news21.html.

2. De Certeau, *Practice,* xiv. Although he does not make this connection, "tactics" are akin to the ancient Greek concept of *kairos,* roughly involving a rhetorical appreciation for discovering the "timely," as well as what is contingently "appropriate."

3. Morris, "Banality in Cultural Studies," 29.

4. "A tactic insinuates itself into the other's place, fragmentarily, without taking it over in its entirety, without being able to keep it at a distance." De Certeau, *Practice,* xix.

5. Massey, *Space, Place, and Gender,* 3.

6. Bindé, "Toward an Ethic of the Future," 51, 52, 51.

7. "The Precautionary Principle," *Rachel's Environment and Health Weekly,* no. 586 (February 19, 1998), http://www.monitor.net/rachel/r586.html.

8. Steingraber, "Myth of Living Safely."

9. Pezzullo, "Performing Critical Interruptions."

10. Environmental justice scholar and activist Beverly Wright provided a similar reply on a toxic tour of Cancer Alley to a "young Nigerian man" after he expressed his disbelief of the atrocious environmental conditions allowed to exist even in the United States: "It is done over and over again and to the same people." Wright, "Race, Politics, and Pollution," 135–36.

11. Peterson, *Sharing the Earth,* 131.

12. Haddow interview.

13. Communities that host toxic tours tend to express the belief that if those in official decision-making positions would simply spend more time in their community, they would eventually agree with the community's perspective. Further, even when a toxic tour is hosted, communities tend to prefer "more time." After a 1998 toxic tour of southern Louisiana, for example, the response was that more time was needed: "Citizen groups and environmental organizations have helped to plan the four-hour site tour of Cancer Alley for the NEJAC. Because of time constraints only a segment of Cancer Alley will be seen on the tour. . . . The Louisiana Citizen Committee for Participation in the NEJAC is urging NEJAC members to return to Louisiana." Environmental Justice Resource Center at Clark Atlanta University, "Communities Help Plan Official NEJAC Fact Finding Tour, But Say Not Enough Time Given to See Louisiana's Environmental Crisis," 1998, http://www.ejrc.cau.edu/louisananejac.htm.

14. "According to democratic theorist Cornelius Castoriadis, public time represents 'the emergence of a dimension where the collectivity can inspect its own past as the result of *its own actions,* and where an indeterminate future opens up as domain for its activities' (Castoriadis, 1991: 113–4). For Castoriadis, public time puts into question established institutions and dominant authority." Giroux, "The Politics of Emergency," quoting from Cornelius Castoriadis, "The Greek Polis and the Creation of Democracy," *Philosophy, Politics, Autonomy: Essays in Political Philosophy* (New York: Oxford University Press, 1991).

15. Mouffe, "Hegemony and New Political Subjects," 96.

16. Bindé, "Toward an Ethic of the Future," 57–58.

17. Pratt, *Imperial Eyes,* 6–7, qtd. in Clifford, *Routes,* 192.

18. Shohat and Stam, "From the Imperial Family," 166.

19. Laclau and Mouffe, *Hegemony and Socialist Strategy* (1st ed.), 176.

20. Conquergood, "Rethinking Ethnography," 187.

21. Conquergood, "Beyond the Text," 28.

Epilogue

1. Press release in author's possession.

2. Mark Schleifstein, "Activists' Ally Snared in Security Net: Students' Photos of Refinery Cost Man His State Job," *New Orleans Times-Picayune,* April 5, 2005; "Louisiana Environmental Official Says He Was Forced to Retire," *Associated Press Newswire,* April 5, 2005.

3. Quoted by permission.

4. Further, current proposals are aimed at *weakening* regulations on the disclosure of toxic chemical pollution through limiting the Toxic Release Inventory.

5. Bill Moyers NOW, "Homeland Insecurity," March 21, 2003, http://www.pbs.org/now/science/chemsafe.html.

6. "Fact Sheet on Senator Corzine's Chemical Security Legislation," http://corzine.senate.gov/priorities/chem_sec.html.

7. "Hurricane Katrina Response: Current Activities," http://www.epa.gov/katrina/activities.html#sep15; Associated Press, "More New Orleans Water Test Results Released: Two New Rounds of Sampling Corroborates Bacteria, Chemical Concerns," MSNBC.com, September 15, 2005; Felicity Barringer and Michael Janofsky, "E.P.A. Struggles to Determine Extent of Hazards in Sludge," *New York Times,* nytimes.com, September 15, 2005; Marla Cone, "Toxic Threat Still Vague but Ominous, EPA Says," latimes.com, September 15, 2005.

Bibliography

The Accidental Tourist. Dir. Lawrence Kasdan. Warner Brothers, 1988. Videocassette.

Adams, Carol J. *The Pornography of Meat.* New York: Continuum International, 2003.

———. *The Sexual Politics of Meat: A Feminist-Vegetarian Critical Theory.* 10th anniv. ed. New York: Continuum International, 1989.

Alcoff, Linda. "The Problem of Speaking for Others." *Cultural Critique* 17 (Winter 1991): 5–31.

Allen, Barbara L. *Uneasy Alchemy: Citizens and Experts in Louisiana's Chemical Corridor Disputes.* Cambridge: MIT Press, 2003.

Allen, Theodore W. *The Invention of the White Race: Racial Oppression and Social Control.* Vol. 1. London: Verso, 1993.

American Cancer Society. *Cancer Facts and Figures 2001.* New York: American Cancer Society, 2001.

Anderson, Benedict. *Imagined Communities: Reflections on the Origin and Spread of Nationalism.* 1983. London: Verso, 1991.

Andrews, Richard N. L. *Managing the Environment, Managing Ourselves: A History of American Environmental Policy.* New Haven: Yale University Press, 1999.

Anzaldúa, Gloria. *Borderlands / La Frontera: The New Mestiza.* 2nd ed. 1987. San Francisco: Aunt Lute Books, 1999.

Aristotle. *The Rhetoric and the Poetics of Aristotle.* Trans. W. Rhys Roberts and Ingram Bywater. 1954. New York: Random House, 1984.

Arora, Ashish, R. Landon, and Nathan Rosenberg. *Chemicals and Long-Term Economic Growth: Insights from the Chemical Industry.* New York: Wiley-Interscience, 1998.

Austin, J. L. *How to Do Things with Words.* Ed. J. O. Urmson and Marina Sbisá. 2nd ed. Cambridge: Harvard University Press, 1962.

Baker, Steve. *Picturing the Beast: Animals, Identity, and Representation.* Champaign-Urbana: University of Illinois Press, 2001.

Bakhtin, Mikhail. *Rabelais and His World.* Trans. Hélène Iswolsky. Bloomington: Indiana University Press, 1984.

Baldwin, James. *The Evidence of Things Not Seen.* New York: Henry Holt, 1985.

———. *The Fire Next Time.* New York: Laurel, 1962.

Bauer, Irmgard L. "Tourism and the Environment, the Other Side of the Coin." *Tourist Studies* 1.3 (2001): 297–314.

Bauman, Richard. "Performance." In *Folklore, Cultural Performances, and Popular Entertainments: A Communications-Centered Handbook,* ed. Bauman, 41–49. New York: Oxford University Press, 1992.

Bauman, Zymunt. "From Pilgrim to Tourist—or a Short History of Identity." In *Questions of Cultural Identity,* ed. Stuart Hall and Paul du Gay, 18–36. London: Sage, 1996.

Beardsworth, Alan, and Alan Bryman. "The Wild Animal in Late Modernity: The Case of the Disneyization of Zoos." *Tourist Studies* 1, no. 1 (2001): 83–104.

Behar, Ruth. *The Vulnerable Observer: Anthropology That Breaks Your Heart.* New York: Beacon Press, 1997.

Bindé, Jérôme. "Toward an Ethic of the Future." *Public Culture* 12, no. 1 (2000): 51–72.

Bishop, Paul L. *Pollution Prevention: Fundamentals and Practice.* Boston: McGraw-Hill, 2000.

Blair, Carole. "Challenges and Openings in Rethinking Rhetoric: Contemporary U.S. Memorial Sites as Exemplars of Rhetoric's Materiality." In *Rhetorical Bodies: Toward a Material Rhetoric,* ed. Jack Selzer and Sharon Crowley, 16–57. Madison: University of Wisconsin Press, 1999.

Bookspan, Shelley, ed. "Junk It, or Junket? Tourism and Historic Preservation in the Postindustrial World." *Public Historian* 23, no. 2 (2001): 5–138.

Bourdieu, Pierre. *Distinction: A Social Critique of the Judgment of Taste.* Trans. Richard Nice. Reprint. Cambridge: Harvard University Press, 1987.

Bowman, Michael S. "Performing Southern History for the Tourist Gaze: Antebellum Home Tour Guide Performances." In *Exceptional Spaces: Essays in Performance and History,* ed. Della Pollock, 142–58. Chapel Hill: University of North Carolina Press, 1998.

Brady, Judith. *One in Three: Women with Cancer Confront an Epidemic.* Pittsburgh: Cleis Press, 1991.

Breast Cancer Oral History Action Project. *Who Holds the Mirror? The Mural, Oral Histories, and Pedagogy of the Breast Cancer Oral History Action Project.* Berkeley, Calif.: Breast Cancer Oral History Action Project, 1998.

Brown, Phil, and Edwin J. Mikkelsen. *No Safe Place: Toxic Waste, Leukemia, and Community Action.* 1990. Berkeley: University of California Press, 1997.

Bruner, Edward M. *Culture on Tour: Ethnographies of Travel.* Chicago: University of Chicago Press, 2005.

Bryant, Bunyan. *Environmental Justice: Issues, Policies, and Solutions.* Washington, D.C.: Island Press, 1995.

Bullard, Robert D., ed. *Confronting Environmental Racism: Voices from the Grassroots.* Boston: South End Press, 1993.

———. *Unequal Protection: Environmental Justice and Communities of Color.* San Francisco: Sierra Club Books, 1994.

Bullard, Robert D., and Beverly H. Wright. "The Quest for Environmental Equity: Mobilizing the African-American Community for Social Change." In *American Environmentalism: The U.S. Environmental Movement, 1970–1990,* ed. Riley E. Dunlap and Angela G. Mertig, 39–49. New York: Taylor and Francis, 1992.

Bullis, Connie. "Retalking Environmental Discourses from a Feminist Perspective: The Radical Potential of Ecofeminism." *The Symbolic Earth: Discourse and Our Creation of the Environment,* ed. Jimmie G. Cantrill and Christine L. Oravec, 123–48. Lexington: University Press of Kentucky, 1996.

Burke, Kenneth. *A Rhetoric of Motives.* 1950. Berkeley: University of California Press, 1969.

Butler, Judith. *Bodies That Matter: On the Discursive Limits of "Sex."* London: Routledge, 1993.

Carson, Rachel. *Silent Spring.* Boston: Houghton Mifflin, 1962.

Cartwright, Lisa. "Community and the Public Body in Breast Cancer Media Activism." *Cultural Studies* 12, no. 2 (1998): 117–38.

Castells, Manuel. *The Power of Identity.* Malden, Mass.: Blackwell, 1997.

Castoriadis, Cornelius. *Philosophy, Politics, Autonomy: Essays in Political Philosophy.* New York: Oxford University Press, 1991.

Chakrabarty, Dipesh. "Open Space/Public Space: Garbage, Modernity, and India." *South Asia* 16 (1991): 15–31.

Chaloupka, William. *Everybody Knows: Cynicism in America.* Minneapolis: University of Minnesota Press, 1999.

Chambers, Iain. *Migrancy, Culture, Identity.* London: Routledge, 1994.

Chicago Surrealist Group. "Three Days That Shook the New World Order: The Los Angeles Rebellion of 1992." In *Race Traitor,* ed. Noel Ignatiev and John Garvey, 1–17. New York: Routledge, 1996.

Chideya, Farai. *Don't Believe the Hype: Fighting Cultural Misinformation about African Americans.* New York: Plume Books, 1995.

Christiansen, Adrienne E., and Jeremy J. Hanson. "Comedy as Cure for Tragedy: ACT UP and the Rhetoric of AIDS." *Quarterly Journal of Speech* 82 (1996): 157–70.

A Civil Action. Dir. Steven Zaillian. Buena Vista Pictures, 1998. Videocassette.

Clark, Gregory. *Rhetorical Landscapes in America: Variations on a Theme from Kenneth Burke.* Columbia: University of South Carolina Press, 2004.

Clifford, James. *Routes: Travel and Translation in the Late Twentieth Century.* Cambridge: Harvard University Press.

———. "Traveling Cultures." In *Cultural Studies,* ed. Cary Nelson, Paula A. Treichler, and Lawrence Grossberg, 96–112. New York: Routledge, 1986.

Cohen, Erik. "The Tourist Guide: The Origins, Structure and Dynamics of a Role." *Annals of Tourism Research* 12 (1985): 5–29.

Cohen-Cruz, Jan. *Radical Street Performance: An International Anthology.* London: Routledge, 1998.

Colborn, Theo, Dianne Dumanoski, and John Peterson Myers. *Our Stolen Future: Are We Threatening Our Fertility, Intelligence, and Survival? A Scientific Detective Story.* New York: Plume, 1996.

Cole, Luke W., and Sheila R. Foster. *From the Ground Up: Environmental Racism and the Rise of the Environmental Justice Movement.* New York: New York University Press, 2001.

Condit, Celeste Michelle, Deirdre Moira Condit, and Paul J. Achter. "Human Equality, Affirmative Action, and Genetic Models of Human Variation." *Rhetoric and Public Affairs* 4, no. 1 (2001): 85–108.

Conquergood, Dwight. "Beyond the Text: Toward a Performative Cultural Politics." In *The Future of Performance Studies: Visions and Revisions,* ed. Sheron J. Dailey, 25–36. Annandale, Va.: National Communication Association, 1998.

———. "Ethnography, Rhetoric, and Performance." *Quarterly Journal of Speech* 78 (1992): 80–97.

———. "Performing as a Moral Act: Ethical Dimensions of the Ethnography of Performance." *Literature in Performance* 5 (1982): 1–13.

———. "Rethinking Ethnography: Towards a Critical Cultural Politics." *Communication Monographs* 58 (1991, June): 179–94.

Cox, J. Robert. "Cultural Memory and Public Moral Argument." *The Van Zelst Lecture in Communication.* Evanston, Ill.: Northwestern University. Unpublished. 1987, May 19.

Crang, Philip. "Performing the Tourist Product." In *Touring Cultures: Transformations of Travel and Theory,* ed. Chris Rojek and John Urry, 137–54. London: Routledge, 1997.

Crawshaw, Carol, and John Urry. "Tourism and the Photographic Eye." In *Touring Cultures: Transformations of Travel and Theory,* ed. Chris Rojek and John Urry, 176–95. New York: Routledge, 1997.

Crocodile Dundee. Dir. Peter Faiman. Paramount Pictures, 1986. Videocassette.

Crouch, David, and Luke Desforges. "The Sensuous in the Tourist Encounter; Introduction: The Power of the Body in Tourist Studies." *Tourist Studies* 3, no. 1 (2003): 5–22.

Crowley, Sharon. Afterword. In *Rhetorical Bodies: Toward a Material Rhetoric,* ed. Jack Selzer and Sharon Crowley, 357–66. Madison: University Press of Wisconsin, 1999.

Cvetkovich, Ann, and Douglas Kellner, eds. *Articulating the Global and the Local: Globalization and Cultural Studies.* Boulder, Colo.: Westview Press, 1997.

Darnovsky, Marcy. "Green Living in a Toxic World: The Pitfalls and Promises of Everyday Environmentalism." In *Reclaiming the Environmental Debate: The Politics of Health in a Toxic Culture,* ed. Richard Hofrichter, 219–37. Cambridge: MIT Press, 2000.

Davis, Susan G. *Spectacular Nature: Corporate Culture and the Sea World Experience.* Berkeley: University of California Press, 1997.

de Certeau, Michel. *The Practice of Everyday Life.* Trans. Stephen Rendall. Berkeley: University of California Press, 1984.

De Falco, Tom. *The Hulk: The Incredible Guide.* New York: Dorling Kindersley, 2003.

DeLuca, Kevin Michael. *Image Politics: The New Rhetoric of Environmental Activism.* New York: Guilford Press, 1999.

———. "Unruly Arguments: The Body Rhetoric of Earth First!, ACT UP, and Queer Nation." *Argumentation and Advocacy* 36 (1999): 9–21.

Depoe, Stephen P., and John W. Delicath. Introduction. In *Communication and Public Participation in Environmental Decision Making,* ed. Stephen P. Depoe, John W. Delicath, and Marie-France Aepli Elsenbeer, 1–10. Albany: State University of New York Press, 2004.

Derrida, Jacques. *Speech and Phenomena and Other Essays on Husserl's Theory of Signs.* Trans. D. B. Allison. Evanston, Ill.: Northwestern University Press, 1973.

——. *Writing and Difference.* Trans. A. Bass. Chicago: University of Chicago Press, 1978.

Descartes, René. *Discourse on Method and Meditations on First Philosophy.* 4th ed. 1964. Indianapolis: Hackett, 1998.

Desmond, Jane C. *Staging Tourism: Bodies on Display from Waikiki to Sea World.* Chicago: University of Chicago Press, 1999.

Diamond, Elin. Introduction. In *Performance and Cultural Politics,* ed. Elin Diamond, 1–12. London: Routledge, 1996.

Di Chiro, Giovanna. "Bearing Witness or Taking Action? Toxic Tourism and Environmental Justice." In *Reclaiming the Environmental Debate: The Politics of Health in a Toxic Culture,* ed. Richard Hofrichter, 275–300. Cambridge: MIT Press, 2000.

——. "Beyond Ecoliberal 'Common Futures': Environmental Justice, Toxic Touring, and a Transcommunal Politics of Place." In *Race, Nature, and the Politics of Difference,* ed. Donald S. Moore, Jake Kosek, and Anand Pandian, 204–32. Durham, N.C.: Duke University Press, 2003.

——. "Defining Environmental Justice: Women's Voices and Grassroots Politics." *Socialist Review* 22, no. 4 (1992): 92–130.

——. "Nature as Community: The Convergence of Environment and Social Justice." In *Uncommon Ground: Rethinking the Human Place in Nature,* ed. William Cronon, 298–320. New York: Norton, 1996.

Dirlik, Arif. "The Global in the Local." In *Global / Local: Cultural Production and the Transnational Imaginary,* ed. Rob Wilson and Wimal Dissanayake, 21–45. Durham, N.C.: Duke University Press, 1996.

Douglas, Mary. *Purity and Danger: An Analysis of Concepts of Pollution and Taboo.* New York: Frederick A. Praeger, 1968.

Douglas, Mary, and Aaron Wildavsky. *Risk and Culture: An Essay on the Selection of Technological and Environmental Dangers.* Berkeley: University of California Press, 1982.

Dowie, Mark. *Losing Ground: American Environmentalism at the Close of the Twentieth Century.* Cambridge: MIT Press, 1995.

Dunlap, Riley E., and Angela G. Mertig. *American Environmentalism: The U.S. Environmental Movement, 1970–1990.* New York: Taylor & Francis, 1992.

Dyer, Richard. *White.* New York: Routledge, 1997.

Echtner, Charlotte M., and Anshuman Prasad. "The Context of Third World Tourism Marketing." *Annals of Tourism Research* 30, no. 3 (2003): 660–82.

Edensor, Tim. "Staging Tourism: Tourists as Performers." *Annals of Tourism Research* 27, no. 2 (2000): 322–44.

———. *Tourists at the Taj: Performance and Meaning at a Symbolic Site.* London: Routledge, 1998.

Eisenstein, Zillah R. *Manmade Breast Cancers.* Ithaca, N.Y.: Cornell University Press, 2001.

Eliasoph, Nina. *Avoiding Politics: How Americans Produce Apathy in Everyday Life.* Cambridge: Cambridge University Press, 1998.

Enloe, Cynthia. *Bananas, Beaches, and Bases: Making Feminist Sense of International Politics.* Berkeley: University of California Press, 1989.

———. *Maneuvers: The International Politics of Militarizing Women's Lives.* Berkeley: University of California Press, 2000.

Environmental Justice. Prod. Jesus People Against Pollution. January 31, 1995. Videocassette.

Erin Brockovich. Dir. Steven Soderbergh. Columbia TriStar Film Distributors International, 2000. Videocassette.

Escobar, Arturo. *Encountering Development: The Making and the Unmaking of the Third World.* Princeton, N.J.: Princeton University Press, 1995.

Farrell, Thomas B. *Norms of Rhetorical Culture.* New Haven: Yale University Press, 1993.

Fenceline: A Company Town Divided. Dir. Slawomir Gruberg. LOGTV, Ltd. Of Spencer, 2002. Videocassette.

Ferris, Deeohn. "A Call for Justice and Equal Environmental Protection." In *Unequal Protection: Environmental Justice and Communities of Color,* ed. Robert D. Bullard, 298–320. San Francisco: Sierra Club Books, 1994.

Field, Roger C. "Risk and Justice: Capitalist Production and the Environment." In *The Struggle for Ecological Democracy: Environmental Justice Movements in the United States,* ed. Daniel Faber, 81–103. New York: Guilford, 1998.

Fine, Elizabeth C., and Jean Haskell Speer. "Tour Guide Performances as Sight Sacralization." *Annals of Tourism Research* (1985): 73–95.

Fitts, Karen. "The Pathology and Erotics of Breast Cancer." *Discourse* 21, no. 2 (1999): 3–20.

Foley, Malcolm, and John Lennon. *Dark Tourism: The Attraction of Death and Disaster.* New York: Int. Thomson Business Press, 2000.

Frankenberg, Ruth. *The Social Construction of Whiteness: White Women, Race Matters.* Minneapolis: University of Minneapolis Press, 1993.

Franklin, Adrian. *Tourism: An Introduction.* London: Sage, 2003.

Franklin, Adrian, and Mike Crang. "The Trouble with Tourism and Travel Theory?" *Tourist Studies* 1, no. 1 (2001): 5–22.

Freeze, R. Allan. *The Environmental Pendulum: A Quest for the Truth about Toxic Chemicals, Human Health, and Environmental Protection.* Berkeley: University of California Press, 2000.

Frow, John. *Time and Commodity Culture: Essays in Cultural Theory and Postmodernity.* Oxford: Clarendon Press, 1997.

Fuoss, Kirk W. *Striking Performances / Performing Strikes.* Jackson: University Press of Mississippi, 1997.

Get on the Bus. Dir. Spike Lee. Columbia Pictures and Sony Pictures Entertainment, 1996. Videocassette.

Gibbs, Lois Marie. *Dying from Dioxin: A Citizen's Guide to Reclaiming Our Health and Rebuilding Democracy.* Boston: South End Press, 1995.

Giroux, Henry. "The Politics of Emergency versus Public Time: Terrorism and the Culture of Fear." In "The University Culture Machine," special issue of *Culture Machine: The Journal* 2 (2000). Ed. Gary Hall and Simon Wortham. http://culturemachine.tees.ac.uk/frm_f1.htm.

Goldfarb, Jeffrey C. *The Cynical Society: The Culture of Politics and the Politics of Culture in American Life.* Chicago: University of Chicago Press, 1992.

Goldman, Robert, and Stephen Papson. *Sign Wars: The Cluttered Landscape of Advertising.* New York: Guilford Press, 1996.

Gottlieb, Robert. *Forcing the Spring: The Transformation of the American Environmental Movement.* Washington, D.C.: Island Press, 1993.

Graburn, Nelson H. H. "Tourism: The Sacred Journey." In *Hosts and Guests: The Anthropology of Tourism,* ed. Valene L. Smith, 21–36. 2nd ed. Philadelphia: University of Pennsylvania Press, 1989.

Gramsci, Antonio. *Selections from the Prison Notebooks.* Ed. and trans. Quintin Hoare and Geoffrey Nowell Smith. 1997. New York: International Publishers, 1971.

Green: A Film about Environmental Injustice. Dir. Laura Dunn. Two Birds Film, 2000. Videocassette.

Greider, William. *One World, Ready or Not: The Manic Logic of Global Capitalism.* New York: Simon and Schuster, 1997.

Grossberg, Lawrence. "On Postmodernism and Articulation: An Interview with Stuart Hall." In *Stuart Hall: Critical Dialogues in Cultural Studies,* ed. David Morley and Kuang-Hsing Chen, 131–50. New York: Routledge, 1996.

——. *We Gotta Get Out of This Place: Popular Conservatism and Postmodern Culture.* London: Routledge, 1992.

Grossman, Karl. "The People of Color Environmental Summit." In *Unequal Protection: Environmental Justice and Communities of Color,* ed. Robert D. Bullard, 272–97. San Francisco: Sierra Club Books, 1994.

Grosz, Elizabeth. *Volatile Bodies: Toward a Corporeal Feminism.* Bloomington: Indiana University Press, 1994.

Hall, Colin Michael, and Stephen John Page. *The Geography of Tourism and Recreation: Environment, Place, and Space.* London: Routledge, 1999.

Hall, Rachel. " 'It Can Happen to You': Rape Prevention in the Age of Risk Management." *Hypatia: A Journal of Feminist Philosophy* 19.3 (2004): 1–19.

Hall, Stuart. "Encoding/Decoding." In *Culture, Media, Language: Working Papers in Cultural Studies, 1972–79,* ed. Centre for Contemporary Cultural Studies, 128–239. 1973. London: Unwin Hyman, 1980.

——. "The Local and the Global: Globalization and Ethnicity." In *Culture, Globalization, and the World-System: Contemporary Conditions for the Representation of Identity,* ed. Anthony D. King, 19–40. Binghamton, N.Y.: SUNY Art Department, 1991.

——. "Notes on Deconstructing 'the Popular.' " In *Cultural Theory and Popular Culture: A Reader,* ed. John Storey, 42–53. Athens: University of Georgia Press, 1998.

——. *Representation: Cultural Representations and Signifying Practices.* London: Sage, 1997.

——. "Signification, Representation, Ideology: Althusser and the Post-Structuralist Debates." *Critical Studies in Mass Communication* 1 (1985, June): 91–114.

Harte, John, Cheryl Holdren, Richard Schneider, and Christine Shirley. *Toxics A to Z: A Guide to Everyday Pollution Hazards.* Berkeley: University of California Press, 1991.

Hawkins, Joan. *Cutting Edge: Art Horror and the Horrific Avant-Garde.* Minneapolis: University of Minnesota Press, 2000.

Helvarg, David. *The War against the Greens: The "Wise-Use" Movement, the New Right, and Anti-Environmental Violence.* 1994. San Francisco: Sierra Club Books, 1997.

Henry, Wesley R. "Carrying Capacity, Ecological Impacts and Visitor Attitudes: Applying Research to Park Planning and Management." In *Ecotourism and Sustainable Development in Kenya: The Proceedings of the Kenya Ecotourism Workshop Held September 13–17, 1992,* ed. C. G. Gakahu and B. E. Goode, 49–62. Nairobi, Kenya: Wildlife Conservation International, 1992.

Higgins, Robert R. "Race, Pollution, and the Mastery of Nature." *Environmental Ethics* 16 (Fall 1994): 251–64.

Highmore, Ben. *The Everyday Life Reader.* London: Routledge, 2002.

Hofrichter, Richard. "Cultural Activism and Environmental Justice." In *Toxic Struggles: The Theory and Practice of Environmental Justice,* ed. Hofrichter, 85–97. Philadelphia: New Society Publishers, 1993.

———. Introduction. In *Toxic Struggles: The Theory and Practice of Environmental Justice,* ed. Hofrichter, 1–11. Philadelphia: New Society Publishers, 1993.

———. "Introduction: Critical Perspectives on Human Health and the Environment." In *Reclaiming the Environmental Debate: The Politics of Health in a Toxic Culture,* ed. Hofrichter, 1–15. Cambridge: MIT Press, 2000.

Holden, Andrew. "In Need of New Environmental Ethics for Tourism?" *Annals of Tourism Research* 30.1 (2003): 94–108.

Honey, Martha. *Ecotourism and Sustainable Development: Who Owns Paradise?* Washington, D.C.: Island Press, 1999.

Hurley, Andrew. *Environmental Inequalities: Class, Race, and Industrial Pollution in Gary, Indiana, 1945–1980.* Chapel Hill: University of North Carolina Press, 1995.

Ignatiev, Noel. *How the Irish Became White.* London: Routledge, 1996.

Ivie, Robert L. *Democracy and America's War on Terror.* Tuscaloosa: University of Alabama Press, 2005.

Jacoby, Russell. *The End of Utopia: Politics and Culture in an Age of Apathy.* New York: Basic Books, 2000.

Johnston, Lynda. "(Other) Bodies and Tourism Studies." *Annals of Tourism Research* 28, no. 1 (2000): 180–201.

Jordan, June. "Report from the Bahamas." In *Visions of America: Personal Narratives from the Promised Land,* ed. W. Brown and A. Ling, 305–15. 1982. New York: Persea Books, 1993.

Kaplan, Caren. *Questions of Travel: Postmodern Discourses of Displacement.* Durham, N.C.: Duke University Press, 1996.

Kaplan, Temma. *Crazy for Democracy: Women in Grassroots Movements.* New York: Routledge, 1997.

Karon, Louis A. "Presence in the New Rhetoric." *Philosophy and Rhetoric* 9, no. 2 (1976): 96–111.

Kelley, Robin D. G. *Race Rebels: Culture, Politics, and the Black Working Class.* New York: Free Press, 1994.

Kennedy, Robert F., Jr. *Crimes against Nature: How George W. Bush and His Corporate Pals Are Plundering the Country and Hijacking Our Democracy.* New York: Harper-Collins, 2004.

Khan, Maryam. "ECOSERV: Ecotourists' Quality Expectations." *Annals of Tourism Research* 30.1 (2003): 109–24

Kim, Sung-kwon Hong Jae-hyun, and Seong-il Kim. "Implications of Potential Green Tourism Development." *Annals of Tourism Research* 30.2 (2003): 323–41.

Kincaid, Jamaica. *A Small Place.* New York: Farrar, Straus & Giroux, 1988.

King, Samantha. "An All-Consuming Cause: Breast Cancer, Corporate Philanthropy, and the Market for Generosity." *Social Text* 19, no. 4 (2001): 115–43.

Kirshenblatt-Gimblett, Barbara. *Destination Culture: Tourism, Museums, and Heritage.* Berkeley: University of California Press, 1998.

Kirshenblatt-Gimblett, Barbara, and Edward M. Bruner. "Tourism." In *Folklore, Cultural Performances, and Popular Entertainments,* ed. Richard Bauman, 300–308. New York: Oxford University Press, 1992.

Klawiter, Maren. "From Private Stigma to Global Assembly." In *Global Ethnography: Forces, Connections, and Imaginations in a Postmodern World,* ed. Michael Buraway, Joseph A. Blum, Sheba George, Zsuza Gille, Teresa Gowan, Lynne Haney, Maren Klawiter, Steve H. Lopez, Seán O Riaian, and Millie Thayer, 299–334. Berkeley: University of California Press, 2000.

———. "Racing for the Cure, Walking Women, and Toxic Touring: Mapping Cultures of Action within the Bay Area Terrain of Breast Cancer." *Social Problems* 46, no. 1 (1999): 104–26.

Kouis, Maria. "Tourism and the Environment: A Social Movements Perspective." *Annals of Tourism Research* 27.2 (2000): 468–89.

Laclau, Ernesto. *New Reflections on the Revolution of Our Time.* London: Verso, 1990.

Laclau, Ernesto, and Chantal Mouffe. *Hegemony and Socialist Strategy: Towards a Radical Democratic Politics.* London: Verso, 1985.

———. *Hegemony and Socialist Strategy: Towards a Radical Democratic Politics.* 2nd ed. London: Verso, 2001.

Laid to Waste: A Chester Neighborhood Fights for Its Future. Dir. Robert Bahar and George McCollough. Philadelphia: DUTV-Cable 54, 1996. Videocassette.

Larabee, Anne. *Decade of Disaster.* Urbana-Champaign: University of Illinois Press, 1999.

Lavelle, Marriane, and Marcia Coyle. "Critical Mass Builds on Environmental Equity." *National Law Journal,* September 21, 1992, Washington Briefs Sec., 5.

Layne, Linda L. "In Search of Community: Tales of Pregnancy Loss in Three Toxically Assaulted U.S. Communities." *Women's Studies Quarterly* 1–2 (2001): 25–49.

Lefebvre, Henri. *Everyday Life in the Modern World.* Trans. Sacha Rabinovitch. New Brunswick, N.J.: Transaction, 1971.

Leopold, Aldo. *A Sand County Almanac: With Essays on Conservation from Round River.* 1949. New York: Ballantine, 1966.

Lerner, Barron H. *The Breast Cancer Wars: Hope, Fear, and the Pursuit of a Cure in Twentieth-Century America.* Oxford: Oxford University Press, 2001.

Lerner, Steve. *Diamond: A Struggle for Environmental Justice in Louisiana's Chemical Corridor.* Cambridge: MIT Press, 2004.

Leroux, Neil R. "Perceiving Rhetorical Style: Toward a Framework for Criticism." *Rhetoric Society Quarterly* 22 (1992): 29–44.

Levin, David Michael, ed. *Modernity and the Hegemony of Vision.* Berkeley: University of California Press, 1993.

Light, Andrew, and Eric Higgs. "The Politics of Corporate Ecological Restorations: Comparing Global and Local North American Contexts." In *Articulating the Global and the Local: Globalization and Cultural Studies,* ed. Ann Cvetkovich and Douglas Kellner, 102–25. Boulder, Colo.: Westview Press, 1997.

Linenthal, Edward T. *Preserving Memory: The Struggle to Create America's Holocaust Museum.* New York: Penguin, 1995.

Lippard, Lucy R. *The Lure of the Local: Sense of Place in a Multicentered Society.* New York: Free Press, 1997.

———. *On the Beaten Track: Tourism, Art, and Place.* New York: New Press, 1999.

Lorde, Audre. *The Cancer Journals: Special Edition.* 1979. San Francisco: Aunt Lute Books, 1997.

MacCannell, Dean. *Empty Meeting Grounds: The Tourist Papers.* London: Routledge, 1992.

———. "Tourist Agency." *Tourist Studies* 1, no. 1 (2001): 23–37.

———. *The Tourist: A New Theory of the Leisure Class.* 1976. Berkeley: University of California Press, 1999.

Madison, D. Soyini. "Ch. 8: My Desire Is for the Poor to Speak of Me Well." In *Remembering: Oral History Performance,* ed. Della Pollock, 143–66. New York: Palgrave MacMillan, 2005.

———. *Critical Ethnography.* New York: Sage, 2005.

———. "Performing Theory/Embodied Writing." *Text and Performance Quarterly* 19, no. 2 (1999): 107–24.

Madison, D. Soyini, and Judith Hamera, eds., *The Sage Handbook of Performance Studies.* Thousand Oaks, Calif.: Sage, 2005.

Marcus, George E. *Ethnography through Thick and Thin.* Princeton, N.J.: Princeton University Press, 1998.

Margaret's Museum. Dir. Mort Ransen. Astra Cinema, Cinépix Film Properties Inc., Malofilm, 1995. Videocassette.

Markwell, Kevin. "'An Intimate Rendezvous with Nature?' Mediating the Tourist-Nature Experience at Three Tourist Sites in Borneo." *Tourist Studies* 1.1 (2001): 39–57.

Marvin, Carolyn. "The Body of the Text: Literacy's Corporeal Constant." *Quarterly Journal of Speech* 80, no. 2 (1994): 129–49.

Massey, Doreen. *Space, Place, and Gender.* Minneapolis: University of Minnesota Press, 1994.

Matamoros: The Human Face of Globalization. Prod. Kim Haddow and the Sierra Club. Dir. Amanda Boxall. Distributed by The Video Project, 2001. Videocassette.

McGehee, Gard. "Alternative Tourism and Social Movements." *Annals of Tourism Research* 29.1 (2002): 124–43.

McKerrow, Raymie E. "Corporeality and Cultural Rhetoric: A Site for Rhetoric's Future." *Southern Communication Journal* 63 (1998): 315–28.

Miller, William Ian. *The Anatomy of Disgust.* Cambridge: Harvard University Press, 1997.

Mills, Charles W. "Black Trash." In *Faces of Environmental Racism: Confronting Issues of Global Justice,* ed. Laura Westra and Bill E. Lawson, 73–94. 2nd ed. Lanham, Md.: Rowman & Littlefield, 2001.

Morris, Meaghan. "Banality in Cultural Studies." In *Logics of Television: Essays in Cultural Criticism,* ed. Patricia Mellencamp, 14–43. Bloomington: Indiana University Press, 1990.

Moses, Marion. "Farmworkers and Pesticides." In *Confronting Environmental Racism: Voices from the Grassroots,* ed. Robert D. Bullard, 161–78. Boston: South End Press, 1993.

Motavalli, Jim. "Toxic Targets: Polluters That Dump on Communities of Color Are Finally Being Brought to Justice." *E Magazine* 9, no. 4 (1998): 34.

Mouffe, Chantal. *The Democratic Paradox.* London: Verso, 2000.

———. "Hegemony and New Political Subjects: Towards a New Concept of Democracy." In *Marxism and the Interpretation of Culture,* ed. Cary Nelson and Lawrence Grossberg, 32–33. Chicago: University of Illinois Press, 1988.

———. *The Return of the Political.* London: Verso, 1993.

Mullan, Bob, and Gary Marvin. *Zoo Culture.* Champaign-Urbana: University of Illinois Press, 1998.

Mulvey, Laura. "Visual Pleasure and Narrative Cinema." In *Feminism & Film,* ed. E. Ann Kaplan, 34–47. Cambridge: Oxford University Press, 2000.

Murphey, John M. "Presence, Analogy, and *Earth in Balance.*" *Argumentation and Advocacy* 31 (Summer 1994): 1–16.

Nash, Roderick. *Wilderness and the American Mind.* 3rd ed. 1967. New Haven: Yale University Press, 1982.

Neumann, Mark. *On the Rim: Looking for the Grand Canyon.* Minneapolis: University of Minnesota Press, 1999.

Nichols, Bill. *Blurred Boundaries: Questions of Meaning in Contemporary Culture.* Bloomington: Indiana University Press, 1994.

Novotny, Paul. "Popular Epidemiology and the Struggle for Community Health in the Environmental Justice Movement." In *The Struggle for Ecological Democracy: Environmental Justice Movements in the United States,* ed. Daniel Faber, 137–58. New York: Guilford Press, 1998.

Nuttal, Mark. "Packaging the Wild: Tourism Development in Alaska." In *Tourists and Tourism: Identifying with People and Places,* ed. Simone Abram, Jackie D. Waldren, and Don Macleod, 223–38. Oxford: Berg, 1997.

O'Brien, Mary H. "When Harm Is Not Necessary." In *Reclaiming the Environ-*

mental Debate: The Politics of Health in a Toxic Culture, ed. Richard Hofrichter, 113–34. Cambridge: MIT Press, 2000.

O'Connor, John. "The Promise of Environmental Democracy." In *Toxic Struggles: The Theory and Practice of Environmental Justice,* ed. Richard Hofrichter, 47–58. Philadelphia: New Society Publishers, 1993.

Odendahl, Jules. "Embodied Views to the Visual through Interdisciplinary and Reflexive Methodologies." *Text and Performance Quarterly* 23, no. 1 (2003): 87–104.

Oliver, Kelly. *Witnessing: Beyond Recognition.* Minneapolis: University of Minnesota Press, 2001.

Olwig, Kenneth R. "Reinventing Common Nature: Yosemite and Mount Rushmore—A Meandering Tale of a Double Nature." In *Uncommon Ground: Rethinking the Human Place in Nature,* ed. William Cronon, 379–408. New York: Norton, 1996.

Patraka, Vivian M. *Spectacular Suffering: Theatre, Fascism, and the Holocaust.* Bloomington: University of Indiana Press, 1999.

Peña, Devon, and María Mondragon-Valdéz. "The 'Brown' and the 'Green' Revisited: Chicanos and Environmental Politics in the Upper Rio Grande." In *The Struggle for Ecological Democracy: Environmental Justice Movements in the United States,* ed. Daniel Faber, 312–48. New York: Guilford Press, 1998.

Perelman, Chaim. *The New Rhetoric and the Humanities: Essays on Rhetoric and Its Applications.* Trans. E. Griffin-Collart and O. Bird. 1970. Dordrecht, Holland: D. Reidel, 1982.

———. *The Realm of Rhetoric.* Trans. W. Kluback. 1977. Notre Dame, Ind.: University of Notre Dame Press, 1982.

Perelman, Chaim H., and Lucie Olbrechts-Tyteca. *The New Rhetoric: A Treatise on Argumentation.* Trans. J. Wilkinson and P. Weaver. Notre Dame, Ind.: University of Notre Dame Press, 1969.

Peterson, Tarla Rai. *Sharing the Earth: The Rhetoric of Sustainable Development.* Columbia: University of South Carolina Press, 1997.

Pezzullo, Phaedra C. "Articulating Anti-Toxic Activism to 'Sexy' Superstars: The Cultural Politics of *A Civil Action* and *Erin Brockovich.*" *Environmental Communication Yearbook* 3 (2006): 21–48.

———. "Mapping What's Happening on the Ground: Three Toxic Tour Surveys." *EJ Times: The Sierra Club Environmental Justice Newsletter* 2, no. 1 (2001): 7–10.

———. "Performing Critical Interruptions: Rhetorical Invention and Narratives of the Environmental Justice Movement." *Western Journal of Communication* 64, no. 1 (2001): 1–25.

———. " 'Resisting "National Breast Cancer Awareness Month': The Rhetoric of Counterpublics and Their Cultural Performances." *Quarterly Journal of Speech* 89, no. 4 (2003): 345–65.

———. " 'Touring "Cancer Alley,' Louisiana: Performances of Community and Memory for Environmental Justice." *Text and Performance Quarterly* 23, no. 3 (2003): 226–52.

———. "Toxic Tours: Communicating the 'Presence' of Chemical Contamination." In *Communication and Public Participation in Environmental Decision-Making*, ed. Stephen P. Depoe, John W. Delicath, and Marie-France Aepli Elsenbeer, 235–54. Albany: SUNY Press, 2004.

Plato. *Cratylus.* Trans. C. D. C. Reeve. New York: Hackett, 1999.

———. *Gorgias.* Trans. W. C. Helmbold. New York: Prentice Hall, 1952.

———. *Phaedrus.* Trans. Alexander Nehamas and Paul Woodruff. New York: Hackett, 1995.

Pratt, Mary Louise. *Imperial Eyes: Travel Writing and Transculturation.* London: Routledge, 1992.

Pretes, Michael. "Tourism and Nationalism." *Annals of Tourism Research* 30, no. 1 (2003): 125–42.

Proceedings: The First National People of Color Environmental Leadership Summit, Washington, DC, October 24–27, 1991. Distributed by the United Church of Christ Commission for Racial Justice.

Proctor, Robert N. *Cancer Wars: How Politics Shape What We Know and Don't Know about Cancer.* New York: Basic Books, 1995.

Reagan, Bernice Johnson. "Coalition Politics: Turning the Century." In *Home Girls: A Black Feminist Anthology,* ed. Barbara Smith, 356–68. New York: Kitchen Table/Women of Color Press, 1983.

Reich, Michael R. *Toxic Politics: Responding to Chemical Disasters.* Ithaca, N.Y.: Cornell University Press, 1991.

Roach, Joseph. *Cities of the Dead: Circum-Atlantic Performances.* New York: Columbia University Press, 1996.

Roberts, J. Timmons, and Melissa M. Toffolon-Weiss. *Chronicles from the Environmental Justice Frontline.* Cambridge: Cambridge University Press, 2001.

Robinson, Amy. "Forms of Appearance of Value: Homer Plessy and the Politics of Privacy." In *Performance and Cultural Politics,* ed. Elin Diamond, 239–66. London: Routledge, 1996.

Roediger, David R. *The Wages of Whiteness: Race and the Making of the American Working Class.* London: Verso, 1999.

Roger & Me. Dir. Michael Moore. Warner Brothers, 1989. Videocassette.

Roosevelt, Theodore R. *Theodore Roosevelt: An Autobiography.* 1913. New York: Scribner, 1920.

Rothman, Hal K. *The Devil's Bargain: Tourism in the Twentieth Century American West.* Lawrence: University of Kansas Press, 1998.

Russo, Antonio Paolo. "The Vicious Circle of Tourism Development in Heritage Cities." *Annals of Tourism Research* 29, no. 1 (2002): 165–82.

Russo, Mary. *The Female Grotesque: Risk, Excess and Modernity.* New York: Routledge, 1994.

Sanderson, Peter. *X-Men Updated Ed.: The Ultimate Guide.* New York: Dorling Kindersley, 2003.

Sandler, Ronald, and Phaedra C. Pezzullo, eds. *Environmental Justice and Environmentalism: The Social Justice Challenge to Environmentalism.* Cambridge: MIT Press, forthcoming 2006.

Sayre, Henry M. "Pursuing Authenticity: The Vernacular Moment in Contemporary American Art." In *Eloquent Obsessions: Writing Cultural Criticism,* ed. Marianna Torgovnick, 107–27. Durham, N.C.: Duke University Press, 1994.

Scarry, Elaine. *The Body in Pain: The Making and Unmaking of the World.* New York: Oxford University Press, 1985.

Schechner, Richard. *Performance Theory.* London: Routledge, 1988.

Schwab, Jim. *Deeper Shades of Green: The Rise of Blue-Collar and Minority Environmentalism in America.* San Francisco: Sierra Club Books, 1994.

Segrest, Margaret. *Memoir of a Race Traitor.* Boston: South End Press, 1994.

Setterberg, Fred, and Lonny Shavelson. *Toxic Nation: The Fight to Save Our Communities from Chemical Contamination.* New York: Wiley, 1993.

Shildrick, Margrit. *Embodying the Monster: Encounters with the Vulnerable Self.* New York: Sage, 2002.

Shohat, Ella, and Robert Stam. "From the Imperial Family to the Transnational Imaginary: Media Spectatorship in the Age of Globalization." In *Global / Local: Cultural Production and the Transnational Imaginary,* ed. Rob Wilson and Wimal Dissanayake, 145–70. Durham, N.C.: Duke University Press, 1996.

Smith, Christian. *Resisting Reagan: The U.S. Central America Peace Movement.* Chicago: University of Chicago Press, 1996.

Solnit, Rebecca. *Wanderlust: A History of Walking.* New York: Penguin, 2000.

Sontag, Susan. *Illness as Metaphor and AIDS and Its Metaphors.* New York: Farrar, Straus, and Giroux, 1977.

———. *Regarding the Pain of Others.* New York: Farrar, Straus, and Giroux, 2003.

Stallybrass, Peter, and Allon White. *The Politics and Poetics of Transgression.* Ithaca, N.Y.: Cornell University Press, 1986.

Stauber, John, and Sheldon Rampton. *Toxic Sludge Is Good for You! Lies, Damn Lies, and the Public Relations Industry.* Monroe, Maine: Common Courage Press, 1995.

Steingraber, Sandra. *Living Downstream: A Scientist's Personal Investigation of Cancer and the Environment.* New York: Random House, 1997.

———. "The Myth of Living Safely in a Toxic World." *In These Times,* April 2001. Third World Traveler Website. http://www.thirdworldtraveler.com/Environment/Myth_LivingToxicWorld.html.

———. "The Social Production of Cancer: A Walk Upstream." In *Reclaiming the Environmental Debate: The Politics of Health in a Toxic Culture,* ed. Richard Hofrichter, 19–38. Cambridge: MIT Press, 2000.

Strange, Carolyn, and Michael Kempa. "Shades of Dark Tourism: Alcatraz and Robben Island." *Annals of Tourism Research* 90.2 (2003): 386–405.

Striphas, Ted. "Communication as Translation." In *Communication as . . . : Perspectives on Theory,* ed. Gregory J. Shepherd, Jeffrey St. John, and Ted Striphas, 232–41. Thousand Oaks, Calif.: Sage, 2006.

The Sunshine State. Dir. John Sayles. Sony Pictures Classics, 2002. Videocassette.

Tarbell, Alice, and Mary Arquette. "Akwesasne: A Native American Community's Resistance." In *Reclaiming the Environmental Debate: The Politics of Health in a Toxic Culture,* ed. Richard Hofrichter, 93–112. Cambridge: MIT Press, 2000.

Taylor, Diana. *Disappearing Acts: Spectacles of Gender and Nationalism in Argentina's "Dirty War."* Durham, N.C.: Duke University Press, 1997.

Trent, Barbara. "Media in a Capitalist Culture." In *The Culture of Globalization,* ed. Fredric Jameson and Masao Miyoshi, 230–46. Durham, N.C.: Duke University Press, 1998.

Turner, Victor. *The Anthropology of Performance.* New York: PAJ Publications, 1986.

———. *From Ritual to Theatre: The Human Seriousness of Play.* New York: Performing Arts Journal Press, 1982.

Tyler, Anne. *The Accidental Tourist*. 1985. New York: Ballantine, 2002.

United Church of Christ Commission for Racial Justice. *Toxic Wastes and Race in the United States*. Ed. B. A. Goldman and L. Fitton. New York: United Church of Christ, 1987.

Urry, John. *The Tourist Gaze*. London: Sage, 1990.

U.S. General Accounting Office [GAO]. *Siting of Hazardous Waste Landfills and Their Correlation with Racial and Economic Status of Surrounding Communities*. Washington, D.C.: GAO, 1983.

Vacation. Dir. Harold Ramis. Warner Brothers, 1983. Videocassette.

Waitt, Gordon, Ruth Lane, and Lesley Head. "The Boundaries of Nature Tourism." *Annals of Tourism Research* 30.3 (2003): 523–45.

Warford, Mark, ed. *Greenpeace Witness: Twenty-five Years on the Environmental Front Line*. London: Andre Deutsch, 1997.

Wargo, John. *Our Children's Toxic Legacy: How Science and Law Fail to Protect Us from Pesticides*. New Haven: Yale University Press, 1998.

Wendell, Susan. *The Rejected Body: Feminist Philosophical Reflections on Disability*. New York: Routledge, 1996.

Williams, Juan. *Eyes on the Prize: America's Civil Rights Years, 1954–1965*. New York: Penguin Books, 1988.

Williams, Linda J. "Film Bodies: Gender, Genre, and Excess." In *Film Genre Reader II*, ed. Barry Keith Grant, 140–58. Austin: University of Texas Press, 1995.

Williams, Raymond. "Base and Superstructure in Marxist Cultural Theory." *New Left Review* 82 (1973): 3–16.

———. *Keywords: A Vocabulary of Culture and Society*. 1976. New York: Oxford University Press, 1983.

———. *Marxism and Literature*. Oxford: Oxford University Press, 1977.

———. *Resources of Hope*. London: Verso, 1989.

Wilson, Rob, and Wimal Dissanayake. *Global/Local: Cultural Production and the Transnational Imaginary*. Durham, N.C.: Duke University Press, 1996.

Wise, J. Macgregor. "Home: Territory and Identity." In *Animations of Deleuze and Guattari*, ed. Jennifer Daryl Slack, 107–27. New York: Peter Lang, 2003.

Wright, Beverly. "Race, Politics, and Pollution: Environmental Justice in the Mississippi River Chemical Corridor." In *Just Sustainabilities: Development in an Unequal World*, ed. Julian Agyeman, Robert D. Bullard, and Bob Evans, 125–45. Cambridge: MIT Press, 2003.

Wright, Beverly H., Pat Bryant, and Robert D. Bullard. "Coping with Poisons in

Cancer Alley." In *Unequal Protection: Environmental Justice and Communities of Color,* ed. Robert D. Bullard, 110–29. San Francisco: Sierra Club Books, 1994.

Yadlon, Susan. "Skinny Women and Good Mothers: The Rhetoric of Risk, Control, and Culpability in the Production of Knowledge about Breast Cancer." *Feminist Studies* 23, no. 3 (1997): 645–77.

Yoshimoto, Mitsuhiro. "Real Virtuality." In *Global/Local: Cultural Production and the Transnational Imaginary,* ed. Rob Wilson and Wimal Dissanayake, 107–18. Durham, N.C.: Duke University Press, 1996.

Young, Iris Marion, "The Ideal of Community and the Politics of Difference." In *Feminism/Postmodernism,* ed. Linda J. Nicholson, 300–323. 1986. New York: Routledge, 1990.

Index